Excellence in Managing Worldwide Customer Relationships

THE GLOBAL WARRIOR SERIES
Series Editor: Thomas A. Cook

Excellence in Managing Worldwide Customer Relationships
Thomas A. Cook (2016)

Growing and Managing Foreign Purchasing
Thomas A. Cook (2016)

Managing Growth and Expansion into Global Markets:
Logistics, Transportation, and Distribution
Thomas A. Cook (2016)

Driving Risk and Spend Out of the Global Supply Chain
Thomas A. Cook (2015)

Mastering the Business of Global Trade: Negotiating Competitive
Advantage Contractual Best Practices, Incoterms®
and Leveraging Supply Chain Options
Thomas A. Cook (2014)

The Global Warrior Series

Excellence in Managing Worldwide Customer Relationships

Thomas A. Cook

CRC Press
Taylor & Francis Group
Boca Raton   London   New York

CRC Press is an imprint of the
Taylor & Francis Group, an **informa** business

CRC Press
Taylor & Francis Group
6000 Broken Sound Parkway NW, Suite 300
Boca Raton, FL 33487-2742

© 2017 by Taylor & Francis Group, LLC
CRC Press is an imprint of Taylor & Francis Group, an Informa business

No claim to original U.S. Government works

Printed on acid-free paper
Version Date: 20161010

International Standard Book Number-13: 978-1-4822-2619-5 (Hardback)

Library of Congress Cataloging-in-Publication Data

Name: Cook, Thomas A., 1953- author.
Title: Excellence in managing worldwide customer relationships / Thomas A. Cook.
Description: Boca Raton, Taylor & Francis Group, [2016] | Series: The global
warrior series ; 5 | Includes bibliographical references and index.
Identifiers: LCCN 2016024614 | ISBN 9781482226195 (alk. paper)
Subjects: LCSH: Customer services--Management. | Customer relations. |
Electronic commerce--Management.| Consumer satisfaction.
Classification: LCC HF5415.5 .C6638 2016 | DDC 658.8/12--dc23
LC record available at https://lccn.loc.gov/2016024614

Visit the Taylor & Francis Web site at
http://www.taylorandfrancis.com

and the CRC Press Web site at
http://www.crcpress.com

Printed and bound in the United States of America by
Edwards Brothers Malloy on sustainably sourced paper

To Hunter Cook, whose dedication to his business is second to none and whose commitment to his clients and attribution to the art of personal training, physical therapy, and nutrition makes me proud every day!

Contents

Foreword

I have always been impressed by Tom's exuberance in global trade, his knowledge, and his proclivity in being able to articulate useful information for all of us who are engaged in international business.

He has authored numerous books, each one a plethora of comprehensive information for exporters, importers, supply chain executives, attorneys, financial personnel, and sales and customer service talent in this industry of buying and selling overseas.

People succeed in international trade who continue to evolve through training, education, and knowledge gain. This book is an excellent resource for growth, information, and skill set development.

Tom plans out the flow of information is an easy-to-comprehend format with lots of detail but structured so it is easy to understand and retain, and more importantly, to utilize in our everyday business activity, which helps us succeed in our careers.

I think you will enjoy this reading, as I have and have always in all of Tom's work, not only in his writing, but in his lecturing, public speaking, and as an advocate for all of us who are wrestling with the day-to-day challenges of international sales, customer service, and business development.

Joe Mantello
FDS, NY

Preface

When I entered global trade as a full-time business pursuit in 1981, global trade was exclusive to larger companies and trading companies. The middle market was just getting their feet wet.

As we approach 2017, a much larger share of companies is expanding globally. Most are in sourcing and purchasing, but many others are finding growth in exports and foreign markets.

Many products grown, produced, refined, and manufactured in North America have great panache in overseas markets and are in great demand. Many products demand a higher profit on foreign shores as compared to domestic more seasoned and matured markets.

With all this growth and expansion, corporate personnel can still do a better job protecting their companies' interests by developing strategies of learning and managing into more comprehensive skill sets and resources.

Specifically, this comes into play with corporate personnel engaged in sales, customer service, and business development: three areas that are very different and similar at the same time.

This book dissects all the issues and concerns in these three areas and provides a foundation for executives to follow to avoid pitfalls and maximize a return on investments worthy of the best companies involved in global trade and world dominance.

The formulas, strategies, and plans of action with the proper information flow, skill set development, and ultimately comprehensive execution can mean successful export sales, business development, and excellence in customer service that can compete with any company in the world.

It is not a matter of size, but rather skill set, capability, and ability to work off of a solid foundation of the basics that are reviewed in great detail in every chapter of this book.

This book can be offered as a complete instruction manual for any executive or company looking to expand their business model in overseas markets.

The book identifies the risks, the challenges, and all the issues, but more importantly offers solutions, strategies, and a structure to minimize the impact of all the obstacles and pass them by successfully.

Selling to foreign markets need not be so concerning that it is not a valid strategy for any company here in North America. While the concerns are real and legitimate, the opportunities are vast and are worth the venture.

But managing the venture is what this book is all about. Managing the venture with due diligence, reasonable care, and comprehensive persistence will mitigate the issues and maximize the opportunity for success. And success as a by-product of managed execution is what this book provides!

Thomas A. Cook

The customer's perception is your reality!

Katie Zabrieski

1

The Challenges of Business Development in International Business

We cannot emphasize sufficiently the case that going international creates risk. The challenges are enormous and sometimes overwhelming.

This chapter outlines these issues and their relevance. The balance of this book outlines the strategies and solutions in each following chapter on how to make these issues disappear or at least be minimized to controllable levels.

THE CASE TO GO GLOBAL

Companies need to expand into international markets for a number of reasons:

Market expansion. For North American companies there are potential limits to growth in their domestic markets. Mature Western markets and new and developing countries all present a huge potential in almost an unlimited market penetration and growth opportunity.

U.S.- and Canadian based products are in high demand in most places worldwide. While we are mostly big importers, there is a major demand for most of the products we grow, raise, farm, mine, and manufacture in the North American arena.

It is a misnomer that we are not competitive in global markets. Just the opposite; our products and services are in huge demand.

Selling globally for most companies is or can become a huge part of their overall sales strategy and even grow to become the most profitable area for margin and long-term opportunity.

Additionally, U.S.-based customer service is second to none. We are leaders in robust customer service deliverables and continually demonstrate to the world that we back our products and services with a team of operational staff that performs consistently, reliably, and cost effectively.

It is also a misnomer that we are not adaptable to other foreign cultures. While I would agree that we can do a better job at language and tolerance in the foreign domain, most of our personnel are very flexible when dealing and managing with foreign sales and customer service matters.

At the end of the day, business development on foreign shores potentially becomes an integral part of any business's growth and expansion strategies.

In various chapters, where we discuss e-commerce from the United States, our consumer products are also in huge favor all around the world and many companies are seriously expanding their e-commerce reach globally.

In some companies, e-commerce sales internationally are growing faster than commercial activity with greater margins.

Enhanced profit margins. I have had it argued both ways—exports reduce margin depth and also enhance it. But my experience in exports in over 60 countries in more than a dozen verticals has demonstrated that there is a definite opportunity for margin expansion on foreign shores, particularly in emerging and developing countries in Asia, Africa, the Middle East, and within all of Latin America.

It typically makes the case for creative and intelligent approaches to sales, marketing, and in customer service for those foreign markets, which also includes intense levels of flexibility, tolerance, and patience customized to the nuances of each country and culture around the globe. This will be discussed in detail in Chapters 2 and 3.

Keep in mind that North America and particularly the United States produce an enormous volume of products from natural sources that are in huge demand along with a host of high-tech, pharma, defense, aerospace, and medical equipment, to name a few industrial areas that are favored by many countries and consumers around the world.

Meeting competitive pressures. Every industry vertical and every company within that vertical is always under significant pressure to:

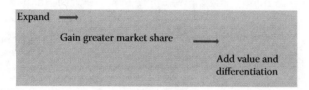

Expand ⟶

Gain greater market share ⟶

Add value and differentiation

Some companies must expand globally to keep pace with their competition so they protect their client base and market share.

An example of this would be a smaller industrial products company that is successful in their domestic sales but is now is faced with the threat of competitors who can service the international needs of their existing domestic clients.

As their clients grow their businesses overseas they have supply needs to these foreign locations. There is now an expectation that you can service these foreign locations just as you do for all their domestic facilities.

Your competitors that currently have that global reach are talking to your clients. This forces you into the global arena just to maintain and develop with your clients' needs.

This is a "reactive" reasoning process, which is not as productive as a process that preempts and anticipates clients' needs, but it does often work to keep clients happy.

Business development risk management. Risk management is a growing and integral management task in any business model.

The risk associated with sales, business development, and customer service is that if we only are in our domestic market, what happens when the economy in that market goes south? What happens if one competitor buys up another competitor and creates certain leverages? What happens if we lose market share? How do we combat these potential risks?

One option is to provide a "balanced approach" and have a certain percentage of sales outside of our domestic market. This provides a "risk management" approach as we are "spreading out" potential areas of concern and exposure to a greater demographic.

It both reduces risk and creates opportunity at the same time!

Risk management is a healthy part of any sales,
business development, or customer service program.

The author contends that as we approach 2018, risk management will become an integral part of every aspect of how a company does business, including customer service and more particularly the supply chain in the international arena.

CHALLENGES OF GOING GLOBAL

Where there is opportunity in foreign sales there is also risk. The key is to identify the risks, mitigate them, and increase the odds for success.

We need to understand the generic risks, which are outlined below:

Ocean shipping is fraught with risk and exposure. Understanding and mitigating risk should be a central focus for all foreign initiatives.

Twenty-One Challenges of Going Global:

1. Physical issues
2. Geographic constraints
3. Economic conditions
4. Political risks
5. Cultural issues
6. Legal differences
7. Establishing a foundation
8. Time differences
9. Performance standards
10. Language differences
11. Payment terms
12. Intellectual property rights (IPR)
13. Transportation and logistics
14. Customs entry
15. Trade compliance
16. Last mile delivery
17. Terrorism and security
18. Regulatory
19. INCOTerms

20. Across-the-globe training
21. Risk management

The challenges of global trade are expansive, as is our physical planet, but manageable through best practices.

Physical Issues

When goods move internationally they can travel over 15,000 miles, in all sorts of weather conditions, modes of transit, and geographic challenges.

Steps must be taken to properly mark, label, and package the shipments for the intended journey. Contemplation must be made as to what risks will be faced when determining all the available packing and marking options.

Many insurance companies and underwriting agencies report that on average anywhere from 1% to as high as 5% of freight transiting internationally can be lost or damaged.

Rough handling, improper packing, water damage, and poor choice of shipping options are primary culprits, as depicted in these two photos.

Geographic Constraints

In the past 25 years the world has become significantly smaller with respect to global trade. Some supply chains deliver on all seven continents and to almost every nook and cranny where people and businesses are domiciled.

In some cases, these supply chains can deliver the same day or the next day depending on where the origin and destinations are located and timing of product availability.

The challenges of distance, geographic variables, and shipping constraints possess potential pitfalls.

Most exporters and importers utilize the skill sets of freight forwarders and other types of transportation providers to navigate through these challenges and pitfalls to make for the best opportunity for a favorable outcome.

Economic Conditions

The economies of the world change every decade, year, month, day, and even hour. There are cycles that have reoccurred over the past 100 years and there are aberrations such as the global recession of 2009.

Executives engaged in export sales need to pay attention to economic conditions globally and certainly in those markets they are currently serving and those in which they are looking to develop future sales.

In larger companies this monitoring activity can be a full-time job, and in smaller and medium-sized operations, it is usually a part-time responsibility.

Regardless, it is an important topic to have as a central focus in export management.

Not paying attention to economic uncertainties can lead to loss of markets, customers, sales, profits, and receivables.

There are both short- and long-term consequences to aberrant economic circumstances.

Conversely, when economics improve, not paying attention and expanding business development initiatives can reduce opportunities.

Economic growth and expansion typically translates into export opportunities for American companies along with operations in all countries around the globe.

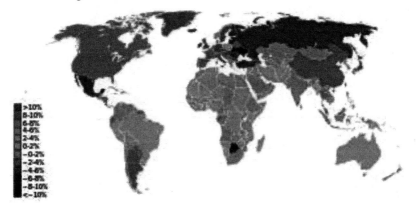

Global gross domestic product (GDP) growth improves the overall economy and creates export opportunities.

The real challenge for companies is not how to react to economic change but to spend time and resources in understanding economic change so it can be predicted better, allowing for preemptive actions as a result of anticipating correctly.

This then affords time to adapt, modify, and tweak proactively, optimizing more favorable results as economic changes occur for the better or worse.

We know from an absolute historical perspective that economic conditions change.

The ability to anticipate these changes would be very beneficial so action steps can be taken to various extremes to be conservative or liberal in your international business development strategies.

This allows expansion or retraction prior to need so the impact is either heightened or lessened based on preemptive actions.

This is a "risk management" as well as a general business development strategy to achieve better results.

Political Risks

Political risk events in Cuba, Sudan, Syria, and Ukraine are recent examples of C, N, E, and D risks facing companies operating in the world arena.

The politics of the world change daily. Most political changes are concerning for global trade. But in rare instances it is a boon.

The international executive who pays attention to global politics will always be in a better position to react proactively in qualified anticipation of potentially threatening circumstances.

As we enter 2017 the threat of North Korean nuclear proliferation, terrorism, specifically ISIS, and economic declines that impact political issues are but a few of the serious challenges in the political arena.

Specific consequences of these issues can be categorized as confiscation, nationalization, expropriation, and deprivation. These acts on a political level are ways in which hostile governments seize assets or prevent global companies from operating in their countries.

These risks, sometimes categorized as C, N, E, and D, have threatened Western interests repeatedly since the 1800s.

Cultural Issues

Negotiating deals with Middle Eastern interests will fail greatly if you do not pay attention to all the cultural behaviors and customs that dictate successful sensibilities with your trading

Every country in the world is identified by its culture. In larger countries like China, the United States, Brazil, and Russia, this can be further differentiated by geographic boundaries, provinces, states, and the origins of the various peoples in each country.

Culture can dominate behavior, making how you approach sales, customer service, and business development critical to your success.

Failure to pay attention to culture in certain parts of the world will

- Eliminate your company from any opportunity to sell
- Make your process of developing successful relations nearly impossible
- Reduce margins
- Reduce opportunities for tenured relationships and sustainability

There are numerous government, books, and Internet resources available to learn everything you need to know about cultural issues in global trade and how best to approach these areas for the best outturns.

Legal Differences

Most companies don't put enough resources into the legal requirements of global trade in their initial foreign expansion.

> *Getting the right legal advice*
> *can be one of the most*
> *important elements of foreign*
> *sales and customer management*

The typical occurrence is to seek legal help when the fire is burning and not proactively.

You don't want to "lawyer up" to such an extent that the initiative is made less valuable, but you want to consult with legal expertise proactively and responsibly to make sure your basic interests are being protected.

It is important that you obtain legal expertise

- That is knowledgeable in global trade
- Has expertise in international business
- Has a reach into local regulatory issues inside the countries you are going to sell into and provide customer service to

Regulations will vary from country to country and are not one size fits all. You must customize your legal considerations on a country-by-country basis. This will apply to areas such as, but not limited, to

- Import and export regulations
- Other government agency regulations, such as those from the Food and Drug Administration (FDA), U.S. Department of Agriculture (USDA), Center for Disease Control (CDC), Alcohol, Tobacco and Firearms (ATF), in those equivalent agencies in the countries you sell and service to
- Legal consequences, fines, penalties and restrictions
- Contract requirements
- Agency and distribution terms and agreements

An excellent source of international trade legal advice is a New York City attorney, Richard Furman with CMK, at rfurman@cmk.com, 646–625–4000, who I have dealt with for over 25 years.

Establishing a Foundation

Companies competing in global trade need to structure a solid platform or foundation for their business mantra, one that separates them from their competitors and creates a clear agenda that affords business differentiation and leverage. Competition is stiff on a global basis and in most verticals there are numerous players grabbing for both a finite and infinite market share.

Differentiation under a foundation of direction and mission is a must so a company can have the best opportunity to deliver the highest degree of customer service to its client base.

Time Differences

Recognize that the world can operate as much as a whole day ahead or behind and any number of hours in between.

This will modify how and when you communicate internationally and your expectation for responses.

When most personnel enter global trade they become frustrated in customer service deliveries as a result of their clients operating in time zones with a total reversal of operating hours.

Providing customer service in a global economy requires a significant restructuring of hours of operation and meeting customer needs 24/7/365!

Performance Standards

Quality and operating standards vary all over the world. It can be argued who has raised the bar of standards, but westernized countries like the

United States, Germany, and Switzerland have clearly been identified with guidelines that enhance quality and operating standards.

In global customer service, there is an imperative to adjust your standards to meet the local needs of where you are servicing in the world.

In certain countries where the expectation is to raise the bar, then you will succeed when this is accomplished.

In other countries where standards are lower, then it is critical to make an attempt to keep standards high as a product or service differentiator. But keeping competitive as well must also be factored in within certain markets.

the bar" of standards for the diverse markets they sell in.

This subject can be a little dicey and must be carefully maneuvered when making "standards" decisions as the long-term implications could be impacted, particularly in consideration of "corporate branding."

Language Differences

Language is the foundation of global trade and binds international customer service as one of the most important aspects of client relationships.

Thomas A. Cook

We are all familiar with the array of languages spoken in every county around the world and the various dialects within certain countries and regions in which we do business.

English is the primary language that most international businesspeople respond to on every continent.

Having said that, we all must be respectful of three issues:

1. That we should realize that speaking English and quality comprehension of English are two separate subjects. We have encountered numerous problems over the years where we thought the other party understood what we just agreed to. They even acknowledged it.

    But at the end of the day, they really did not comprehend what we said and that was later evidenced when a dispute surfaced.
2. Although English is the language of global trade, there are huge advantages when we can speak and understand the languages of the countries we provide customer service to.

I have witnessed time and time again the advantages and business leverages that can be obtained when there is an ability to speak the language of the country in which you are doing business.

Language skills are important and must not be lost in our educational and training programs.

3. Recognize that differences in language and interpretation will also impact how contracts and agreements are written that cross international borders.

Hence the important need for professional global and local legal representation in the countries we service.

Learn the basics of the languages of the countries in which you do business.

Payment Terms

Getting paid on global sales is a serious challenge. Offering terms makes you more competitive but also opens the door for additional risk.

The risk does not mean that you do not offer competitive terms, but it means that you must "manage" the risks to keep them minimal and to take measures to mitigate proactively.

Payment in advance is preferred but is not competitive. Letters of credit are traditional but come with risk, cost, and administration. Drafts ... time, sight and drawn are reasonable options.

On terms and open accounts are more competitive options that add potential risk into the export transaction.

Intellectual Property Rights

IPR in some countries is as protected as it is in the United States. In other countries, such as China, IPR protections are at a bare minimum and can pose significant exposures to the products and services we offer to Asian customers.

IPR is a very legitimate concern for any company selling and servicing in overseas markets. In some countries, such as, but not limited to, China, this can be a full-time endeavor.

IPR protections must be built into every marketing, business development, and customer service decision in certain foreign markets. Having legal expertise in IPR is of real value and can protect or offer some mitigation of a company's rights in various countries.

> Recognize that in some instances there are no protections for IPR. A risk with certainty that must be calculated into global expansion.

Transportation and Logistics

Moving freight globally creates a whole set of challenges with respect to distances, mode choices, risks, customs, documentation, and so on. This is covered throughout various sections in this book.

Logistics can be a huge expense in landed costs and can make the difference between being competitive or losing money on a transactional basis.

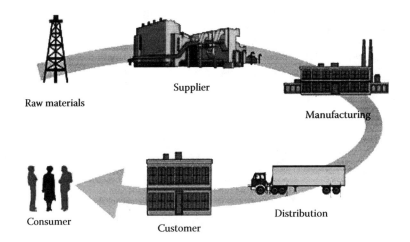

The global supply chain is operated via transportation modes in the science of logistics management. Over the past 25 years this expense has grown significantly as a component of costs of goods sold.

It has also become an integral management function in most companies and part of both strategic planning and tactical and operational functions.

Education and training in global logistics (AMANET.org and NIWT .org) has become increasingly important in providing high levels of customer service for international customers and has grown tenfold in the past 15 years.

Learning your transportation and logistics options is an important ingredient to being competitive in global customer service and expansion.

Customs Entry

One of the trickier challenges of providing global customer service is navigating the risks of "Customs" in all the countries in which we do business.

Customs utilizes dogs in the execution of their responsibilities.
Here puppies are being trained in the "art of strategic sniffing."

When goods, merchandise, and services pass through borders they must clear each country's customs authorities.

The United States customs department is the Customs and Border Protection (CBP). This name has been in place since 2002 after the events of 9/11, when "security" became a large component of customs responsibilities, not only in the United States, but globally as well.

Customs around the world has numerous responsibilities:

- To protect their country from people, goods, or services entering that may be illegal or harmful
- To make sure paperwork, documentation, and regulatory concerns are being met
- Collection and validation of documentation
- Managing security regulations
- Collection of duties and taxes such as value added tax (VAT) and general services tax (GST)
- IPR and gray market protections
- Front line on other government agencies that regulate energy, communications, agriculture, pharma, food, and so on

Managing "Customs" is a huge responsibility and also a big frustration for most personnel who engage with them directly. Failure to comply halts the supply chain from advancing as anticipated.

Larger companies have now created positions in *trade compliance management* that manage this responsibility as its own area of expertise and professional capabilities.

One such company, Dragonfly Global (dragonfly-international.net), specializes in trade compliance management, which can be a significant resource in your arsenal to manage customs responsibilities anywhere in the world.

Trade Compliance

As discussed previously, trade compliance management deals with customs issues but it actually is a much greater capability in most companies.

> Trade compliance is often viewed only as a "regulatory" issue ... but when utilized effectively can also impact the transactional processes in a business to make it more competitive.
>
> **Thomas A. Cook**

- Any customs issues for imports
- Any regulatory concerns in exports
- Manage other government agency requirements, such as in the United States (e.g., FDA, USDA, CDC, ATF, Department of Transportation [DOT])
- Manage landed cost modeling
- For public companies, deal with Sarbanes–Oxley Act of 2002 (SOX) concerns in the supply chain
- Manage free trade agreements
- Harmonized Tariff Schedule of the United States (HTSUS)
- Documentation, record keeping, origin data
- Drawback programs

Last Mile Delivery

When companies move freight internationally, the INCOTerms choice, FOB, DDP, and so on, will determine at what point in the supply chain the seller and buyer are each responsible for handling the freight.

For certain types of shipments, the buyer has an expectation that the seller or exporter will deliver the goods to the final point of utilization or to where it brings utilization or value.

This can be referred to as the "last mile delivery" and in INCOTerms this can be referred to as DDP or DAP, depending on to what extent it is utilized.

The seller would then need to have a service provider or logistics solution to be able to accommodate this need.

In some markets and countries, the last mile delivery is not an easy find, and for particular sizes of shipments, values, verticals, product nuances, and so on, this can be even more difficult.

Last mile delivery needs to be well thought out. Chapter 3 will discuss this in more detail.

Terrorism and Security

The events of 9/11 in the United States changed the world forever and in global supply chains made a huge impact on how companies sell and service companies in foreign markets.

Regulations and security protocols grew in mass and in complexity for companies servicing clients in foreign markets.

In every supply chain, it became necessary to

- Deal with new compliance, security, and terrorist regulations
- Add additional time, resources, and expense to goods moving internationally

- Raise the bar of how corporate staff navigated through supply chain responsibilities with respect to security and terrorism
- Train executives in new controls in security and terrorism
- Have companies enter security programs such as Customs-Trade Partnership Against Terrorism (C-TPAT), Authorized Economic Operator (AEO), and Partners in Protection (PIP)

Customs-Trade
Partnership Against Terrorism

The bottom line is that the events of 9/11 have caused corporations to manage their overseas sales and customer service entwined with security, compliance, and antiterrorist procedures that have added cost, SOPs, and process differentiators to the overall supply chain business model.

This is both a necessary evil and a security enhancement that adds to the overall antiterrorist efforts with regard to international commerce within the United States and throughout the world.

Regulatory

When we do business in the United States there are considerable regulations we have to contend with.

Many of these regulatory requirements follow us when we enter sales and customer service responsibilities on foreign shores.

Sometimes these regulatory issues are much less strict and sometimes significantly stricter. For sure they are different.

We have a basic responsibility in foreign sales and customer service to understand the regulatory requirements in the local country so we can effectively and easily sell to and service our clients' needs.

These regulatory needs may be governed in human resource issues, compliance concerns in pharma, food, cosmetics, customs, or in other regulated areas.

Many times the regulations mirror what happens in the United States, and many times it can be 180 degrees different.

C-TPAT is an important regulatory program!

INCOTerms

INCOTerms are an internationally recognized term of sale, presented by the International Chamber of Commerce (ICC) in Paris, France.

> There are currently 11 INCOTerms: Ex Works, FOB, FCA, FAS, CIF, CIP, CPT, CFR, DAP, DAT, and DDP.
>
> **ICC, Paris France**

The intent is to obtain census from countries belonging to the United Nations in "evening out" and "standardizing" terms of sale for goods and services crossing international borders.

This means that the FOB term in Germany would carry the same definition and shipping implications as the FOB term in China, or the DDP term in New York City would carry the same meaning for those in Sydney.

INCOTerms have changed and are updated approximately every 10 years. In the latest update in 2010, utilization of INCOTerms was expanded to include domestic shipping as well.

In some countries this works suitably, while in others such as the United States it does not.

INCOTerms determine a point in time that the responsibility and costs for a transaction transfer from a seller to a buyer (and internationally, from an exporter to an importer). This is covered in more detail in various chapters.

Terminos internacionales de comersio

Across-the-Globe Training

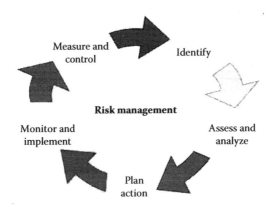

Risk management is a legitimate business process to protect company assets.

NIWT.org

Where does someone learn the skill sets of global trade and international customer service? The majority of personnel are trained on the job! If their instructor or mentor is doing it wrong, that process may continue until it causes great pain!

There is a definite need for training of the necessary skill sets of global trade and international business. Most institutions of higher learning view this subject from a broad view and strategic perspective.

The training need comes from a level that is more tactical and hands-on so execution of shipment activity can be at a purchasing, sales, and operational level.

The National Institute for World Trade (NIWT.org) is one such training institute, along with the American Management Association (AMANET

.org), who specialize in strategic training classes that help train corporate staff in those necessary skill sets.

Customer service is what differentiates one company from another. Training customer service personnel is therefore a critical component of maintaining and developing new clients, increased margins, and overall profitability.

Risk Management

The mindset that protects a company from adverse operating challenges is often referred to as "risk management." It is both an art and science that comprises how company executives view risk and chose one of four steps:

1. Ignore risk, roll the dice, and hope for the best!
2. Budget for risk and the financial consequence
3. Transfer risk to a third party
4. Be proactive and take steps to mitigate risk

The last two steps are usually followed, but many times after steps 1 and 2 have been followed, failure occurs and no one is happy with those consequences.

Risks to a company in global trade can be found in numerous areas that are all outlined in this chapter.

Central areas of concern are financial, liability, and property.

However, business risk in areas of strategic sales, purchasing, and operations can also be of concern and must be weighed in as areas of risk review, evaluation, and risk strategy.

Most companies build risk management in two areas as they mature into larger entities and expand globally:

- Build a risk management department with dedicated risk professionals managing these challenges
- Build a risk management mindset into all of critical management teams so that awareness and due diligence will pay back in efforts to recognize and mitigate risks in their business silos

E-Commerce

The majority of companies with consumer products and services have moved in a direction with E-commerce in their marketing, business development, and growth strategies.

Some companies have moved in a big way or 100% into the world of e-commerce.

E-commerce is gaining huge attraction in all markets around the world

E-commerce poses potential problems around the world where the supply chain infrastructure has not yet caught up with the requirements of e-commerce shipping needs.

E-commerce places demand in areas such as, but not limited to

- Last mile delivery
- Customs clearance
- Duty, tax, and VAT application
- Return shipments
- 24/7 customer service

In more westernized countries like the United States, Great Britain, and Germany there is a more matured process for e-commerce sales and customer service. In countries like Mexico, China, and Saudi Arabia, e-commerce is less matured and faces more difficult challenges.

This is covered in more detail in Chapter 3.

SUMMARY

The challenges as outlined in this chapter are vast, comprehensive, and daunting, but they are also manageable when identified, understood, and managed responsibly and proactively.

The balance of this book will revisit these risks and challenges and offer both strategic and tactical solutions.

> The goal as a company is to have customer service that is not just the best but legendary.
>
> **Sam Walton**
> *Founder of Wal-Mart*

2

Establishing a Robust and Aggressive Export Sales Strategy

One of the bright spots of President Obama's presidency was the Obama Export Initiative. This effort was successful in allowing America to compete in global markets more successfully and increase export sales opportunities.

Exports have a direct impact on our deficit reduction strategies and our overall financial and economic well-being.

An aggressive export strategy must integrate with a robust customer service platform, which is reviewed in this chapter.

WHY A COMPANY CREATES AN EXPORT STRATEGY

As a country we fully understand the importance of export strategy and development. It only works to our national status and sustainability.

Additionally, there is a greater belief that business between nations reduces the opportunities for serious conflict. I think our political relationship with China is a good example of serious differences that are mitigated by strong economic and business ties.

This chapter reviews from a company's perspective why you want exports as part of your business DNA!

Exports should be a critical component of any company's business model.

- Expands markets and reduces business risk
- Diversifies market reach
- Greater margin potential
- Opens new markets where other business advantages may be obtained

Expands Markets and Reduces Business Risk

The United States as a market is not infinite. In some verticals maximum penetration and opportunity have already peaked.

So where does a company grow and expand?

Exports are a very likely and viable option. While international has limitations in some aspects, it is infinite to some extent.

Think about all the countries around the world that have not been touched by your products and services.

The conclusion is that exports can easily expand your markets, sales, and growth opportunities.

When this happens is also has the benefit of reducing business risk. It does this because it allows your portfolio of sales development to be less dependent in one geographic area and spreads the risk to a larger market.

Therefore, export development can be considered a "risk management" strategy.

Developing a successful export strategy is a risk management principle
with numerous levels of benefit to a company's business model.

Diversifies Market Reach

The "diversification" that can take place in multiple markets helps balance out the risk of political, economic, and geophysical challenges that come into play every day or every year of every century in how business interacts from one country to another.

Diversification spreads both opportunity and risk into numerous markets. As one economy worsens, another grows.

- As one market loses population, another increases.
- As one market is hampered by political events, another market flourishes.
- As one market is devastated by serious geophysical events, another market has stability.

Floods can be devastating and in some countries happen like clockwork!

- As one market is consumed by earthquakes, floods, and tsunamis, another market is having the best weather of the last decade.
- As one market is going through hard economic times, another market is having its best stretch of financial prosperity.

There would not be too many economists not in favor of export expansion and all the benefits of that diversification opportunity.

American exports currently have a huge market share but the potential is much larger and can be very much developed further and expanded.

Some Truisms about American Exports

- American products and services are in high demand globally
- It is prestigious for foreign countries to have U.S.-based consumer products in their homes, on their bodies, or in their consumptions
- American "customer service" is by far the best in the world
- Exports from America in certain verticals can be competitive: *electronics, medical equipment, defense-related, pharma, aerospace, industrial products, agriculture, and fresh and processed foods* are but a few of these verticals with great export potential.

Greater Margin Potential

Since the mid-1970s, I have worked with over 1000 companies engaged in international business initiatives, expansion, and in customer service.

It is true that in some verticals, such as but not limited to fossil fuels, fashion, and retail, it is difficult for U.S.-based companies to compete internationally and earn higher than domestic margins. This is not true for the overall greater number of commodities we export and sell overseas.

In areas such as but not limited to aerospace, agriculture, high-end electronics, and medical products, we can be very competitive and earn higher margins overseas then we do on domestic sales.

The domestic market can attract more competition, some locally and some from foreign competition who value the U.S. consumer. The risks in the United States can sometimes be viewed as minimal, therefore attracting more and aggressive competitors.

Some sellers view exports as too risky and do not place any serious relevance on export opportunities.

That negative mindset then creates opportunity for those who entertain both the opportunity and risk. *The favorable consequence can be higher margins.*

Opens New Markets Where Other Business Advantages May Be Obtained

As a company expands into exports those relationships can create other advantages and opportunities.

A Tier 1 automotive industry supplier in Michigan that we worked with had developed an export strategy in the early 2000 period. This export activity created some interesting relationships in foreign markets.

One relationship was a small distributor in Netherlands. The relationship eventually became an acquisition. The Michigan company gaining this foothold in Europe added in funding and expanded the supplier to another eight countries, increasing sales starting from 800,000 USD to over 10,000,000 USD in a 9-year period.

This made what was originally an export client into a subsidiary that allowed it to take advantage of penetration into the euro market.

In another example, a California-based dairy farmer developed an export program to China.

That relationship grew from 500K sales per year to 2.5MM in a 3-year period of time.

When the California company was looking to find capital for a new processing facility, the Chinese buyer was a willing financier and became a private equity investor.

With its own money at stake that Chinese investor opened doors for the California company into other Asian markets where they had interests and influence.

Within a 10-year period, the California company's exports of 500K grew to over 20MM and spread from China to Korea, Cambodia, Thailand, Vietnam, Malaysia, and Indonesia.

Through that expansion it began to cultivate specific products that were of greater interest to Asian cuisine. This gave them significant competitive advantage that led not only to current growth and expansion, but increased margins from 7% to over 19%.

These margins were better than their U.S. sales, which due to competitive pressures saw them dwindle.

Necessary Components to Exporting

There are two basic components of export management and the accompanying customer service to make for successful trade.

INCOTerms and landed cost modeling are two areas that export companies need to pay attention to.

LANDED COST MODELING SOP EXAMPLE

Effective 1 January 2017, all divisions of corporate will utilize a landed cost calculator for import shipments in determining the "true and real" cost(s) to corporate when comparing vendor options in the decision making process.

It is critical that we comprehensively understand what our "total costs" are in making the decisions on where, what, and how much we buy from overseas or domestic suppliers.

- We also need to document this process in our product files, available for review upon request
- Following is an outline of what are landed costs as an overview in general, followed with some additional thoughts on specifically sourcing from China, where the majority of our import shipments originate
- This SOP concludes with a draft calculator that should be utilized as a guide for actually determining landed costs for your products

What Is Landed Cost?

Establishing *landed costs* for the products that a company handles can be difficult and convoluted. All businesses that import or export need to understand what the total cost of goods is for what they are buying or selling. In order to accurately calculate the landed cost, all factors beyond the obvious primary price must be considered. Calculating **landed cost** is critical in understanding what a product actually costs and therefore for what price it can be sold.

This impacts margin considerations, which are one of the most important aspects of managing a business in public and private markets.

A hallmark of excellent customer service in export markets is identifying and managing "landed costs." This helps a company make better decisions to gain competitive advantage and be of greater value to their international customers.

Understanding the components of landed cost and taking constructive steps to impact these components favorably will provide huge advantages from a customer service perspective.

Landed Cost Definition

Landed cost is the total cost of a product once it has arrived at the buyer's door. The list of components that are needed to determine landed costs include the original cost of the item, all brokerage and logistics fees, complete shipping costs, customs duties, tariffs, taxes, insurance, currency conversion, crating costs, and handling fees. Not all of these components are present in every shipment, but all that are must be considered as part of the landed cost.

Clearly it is advantageous to reduce the cost of each or any component of landed cost. Each one will allow the seller to lower the final selling price or increase the margin associated with that sale.

When considering the **landed cost or "true cost"** of any item that is shipped internationally there are components that need to be included. For instance, determining *harmonized system codes* (HS codes) or harmonized tariff system codes (HTS codes) is essential for over 98% of global trade. Once the HS code or HTS code is obtained, the required import duties and tax rates can be established. Accuracy of these harmonized codes is of significant importance as misclassification will result in incorrect tariff rates, incorrect duties, and eventually customs delays and fines. In those instances where customs delays and fines are levied, they will also need to be calculated into the landed cost model.

Global trade management, supply chain management, and international logistics have many moving parts. In this economic climate trade agreements are being forged and modified at a very high rate. *HTS codes* vary from place to place, the cost of fuel can drastically affect shipping costs, currency valuations ebb and flow constantly, and the list of variables goes on and on. Limiting the variables to a manageable few will streamline operations and keep overall cost structures as stable as possible.

Additional variables such as but not limited to quantity purchased, INCO term, insurance, inland freight, and storage/warehousing all impact landed costs, but are often not considered by purchasing and sourcing personnel at the time of product acquisition.

Controlling costs, ensuring timely deliveries, and customs compliance are serious issues that concern every international business. Landed cost is a significant component of all these concerns.

ADDITIONAL CONSIDERATIONS

How to Calculate Landed Cost When Importing from China

As an importer, *made in China* is a good choice for many products that can sell locally or online with a good profit. Although corporate purchases goods from all over the world and the diversity will continue to grow, China presents itself as our largest source of imported goods.

Making sure we are earning the correct margins on merchandise sales from China is a key responsibility of all purchasing and sourcing managers. Additionally, supply chain and logistics considerations must be contemplated, and therefore those corporate managers with these specific responsibilities must be considered as part of the landed cost model.

Congruently, corporate trade compliance consultants must be in the loop, as total costs will be impacted by various areas in import and export trade compliance issues, such as but not limited to vendor choices, INCOTerms, and HTS codes utilized.

> Establishing a "landed cost" model is not just important, it is essential.
>
> **NIWT.org**

But in fact, too many both *seasoned* and new-to-China buyers focus only on product purchase price and then get an ugly surprise when they have an accumulation of additional costs when the goods arrive in their destination country, which they didn't plan for in the budget or when margins were considered.

Finding a supplier and getting a quotation is just the first step. All buyers should calculate a landed cost of the product they are purchasing before actually importing it. *Do not go through the trouble of importing and then finding out you spent more than you can sell it for.*

This outline will help you study and understand the true cost of the product you are buying from China. Let's begin.

What Is Landed Cost?

Landed cost is the total cost of a product once it has arrived at the buyer's door.

This list of components that are needed to determine include *the original cost of the item, all brokerage and logistics fees, complete shipping costs, customs duties, tariffs, taxes, insurance, currency conversion, crating costs, and handling fees.*

Not all of these components are present in every shipment, but all that are must be considered part of the total cost.

You can check through the chart below:

	A	B	C	D	E	F	G	H	I	J	K	L	M
1	INCOTerms	Loading on truck	Export-customs declaration	Carriage to port of export	Unloading of truck in port of export	Loading charges in port of export	Carriage to port of import	Unloading charges in port of import	Loading on truck in port of import	Carriage to place of destination	Insurance	Import-customs clearance	Import taxes
2	EXW	Buyer	Buyer	Buyer	Buyer	Buyer	Buyer	Buyer	Buyer	Buyer	N/A	Buyer	Buyer
3	FCA	Seller	Seller	Seller	Buyer	Buyer	Buyer	Buyer	Buyer	Buyer	N/A	Buyer	Buyer
4	FAS	Seller	Seller	Seller	Seller	Buyer	Buyer	Buyer	Buyer	Buyer	N/A	Buyer	Buyer
5	FOB	Seller	Seller	Seller	Seller	Seller	Buyer	Buyer	Buyer	Buyer	N/A	Buyer	Buyer
6	CFR	Seller	Seller	Seller	Seller	Seller	Seller	Buyer	Buyer	Buyer	N/A	Buyer	Buyer
7	CIF	Seller	Seller	Seller	Seller	Seller	Seller	Buyer	Buyer	Buyer	Seller	Buyer	Buyer
8	DAT	Seller	Seller	Seller	Seller	Seller	Seller	Seller	Seller	Buyer	N/A	Buyer	Buyer
9	DAP	Seller	Seller	Seller	Seller	Seller	Seller	Seller	Seller	Seller	N/A	Buyer	Buyer
10	CPT	Seller	Seller	Seller	Seller	Seller	Seller	Seller	Seller	Seller	N/A	Buyer	Buyer
11	CIP	Seller	Seller	Seller	Seller	Seller	Seller	Seller	Seller	Seller	Seller	Buyer	Buyer
12	DDP	Seller	Seller	Seller	Seller	Seller	Seller	Seller	Seller	Seller	N/A	Seller	Seller

INCOTerms 2010

The INCOTerms rules are intended primarily to clearly communicate the tasks, costs, and risks associated with the transportation and delivery of goods. As you can see, the table shows several fees. Other tables may include the point in time where risk and cost pass between a seller and a buyer.

Of course you can choose DDP. In this case, you don't need to do any calculation by yourself as the seller will provide you with a single cost to get it to your door. That said, DDP can be a more costly term under which to purchase as the seller is going to make certain his or her landed cost includes all potential variables and then some. In many instances, choosing DDP is the most expensive method of purchasing.

That's why most importers will choose FOB, which means that you let the supplier deliver the cargo to the outbound gateway, border crossing, port or airport and you'll take it from there. Imports from China are typically purchased on a FOB or FCA basis.

At that point, you can handle the rest of the process by working together with your international transportation provider, customhouse broker, and/or your freight forwarder.

As an example, there are many variables involved, so use the following as a guide:

- **Cost of goods:** $ variable depending on unit price and quantity.
- **Import assistance company:** $ variable depending on level of service.
- **Freight:** $ variable, depending on volume, ports of exit/entry, time of year, freight company used, and so on. Allow $2000–$5000.
- **Duty:** $ variable percentage of the value customs put on your goods.
- **Tax** (goods and services tax or value-added tax): $ variable percentage of (the customs value of cost of goods + freight + insurance + customs duty).
- **Insurance.**
- **Inland freight.**
- **Other:** This would include Customs clearance, document fees, wharf charges, and so on. Allow another 3% on top of everything else.

So let's just move forward to the most complex part.

IMPORT CUSTOMS DUTIES AND TAXES

One common mistake here is to ask the supplier in China to confirm the taxes and duties in the destination market. Suppliers may not be knowledgeable about how your government would classify the given product and what regulations apply.

U.S. Customs (CBP) regulations holds the importer of record fully responsible for the accuracy of an HTS classification.

Before finding the tariff amount for a particular product, you need to identify the harmonized tariff schedule number for their product.

1. Find the HS Code of Your Products

HS codes (harmonized commodity description and coding system) are part of an international classification system that simplifies the process for customs to locate the specific product among thousands of catalogued numbers and associates an imported product category with a specific import duty rate.

Please note: HS code is also referred to as *tariff codes, customs codes, harmonized codes, export codes, import codes, and harmonized commodity description and coding system codes.* So never get confused. When there's a code representing the product, that's the HS code.

HS codes can vary depending on the country. The code that your supplier provided for you is usually just the beginning. However, using the supplier's first four- to six-digit numbers can assist in providing a hint or clue as to where to find the correct code. Classification requires the review of general notes, section notes, chapter notes, and explanatory notes to ascertain the most accurate code.

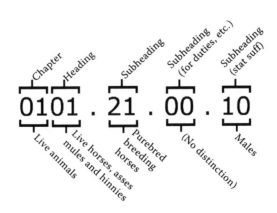

Ideally and to ensure compliance with import regulations, the purchaser should be providing the supplier with the HS code and requesting the HS code be listed on the supplier's commercial invoice. Customs duties and taxes will be calculated by HS code for each product and the declared value (see #2 below) on the commercial invoice.

Knowing the right code of your product is of central importance to your importing process. Without it or using an incorrect code may not only delay customs clearance but could also incur unexpected costs.

2. Declared Value

Customs duties and taxes are percentages calculated based on the customs value. The customs value is based on the declared value, which in turn is stated on the commercial invoice—a document issued by the supplier that is generally used as the basis for customs clearance.

In the United States, the FOB purchase value is what is typically the declared value to U.S. Customs (CBP). While the United States uses the FOB value as the basis for determining valuation, it is important to keep in mind that the transaction value is not always an acceptable method of valuation in the United States and depends on the circumstances of the transaction.

Other countries will have their own variation on what constitutes the correct value to be declared and many times it is a cost, insurance, freight (CIF) value plus other factors. Therefore, it is necessary to find a good customs broker in the destination country to best sort through this crucial element of the customs clearance process.

Duty/Tax Free Amount (de minimis Value)

The de minimis value of the destination country is the declared value of your shipment below which duty and tax will not apply. This means that if you are importing a shipment with a total declared value less than this amount, duty and tax do not apply (certain products may be subject to other types of fees or taxes, such as alcohol and tobacco).

Certain countries have a separate threshold. The list below provides some data from publicly available sources or our practical experiences. We accept that it may not be perfectly accurate or up to date.

- Australia: 1000 AUD
- Canada: 20 CAD

- Europe: 22 EUR
- Japan: 130 USD
- New Zealand: 308 USD (including freight)
- Russia: 10,000 RUB
- Singapore: 307 USD
- South America: 50 USD
- United Kingdom: 15 GBP
- United States: 200 USD

Please note: It's always the importer's responsibility to ensure that the correct declared value is stated on the commercial invoice. This responsibility cannot be shifted to the overseas/foreign supplier.

3. Import Customs Duties

Duty

A duty is a kind of tax, often associated with customs, levied by a state on the import or export of goods in international trade. A duty levied on goods being imported is referred to as an import duty. For the purposes of this book, when duty is mentioned it is referring to all import customs duties.

A free tool online that can provide some assistance can be found at http://www.importcalculator.com/.

- Almost all countries have three levels of duties for origin countries. Below is a screenshot from *Harmonized Tariff Schedule of the United States.*

General	Rates of Duty 1 Special	2
6.7%	Free (A, AU, B, BH, CA, CL, CO, E, IL, JO, KR, MA, MX, OM, P, PA, PE, SG)	90%
4.4%	Free (A, AU, B, BH, CA, CL, CO, E, IL, JO, KR, MA, MX, OM, P, PA, PE, SG)	35%

- Imports from most countries are dutiable at the normal trade relations rates under the General header in Column 1.
- Goods from countries that do not have normal trade relations with the United States are dutiable at the full rates in Column 2.
- Goods from some countries enjoy duty-free status. They are shown under the Special header in Column 1 of the tariff schedule.

You can take the three different rates as most loved (1), most hated (2), and others (general).

The first column (general) is referred to as the "Most Favored Nation," and China is considered a "Most Favored Nation" by most countries. The general notes of the harmonized tariff schedule will indicate which countries are considered Most Favored, Special, and Column 2 countries.

- Between China and some countries, there are preferential duty treatment programs. The document required to accompany these shipments is called a certificate of origin.
  - Certificate of origin form for China-Chile FTA (Form F)
  - Form for the Free Trade Agreement between the Government of China and the Government of New Zealand (Form N)
  - Certificate of origin China-Pakistan FTA (Form P)
  - Certificate of origin Asia-Pacific Trade Agreement (Form B)
  - Asian-China free trade area preferential tariff certificate of origin (Form E)

Duty Calculation

Duty is calculated on the harmonized tariff number and country of origin of the imported item. Some products may enter duty-free even without a preferential tariff treatment program between the country of origin and the country of import. On the other side of the spectrum, some products may have an even higher tariff rate applied if that product being imported is considered to be originating in a country that is "dumping" foreign-made products into the importing country and having an adverse reaction on the domestic market. This may also be found when a foreign government is providing assistance in the form of a subsidy to a foreign manufacturer to enable that manufacturer to sell their product at a reduced fee.

Example: An European Union (EU) importer intends to import women's knit t-shirts (HTS #6106.9000.20) from China.

EU member states have the same customs duty rates on products imported from non-EU countries. An importer only pays customs once, for products imported from China. Custom duties are not added to products sold within the EU. Thus, your Spanish and German customers won't need to pay customs on products that have already entered EU territory.

- Go to http://www.htscode.org/and type in "T-shirt" and search, or just type in "610690." You can try both reverse searches to make sure the HTS code is correct.
- Go to http://ec.europa.eu/taxation_customs/dds2/taric/taric_con sultation.jsp and fill in the "Goods code" and "Country of origin," which are 610690 and China – CN, respectively. Then dig to the final 12%.

  Below is a list of common products and their respective duty rate to EU from China:
  - Wristwatches: 4.5%
  - Tablet PC: 0%
  - Solar panels: 0%
  - Electric bikes: 6%
  - LED bulb lights: 4.7%
  - Peanuts: 12.8%

As previously mentioned there are other types of duties.

For example, if you are an importer in the United States, you are responsible for knowing that your goods from China are subject to antidumping duties (ADDs) or countervailing duties (CVDs). If so, then your customs declaration must include the corresponding type of import duties imposed.

Some ADD or CVD rates may be assessed at 100% of the value of the goods or even higher.

4. Import Taxes

Value-Added Tax (VAT)

A value-added tax (VAT) is a form of consumption tax. From the perspective of the buyer, it is a tax added to the purchase price. From the perspective of the seller, it is a tax only on the value added to a product, material, or service, from an accounting point of view, by a specific stage of the product's manufacture or distribution.

In the EU, for example, different member states have different VAT rates. However, the standard VAT rate applies to most consumer and industrial products imported from China.

Please note: The VAT added on the imports can be offset against the VAT added on sales.

Goods and Services Tax

Goods and services tax (GST) applies to most products imported to Australia, which is 10% on most goods and services transactions. GST is levied on most transactions in the production process, but is refunded to all parties in the chain of production other than the final consumer.

5. Insurance

Cargo insurance will also be a factor in landed cost. Many companies insure their freight through a master cargo insurance policy. This protects merchandise on an "all risk" "warehouse to warehouse" basis. The person in the company responsible for risk management will be most familiar with the particulars of the insurance policy, including terms and conditions, as well as the pricing of the policy.

For landed cost calculation purposes utilize 10/$100 of insured value. If a purchase is valued at $50,000 USD, then the insurance cost is calculated at 50,000 divided by 100 × .10 = $50 USD.

Insurance for imports and exports is often misunderstood. Seek out professional guidance to make sure the risk of physical loss or damage is assessed and the proper insurance protection is in place to minimize financial risk.

6. Inland Freight

Our merchandise will typically arrive at an ocean port, airport, or at the border. It will then move from that point to our final destination somewhere in the United States at a point of sale, value, or utilization.

That inland freight cost must be obtained from our international transportation provider and included in the landed cost model.

Landed Cost Calculator

Category Cost(s)
FOB/FCA cost of merchandise
Pickup at supplier
Inland transportation to a port or airport
Origin terminal and port fees
Export licensing, documentation, and duties
Ocean, air, or truck international freight
Import clearance, documentation, and handling
Duties, taxes, VAT/GST
Terminal and port fees at destination
Customs review
Harbor maintenance fees
Cargo insurance
Inland transportation to importer's location
Storage/warehousing/distribution

Landed Cost Summary

Protecting our profits and growing our business are key responsibilities of everyone involved in sourcing, purchasing, merchandising, logistics, or supply chain.

Making sure we are aware of all our costs, then applying sound practice to lower or costs and risks are all primary responsibilities.

Understanding landed cost modeling is necessary to control margins and accomplish our corporate goals.

Reprinted from *American Shipper Magazine*, April 2016

The Bottom Line with Tom Cook

Landed cost in global trade

Establishing landed costs for the products that a company handles can be difficult and convoluted. All businesses that import or export need to understand what the total cost of goods is for what they are buying or selling. In order to accurately calculate the landed cost, all factors beyond the obvious primary price must be considered. Calculating landed cost is critical in understanding what a product actually costs and, therefore, what it can be sold for.

Landed cost definition

Landed cost is the total cost of a product once it has arrived at the buyer's door. This list of components that are needed to determine landed costs include the original price of the item (converted to U.S. dollars), all customs brokerage and handling charges, complete freight and shipping costs, customs duties, tariffs, taxes, insurance, packaging costs, and surcharges.

The calculation and model for landed cost must be customized to the variables for imports, the accompanying table can be used, recognizing that specific nuances in each supply chain might modify how this list would appear.

The choice of INCOTerm will be a major factor in how costs, responsibilities and risks are distributed between the seller and buyer. It is critical that both parties when agreeing to the use of an INCOTerm that they understand the risks and costs.

Importers into the United States by ocean freight typically buy F.O.B. outbound gateway. In China this might be written as F.O.B. Shanghai.

This means the buyer will assume all risks and costs once the goods are placed onboard the oceangoing vessel in the port of export from overseas. The key words being "risks and costs."

Marine insurance, when thoroughly written offers "all risk," "warehouse-to-ware house" coverage for the buyer at specific terms and a rate of premium to be agreed.

The buyer must take a few steps to impact landed costs:

- Use comprehensive freight forwarders, customs brokers and professional service providers that have expertise and can lend value in the global supply chain.
- Pay attention to the choice of INCOTerm. Many choices give you control over various aspects of the supply chain where you can impact cost.
- Review each line item in the landed cost model to determine where costs can be reduced.
- Mode of transportation will impact landed costs. Many times air freight is used, when ocean freight could be a less expensive option.
- Inland freight expenses can be included in the ocean freight, where there is an opportunity to leverage the larger ocean freight spend to obtain a better inland freight cost.
- Utilization of technology and reducing "paper" in the transaction can reduce ISF, customs clearance and handling charges when automation replaces repetitive human handling of import and export documentation.
- When freight does not have to be consolidated or deconsolidated and can be shipped in units direct from suppler to point of end use, will also reduce costs.
- Negotiating away in a soft freight market with surcharges such as PSS, GRIs, and BAF will also impact landed costs favorably.

- By leveraging your spend with a minimum number of service providers and carriers will place a focus on a smaller group of "partners" that will maximize the opportunity to obtain a better deal.
- Develop a "partnership" mentality with all your service providers and carriers. Favor tenured relationships and work as a "team" in your supply chain. Loyalty and a working mindset will have true rewards in lieu of short-term benefits.

Another huge area that is impacting landed costs is the use of trade programs, such as free trade agreements, foreign trade zones and bonded warehouses, which can substantially lower and impact the cost of buying, selling and shipping goods. A subject for the next Bottom Line.

Just understand that studying landed cost and the variables, and then applying sound cost reduction principles, can make your supply chain operate more competitively.

Cook is a seasoned global supply chain professional, author of 19 books on global trade and managing director of Blue Tiger International. He can be reached at tomcook@bluetigerintl.com.

Landed cost variables

- **Purchase price of goods**—variable depending on unit price and quantity (converted to U.S. dollars).
- **Buying Agents**—variable depending on level of service.
- **Consolidation**—securing LCL shipments into larger shipments and coordinating freight from several suppliers.
- **Transportation**—variable, depending upon choice of mode, carrier, freight rate negotiation and surcharges.
- **Duty**—variable percentage of the value Customs put on your goods, typically origin and HTS number factored.
- **Tax** (Goods and Services Tax or Value Added Tax)—dollar variable percentage of (the Customs value of cost of goods plus freight, plus insurance, plus Customs duty).
- **Insurance Charges**, typically referred to as cargo insurance.
- **Customs Clearance**, ISF, etc.
- **Storage and deconsolidation**.
- **Inland Freight**—from inbound gateway to final destination.
- **Demurrage**—if applicable when potential delays occur.

UNDERSTANDING THE IMPORTANCE OF INCOTerms

INCOTerms are among the most important comprehensions in global trade and customer service management. For export responsibilities it is imperative that you grasp a basic understanding of INCOTerms.

The following outline is an excellent primer for a good foundation and more importantly for execution of your customer service responsibilities in international business.

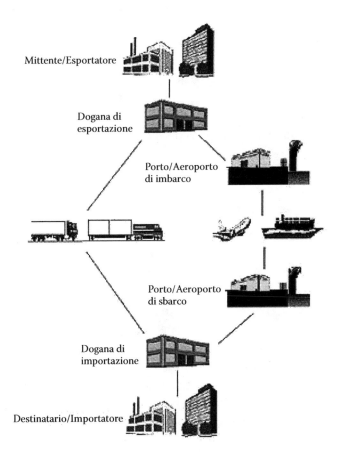

Mittente/Esportatore

Dogana di esportazione

Porto/Aeroporto di imbarco

Porto/Aeroporto di sbarco

Dogana di importazione

Destinatario/Importatore

Moving freight from origin to destination requires a comprehensive understanding of INCOTerms.

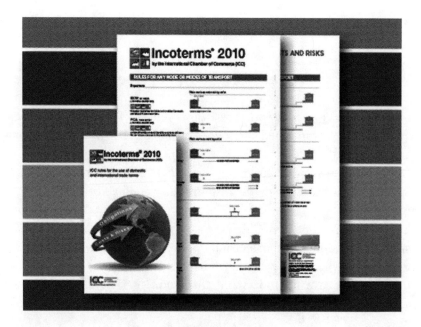

INCOTerms are governed by the ICC in Paris, France (ICCWBO.org). It provides an excellent resource and training options.

The best concept in understanding INCOTerms is that it is a

- Point in Time and Trade …
  - Responsibility
  - Liability

Transfers between a

- Seller <-> Buyer
- Importer <-> Exporter

Costs and Risks—Are the primary areas covered by INCOTerms. We tend to make it more complicated, but it does not need to be. This is oversimplified, but correctly stated.

INCOTerms are a point in time and trade between a seller and a buyer in international business where the responsibility and liability pass between the parties.

The original intent of INCOTerms was to provide a uniform and consistent reference point for exporters and importers to utilize when determining when and where this exchange took place.

It was imperative to understand this point in time and trade as it attempted to provide a reference point in defining costs and risks to both parties.

As INCOTerms evolved through the years to the current 2010 edition, these points are still valid, although the structure, options, and meanings have changed.

In the past and up to today, understanding these costs would impact the decision making regarding various aspects of the transaction, such as but not limited to price, logistics, payment options, title transfer, and so on.

Managing these decisions eventually impacts a company's ability to make the trade and transactions profitable, competitive, and ultimately, sustainable.

The focus of the balance of this chapter is to provide how INCOTerms relates to all these peripheral areas of an international business relationship so one stays out of trouble, but more importantly, how to best leverage options that place your company in the most competitive arena.

When INCOTerms became updated in 2010, this author came to a much greater awareness that they are not an "end-all" to an international commercial transaction, but rather a starting point or reference point for the seller and buyer to utilize to manage cost and risk.

INCOTerms are a serious issue. I always advice that they must be read in a "**detailed way.**" What I mean is that you have to read the prologue, opening pages, definitions, and so forth before you read the leading INCOTerms reference page. Then you must continue to read the INCOTerms following pages to obtain full details, intent and use of.

It is imperative to read the INCOTerms book in a focused and disciplined way. It is not a single page. It is the sum of all the pages, words, explanations, and intents that can only be grasped by thorough and comprehensive reading, analysis, and contemplation.

I have also found that you may need to read it several times, maybe 10 times before you get it. I also have learned about specific INCOTerms by reading about other terms where references are made back and forth that make gray areas a little clearer.

There are wide misnomers about INCOTerms. Most companies and global personnel do not know how to navigate the INCOTerms successfully. In fact, most companies and personnel only begin to grasp the full scope and meaning of INCOTerms when a problem has arisen. Companies that are proactive in understanding the INCOTerms can master the INCOTerms and global trade as well.

Common misnomers of INCOTerms include:

- *They have some legal bearing in most countries*
- *They are a complete global transaction from sale through to payment and defining aspect of a sale or purchase*
- *They calculate when "title or ownership" transfers between the parties*
- *They have merit in domestic transportation*
- *While INCOTerms attempt to identify "risk" they clearly regulate insurance responsibilities*
- *INCOTerms identifies what parties are responsible for trade compliance responsibilities to the government agencies regulating the export/import transaction*
- *INCOTerms by default define origin and delivery points*
- *They provide a clear costing model to both the seller and buyer*
- *FOB has utilization in our domestic business model in all countries*

All these examples demonstrate areas in which INCOTerms are thought to be a solution, but more likely is really only a "reference point" and a lot more has to be considered and ultimately done to protect cost and risk to both parties!

When we say "done" above, we mean actions taken by both or either party in how the transaction is constructed and agreed to, by contract (typically sales or purchase order).

Both parties have numerous options on how the deal is constructed. How they construct the deal will truly determine costs and risks.

This book through the balance of the chapters will provide the "blueprint" to see how best we elect those options that puts our company in the most leveraged, competitive scenario.

In exports typically sales or customer service personnel take leads to an eventual export order. In imports, typically purchasing takes the lead on purchase orders.

It is at that time in the process of the supply chain that this critical element of INCOTerms comes into play.

INCOTerms are often a very misunderstood aspect of trade. Many individuals supported by company protocols relate INCOTerms to insurance, freight, transfer of title, ownership, and revenue recognition, when in fact while INCOTerms are connected to all these issues, with a dotted line, they are very much "independent" functions that impact sales and purchase agreements very differently.

When we create a purchase order or a sales agreement there are a number of issues which are connected that need to be analyzed.

Those issues are not limited to, but primarily are

- Terms of sale
- Terms of payment
- How freight is handled
- How insurance and risk is managed
- When and how title or ownership is transferred
- How and when "revenue" gets recognized
- Who is responsible for trade compliance issues
- Legal jurisdiction
- How disputes are settled
- How company tax issues (IRS or equivalent) are mitigated
- Packaging, marking, and labeling
- Intellectual property rights

The connection between all these issues is that they impact cost and risk for the buyer and seller, importer and exporter, and potentially all the parties engaged in the transaction.

They impact the ultimate profit for the transaction and in the long term set the stage for future potential or demise.

Additionally, we recognize that INCOTerms both by design and default are really only a reference point in an international transaction. The seller and buyer must look at the nuances of the transaction and write their contractual agreements to mirror these nuances and make a best attempt to proactively "handle" the matter within the written language of the documentation.

That means that INCOTerms are not necessarily an "end-all" but only a starting point for gaining common ground in a trade or transaction. The final agreement is supposed to reflect the INCOTerms plus a clearer indication of what else would need to be agreed to. Here is a summary of some of those contractual issues, which are covered in more detail throughout the following chapters in this book.

INCOTerms 101: Demystifying the Misnomers!

An international contract of sale or purchase has several points connected to one another and all are related to the choice of INCOTerms, but at the end of the day, are all separate and distinct concerns of global trade in contract law. They are as follows.

Terms of Sale

The terms of sale are the INCOTerms where risk and costs are distinguished as a "point in time" where that transfer occurs between the seller (the exporter) and the buyer (the importer). Ex Works, FOB, CIF, and DDP are the most common terms utilized in global trade.

The INCOTerms only outline responsibility and liability boundaries between sellers and buyers (exporters and importers) as a standard of cost and risk in a contractual obligation typically found in sales or purchase orders.

INCOTerms are set by choice, by default, or by trade practice. In any method they become part of the agreement between two or more parties that deal with a multitude of issues involved with logistics, insurance, and the passage of risk and costs.

Terms of Payment

How money is transferred between the buyer and the seller is how we determine payment methods, drafts, letters of credit (L/Cs), consignment, and so on. This is irrelevant to what INCOTerms are utilized. But having said that, in Chapter 5 we will see how payment will impact risk to an exporter well beyond the INCOTerms utilized.

How Freight Is Managed

Freight is addressed in the INCOTerms but because we can make other arrangements in the actual sales or purchase agreement we will tend to impact ultimately how freight is handled in an international transaction.

For example, we can always make freight charges prepaid or collect. We can always amend the INCOTerms to include loading, movement to a forwarder, and so on.

How Insurance and Risk Is Managed

Risk is determined by the INCOTerms chosen. But having said that, when other parameters are raised, how a contract is ultimately structured can impact how risk is perceived and realized to either the seller or the buyer.

In a FOB export sale where the buyer has payment terms after the goods arrive at their facility overseas, the goods are lost or damaged and the customer refuses to make payment in full, citing the some of the goods arrived lost or damaged.

The exporter now has a risk of loss or damage after delivery on board an ocean-going vessel, contrary to the intent of the INCOTerms FOB because they have not yet received payment.

When and How Title or Ownership Is Transferred

Title is not controlled by INCOTerms. It has to be addressed elsewhere in the contract of sale or purchase. We strongly recommend that "title" or "ownership" not be passed to the buyer until payment in full has been received against the seller's performance to deliver.

How and When "Revenue" Gets Recognized

It is important to completely understand the laws in the countries you ship to and from in terms of how revenue regulations are applied. The consequences could be severe when revenue recognition is done incorrectly.

Revenue recognition is different in every country and the controlling body that impacts accounting regulations, whether we are discussing the Internal Revenue Service, Securities and Exchange Commission, China QI, EU, or HM Revenue, to name a few governing bodies.

The issue gets more convoluted for related companies shipping internationally between common parties.

Who Is Responsible for Trade Compliance Issues

INCOTerms do state which party to the transaction is responsible for either export or import formalities. This could be part of the overall trade compliance responsibilities, which differ greatly from one country to another.

The events of 9/11 have greatly impacted the trade compliance and security guidelines for shipping to and from the United States.

The 2010 INCOTerms edition was greatly enhanced when it included trade compliance and security initiatives into its definitions.

More specifically, this relates to the importer's security filing (ISF) for inbound freight into the United States from overseas origins. It requires the seller in the foreign country of origin to provide information to the buyer in the United States what they transmitted to U.S. Customs prior to the goods being loaded on board the ocean-going vessel destined for a U.S. port of entry.

The new INCOTerms now includes these security concerns as part of a seller's or buyer's responsibility in the transaction.

Legal Jurisdiction

All contracts should have a provision not influenced by the choice of INCOTerms that outlines what jurisdiction(s) the contract is written in and what regulatory bodies are involved in managing the contractual obligations. Examples include: covered under the laws of Republic of Egypt, the United States, United Kingdom, and People's Republic of China.

How Disputes Are Settled

All contracts need to have provisions on where disputes will be settled. This will usually tie into the jurisdiction, but not necessarily so. For example, you may have a contract between a Belgian and an Italian company, but have contractual wording that settles disputes in arbitration in Zurich, Switzerland.

Another example may be a contract for shipments being exported from France to Japan, with both parties agreeing in the event of a dispute arising that disputes will be settled in Japan.

Settlement is a negotiated issue that eventually both parties must agree on and then commit to writing as part of their sales or purchase contract/agreement.

This area has no direct relationship to the INCOTerms utilized.

How Company Tax Issues (IRS or Equivalent) Are Mitigated

Taxes are determined typically by the country or governing body where the transaction is occurring. If they become part of a sale or purchase contract there would be a clause referring to who has the obligation to pay VAT, GST, and/or other related charges.

There are also tax issues relating to how a government taxes a company for profits, such as the IRS in the United States, which is potentially impacted by how sales and purchases are structured inclusive of the use of INCOTerms.

European countries have provisions for obtaining VAT refunds.

While the INCOTerms utilized addresses this in their intent to provide cost and risk to a certain point in time, most companies have learned from experience that they are better off in most contracts to outline in detail who is responsible for any taxes or duties, particularly those where refunds may be available, such as with VAT and GST.

Tax issues in global trade are typically complex with lots of interpretation and leeway as to how the regulations apply.

It is critical to obtain tax assistance from external professionals such as lawyers, accountants, and consultants.

A decision on one end of a transaction on what INCOTerms to utilize may impact the tax implications for the other party, making collaboration between sellers and buyers imperative.

Packaging, Marking, and Labeling

While packing, marking, and labeling are discussed in INCOTerms, the issue is not made as clear as it should be. First, INCOTerms do not address stowage or handling of goods. They do mention packing to comply with any requirements under the contract of sale and those fit for transportation, but neither is defined.

Parties to the contract of sale or purchase need to outline in detail exactly what the shipper needs to do to properly pack, mark, and label the goods for transit and to comply with customs regulations on marking, as well as packaging for market access.

When transport conveyances are utilized such as ocean and air containers, it is important to add guidance and instruction on cargo stowage, blocking, and bracing.

Intellectual Property Rights

The protection of patents, trademarks, and other proprietary rights is not addressed by INCOTerms. It is necessary for those entering the sales or purchase agreement to address these concerns very specifically.

Companies engaged in global trade also must be aware of how local governments deal with IPR issues and how they support the protection of IPR matters for foreign entities doing business in their country.

This is covered in more detail in Chapter 5 and is another important component of global trade that is not addressed by INCOTerms.

What We Need to Know about INCOTerms 2010

INCOTerms 2010 is defined by 11 rules reducing the previously utilized 13 rules in INCOTerms 2000.

The 2010 edition introduced two new rules, "Delivered at Terminal" (DAT) and "Delivered at Place" (DAP), which replace four rules of the prior version "Delivered at Frontier" (DAF), "Delivered Ex Ship" (DES), "Delivered Ex Quay" (DEQ), and "Delivered Duty Unpaid" (DDU).

In the 2000 edition, the rules were divided into four categories (E, F, C, and D), but the new 11 predefined terms of INCOTerms 2010 are subdivided into two categories based only on method of delivery. The larger group of seven rules applies regardless of the method of transport, with the smaller group of four being applicable only to sales that solely involve transportation over water.

Rules for Any Mode(s) of Transport

The seven rules defined by INCOTerms 2010 for any mode(s) of transportation are in summary form below.

Ex Works (EXW): Named Place of Delivery

The seller makes the goods available at its premises. This term places the maximum obligation on the buyer and minimum obligations on the seller. The Ex Works term is often used when making an initial quotation for the sale of goods without any costs included. EXW means that a seller has the goods ready for collection at his or her premises (works, factory, warehouse, plant) on the date agreed upon. The buyer pays all transportation costs and also bears the risks for bringing the goods to their final destination. The seller doesn't load the goods on collecting vehicles and doesn't clear them for export. If the seller does load the goods, he or she does so at buyer's risk and cost. If parties wish the seller to be responsible for the loading of the goods on departure and to bear the risk and all costs of such loading, this must be made clear by adding explicit wording to this effect in the contract of sale.

Free Carrier (FCA): Named Place of Delivery

The seller hands over the goods, cleared for export, into the disposal of the first carrier (named by the buyer) at the named place. The seller pays for carriage to the named point of delivery and risk passes when the goods are handed over to the first carrier.

Carriage Paid to (CPT): Named Place of Destination

The seller pays for carriage to the named place of destination. Risk transfers to buyer upon handing goods over to the first carrier.

Carriage and Insurance Paid to (CIP): Named Place of Destination

The containerized transport/multimodal equivalent of CIF. The seller pays for carriage and insurance to the named place of destination, but risk passes when the goods are handed over to the first carrier.

Delivered at Terminal (DAT): Named Terminal at Port or Place of Destination

The seller pays for carriage to the terminal, except for costs related to import clearance, and assumes all risks up to the point that the goods are unloaded at the terminal.

Delivered at Place (DAP): Named Place of Destination

The seller pays for carriage to the named place, except for costs related to import clearance, and assumes all risks prior to the point that the goods are ready for unloading by the buyer.

Delivered Duty Paid (DDP): Named Place of Destination

The seller is responsible for delivering the goods to the named place in the country of the buyer and pays all costs in bringing the goods to the destination, including import duties and taxes. This term places the maximum obligations on the seller and minimum obligations on the buyer.

Rules for Sea and Inland Waterway Transport

The four rules defined by INCOTerms 2010 for international trade where transportation is entirely conducted by water are

Free Alongside Ship FAS: Named Port of Shipment

The seller must place the goods alongside the ship at the named port and clear the goods for export. Suitable only for maritime transport but not for multimodal sea transport in *containers* (see INCOTerms 2010, ICC publication 715). This term is typically used for break bulk, heavy-lift, or bulk liquid cargoes.

Free on Board (FOB) Named Port of Shipment

The seller must load the goods on board the vessel nominated by the buyer. Cost and risk are passed from seller to buyer when the goods are actually on board of the vessel. The seller must clear the goods for export. The term is applicable for maritime and inland waterway transport only but not for multimodal sea transport in containers (see INCOTerms 2010, ICC publication 715). The buyer must instruct the seller about the details of the vessel and the port where the goods are to be loaded, and there is no reference to, or provision for, the use of a carrier or forwarder.

Cost and Freight (CFR): Named Port of Destination

The seller must pay the costs and freight to bring the goods to the port of destination. However, risk is transferred to the buyer once the goods are loaded on the vessel. Maritime transport only and insurance for the goods is not included. This term was formerly known as C&F.

Cost, Insurance, and Freight CIF: Named Port of Destination

Exactly the same as CFR except that the seller must in addition procure and pay for the insurance. Maritime transport only.

The four terms that were eliminated the 2000 edition of INCOTerms:

- Delivered at Frontier (DAF)
- Delivered Ex Ship (DES)
- Delivered Ex Quay (DEQ)
- Delivered Duty Unpaid (DDU)

DAF, DES, and DEQ were terms that were rarely utilized and reflect terms that had a place in international trade years ago, when freight was moved differently.

DDU, however, was a term that had great use and a real value in global trade transactions. It has been replaced by the Delivered at Place (DAP).

The switch from DDU to DAP is an ongoing process for a lot of companies who operate globally. In Chapter 3 when we look at best practices we will review how best to manage these changes and incorporate them into supply chain management.

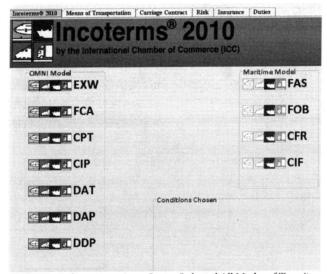

INCOTerms has two sections: Ocean Only and All Modes of Transit

Various Modes of Transit

A good change by the drafting committee afforded the new edition to be set into two sections.

The INCOTerms 2010 is structured into these two sections:

- Those for sea and inland waterway only: FAS, FOB, CFR, and CIF
- Those for all modes: EXW, FCA, CPT, CIP, DAT, DAP, and DDP

It is important to note the following:

Transactions by air, rail, truck, and nonvessel need to be referencing INCOTerms in the first section allowing multimodal transport. As these sections also allow sea and inland waterway, they would also be a potentially good choice across the board, allowing a broader term to be utilized, and then possibly avoiding confusion. It goes to say that the terms' specific details need to be reviewed to be assured that this will work in your supply chain.

Example: A supplier in Genoa, Italy, plans to export by air from Rome to a customer in Seoul, South Korea.

The seller utilizes a commercial invoice stating FOB Rome, Leonardo da Vinci Airport. This would be the misuse of an INCOTerms that is designed for sea and inland waterway only.

But if the company had a policy for exports from its plant in Genoa that utilized FCA, this would have application for both air and sea and help avoid this type of error.

FOB "On Board"

The FOB term in the 2010 edition had numerous changes. The one being discussed here references the issue of "On Board" versus "when the goods pass the ships rail" in the 2000 edition.

That point in time where responsibility and liability pass from the seller to the buyer in the 2000 edition could clearly be observed when the cargo passed the ships rail moving onto the vessel.

In the real world we all know that a majority of sea freight moves in ocean containers, typically 20- and 40-foot varieties. But we also know that a considerable amount of freight moves by break bulk, roll-on/roll-off, and in other modes.

Freight in those situations will move across the rail, but potentially at a later time frame and distance will be moved and secured into position. So the question is raised as to what then does **"ON BOARD"** mean? Is it when it passes the rail, stevedored into position, secured, and so forth?

The information flow always reminds us that INCOTerms are a reference point and not an end all in an international commercial transaction.

In the case of FOB on a break bulk shipment, this would mean that the purchase order from the buyer should clearly express what they require from the shipper in loading the goods ON BOARD the vessel, and/or the seller/shipper clearly describes on the commercial invoice what it will plan to do to meet the ON BOARD requirement.

Example: An exporter from Sydney sells a 60-foot sailing yacht to a buyer in Singapore. The terms of sale are FOB Sydney and the goods will be shipped on an ocean-going vessel direct from Sydney Harbor to the port of Singapore.

The FOB term means that the seller delivers once the goods are placed on the vessel. But functionally, this is not as easily as it seems. The nature of the shipment places the yacht in a cradle, spanning some 70 feet long by 20 feet wide, 38 feet high, and weighing some 32 tons.

The cradle will be nestled and secured on deck before the ship sails by the Sydney longshoreman and stevedores engaged by the ocean freight carrier or steamship line.

If the intent of the buyer is to have the seller make delivery once the goods are ON BOARD in final position and then secured by lashing by the professionals and approved by the captain of the vessel, then they need to build those terms in their PO and have the seller (exporter) in Sydney agree to those terms.

There will be additional costs for all this labor that should be reflected in the overall FOB price between the two parties, typically prepaid by the seller and recouped when payment is received.

The bottom line here is that both parties must be wary of an ocean-going FOB transaction where noncontainerized freight is being handled and they must specify the intent of their expectations on just what they want ON BOARD to mean in that transaction or agreement.

As time passes and we see litigation and cases adjudicated, we will learn more about this interpretation. Meanwhile, use this term cautiously on break bulk freight.

Domestic Use

The author believes that the original architects of INCOTerms placed the intent that they were designed for goods passing through international borders and not for internal country shipments or for domestic transportation needs.

The 2000 edition stated the intent was for goods crossing international borders but allowed for domestic utilization.

It is important to note that while it allowed for domestic that was then not a "license" to utilize for domestic.

But in the 2010 edition, written on the cover the words are added for "domestic and international trade." This has changed how companies engaged in global trade view and utilize INCOTerms. Many companies have begun to incorporate them into their overall sales strategies and procedures for both domestic and international.

Many countries around the globe benefit from INCOTerms in domestic utilization but are unsure of their immediate application for domestic trade in the United States.

In the United States prior to 2004, the UCC, governance in all 50 states except Louisiana had provisions in their shipping terms. FOB was a "place" most widely utilized; FOB Origin or FOB Destination.

Very simplified, FOB Origin meant that the price paid was for the buyer to "come and pick the freight up." FOB Destination meant that the price paid included delivery to the agreed destination.

In 2004, these provisions were recommended to be abolished from the UCC. The problem with that is not many states adopted this change so a quandary exists that this UCC provision of FOB Origin and Destination still has application in most states and it is still accepted in practice as a shipping term in most American domestic contracts.

The author is stating that it is still acceptable for a U.S. company to utilize this UCC provision for FOB Origin and Destination in its domestic sales or purchase contracts but recognizing that at some point in time down the road it is likely to be eliminated formally. When? We do not know.

This particular issue does not necessarily impact domestic shippers in other countries around the globe.

In the United States, it is ok to utilize INCOTerms 2010 for domestic sales, but we must realize that the complications of how INCOTerms have been designed make the FOB term mostly not viable. The author believes that the main reason for the change of INCOTerms to include "domestic" was because of considerations in the European community and not the United Sates.

The FCA term has domestic viability in the United States, but this whole subject must be carefully and judiciously thought out to assure that any changes work both internally and externally with suppliers and customers.

UCC GUIDELINES ON THE FOB TERM
IN THE UNITED STATES

§ 2-319. F.O.B. and F.A.S. Terms.

(1) Unless otherwise agreed the term F.O.B. (which means "free on board") at a named place, even though used only in connection with the stated price, is a delivery term under which

(a) when the term is F.O.B. the place of shipment, the seller must at that place ship the goods in the manner provided in this Article (Section 2-504) and bear the expense and risk of putting them into the possession of the carrier; or

(b) when the term is F.O.B. the place of destination, the seller must at his own expense and risk transport the goods to that place and there tender delivery of them in the manner provided in this Article (Section 2-503);

(c) when under either (a) or (b) the term is also F.O.B. vessel, car or other vehicle, the seller must in addition at his own expense and risk load the goods on board. If the term is F.O.B. vessel the buyer must name, the vessel and in an appropriate case the seller must comply with the provisions of this Article on the form of bill of lading (Section 2-323).

(2) Unless otherwise agreed the term F.A.S. vessel (which means "free alongside") at a named port, even though used only in connection with the stated price, is a delivery term under which the seller must

(a) at his own expense and risk deliver the goods alongside the vessel in the manner usual in that port or on a dock designated and provided by the buyer; and

(b) obtain and tender a receipt for the goods in exchange for which the carrier is under a duty to issue a bill of lading.

(3) Unless otherwise agreed in any case falling within subsection (1)(a) or (c) or subsection (2) the buyer must reasonably give any needed instructions for making delivery, including when the term is F.A.S. or F.O.B. the loading berth of the vessel and in an appropriate case its name and sailing date. The seller may treat the failure of needed instructions as a failure of cooperation under this Article (Section 2-311). He may also at his option move the goods in any reasonable manner preparatory to delivery or shipment.

(4) Under the term F.O.B. vessel or F.A.S. unless otherwise agreed the buyer must make payment against tender of the required documents and the seller may not tender nor the buyer demand delivery of the goods in substitution for the documents.

INCOTerms vs the Uniform Commercial Code

Trade practitioners in the U.S. will be aware that the terms FOB, CIF and so on are defined within the United States federal Uniform Commercial Code (UCC). First published in 1952, UCC covers many aspects of commercial contracts. It contains "shipment and delivery" provisions that have similar aims to those of the INCOTerms rules.

Some UCC expressions have the same three-letter abbreviations as those within the INCOTerms system; but their definitions are totally different. Notoriously, "FOB" can have a number of different meanings within UCC, most of which do not correspond with the ICC INCOTerms FOB definition.

The situation is confused further by variations between different US states. In 2004, there was a major revision of the UCC, which abolished many of these terms. However, for reasons unrelated to its "shipment and delivery" provisions, many states have failed to adopt the 2004 revision; so in these states, the former UCC revision remains law.

Companies in the US are therefore faced with the prospect of mastering two versions of the UCC for use with domestic transactions, plus ICC INCOTerms rules for use with cross-border transactions.

EX Works and DAP are also excellent options. EX Works could replace FOB origin and DAP could replace FOB destination with some minor differences. But technically any INCOTerms 2010 could be utilized.

The key is utilizing the INCOTerms that meets both parties' intents and that they both agree to recognize the risks and costs associated for both.

It is also very important to note that **the 2010 FOB INCOTerms should not be utilized for domestic trade as the intent per the section it is in and the wording, for sea and inland waterway only, unless you will be utilizing those water modes for inland transportation, which is typically unlikely.**

All companies need to tread carefully when choosing INCOTerms 2010 for domestic utilization. There are logistics and financial and legal considerations in moving from the standard UCC terms to INCOTerms 2010.

This author has determined by practice and current typical situations in corporate America that UCC stills has validity while INCOTerms 2010 has validity but still some "gray areas" to its use, so move forward thinking out options that work best for your supply chain, and acknowledge that you now have options.

BEST PRACTICES IN CUSTOMER SERVICE ON EXPORT SALES

*A huge differentiator from one company to another is how "customer service" is managed. This section views the challenges of dealing with customers on a global basis and then more importantly offers guidance on a **Best Practices** approach to make your customer service the high point of your export operations.*

Challenges of Global Customer Service

There is no question regarding the significant challenges facing export customer service personnel.

Besides all the macro issues we outlined in Chapter 1, there are a number of specific customer services issues we need to contend with:

- Differences in culture and language
- Difference in time
- Difference in contract law

- Accommodating market demands
- Customer expectations
- Return shipping

Differences in Culture and Language

The difference in culture and language between English and the numerous countries we do business in is huge.

Although English is generally the "language of the business world" there are significant benefits to being able to speak the languages of the countries you do business in.

Even rudimentary understanding will be ok. Just being able to say hello, goodbye, and thank you in the various languages of the countries you do business with will have payback in spades.

As a general statement American businesspeople can learn to be more respectful of foreign languages. Do not always expect English to be spoken!

We should learn the basic cultures of the places we sell to. With the Internet and various web-based resources, it is pretty simple to find out the basic cultures of any place in the world.

We need to focus on cultural issues that could impact relationships or have business implications.

The business world outside the United States is more driven by relationships than here in America.

Developing that relationship and spending time, money, and resources will go a long way in helping to facilitate better customer service being delivered.

Many times a relationship in foreign cultures is just as important an issue itself as the quality of the product and/or service being exported.

It is easier to develop the relationship when there is a basic understanding of culture and language skill sets.

Difference in Time

If we are in New York and our customer is in Korea and we speak to them at 7 PM on Friday evening, recognize that it could be 7 AM on Saturday morning where they are in Korea.

Twelve hours ahead and a new day!

If we are in Chicago dealing with a customer in Italy at 12 noon on Monday afternoon, it could be 7 PM that evening where they are located. We are getting ready for lunch and they are just finishing dinner.

This puts pressure on our customer service team to operate during off hours to accommodate client needs.

Difference in Contract Law

Part of our responsibilities in customer service is to develop sales, agency, and distribution agreements with our foreign clients. Therefore, we need to have a basic understanding of contract law in the various countries in which we operate.

Additionally, we need to have legal resources to assist us from a legal standpoint to assure that we are in compliance with all local statutes and regulations.

A customer service team that is engaged in export sales and business development will always be in a better and more secure position with agreements in place that can sustain potential prosecution and trial demands in that local country as well as here in the United States.

Accommodating Market Demands

Market demands can be characterized as local nuances required for a product specification, qualities, or differences needed to sell and service in that specific market.

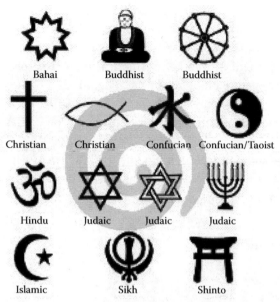

For example, a U.S.-based food company is looking to sell certain food products into Asia. Knowledge that the Asian market prefers products that are a little sweeter than what we may like in the West is an important factor of which to be aware. Therefore, the U.S. company would need to make certain there is additional sweetener added to its marinades, processed foods, and so forth when selling to Asian markets.

Another example might be the requirement to include CE markings on consumer electronics sold to European countries in lieu of the UL certification and markings we have here in the United States.

A final example may be the need for an import license and/or permit to be obtained prior to import in that destination country. This may require the exporter to create additional paperwork prior to export including proforma invoices and providing other information for the importer to obtain their import license.

Customer Expectations

Global customers have service demands both similar to U.S.-based companies and ones that are very different. Those exporters who accommodate these demands and expectations will be in the best position to develop, sustain, and grow their client relationships.

An example of a client expectation is being sensitive to their religious and cultural ceremonies. Holidays and observances such as Ramadan in the Middle East, Chinese New Year in Asia, Yom Kippur in Israel and the United States, Mardi Gras in Latin America, and Christmas in the United States and Europe are but a few of the religious and cultural events that happen every year. We may be asked both to recognize their holidays and close down operations and then be patient as the companies reopen business activities.

This can be difficult to accommodate as these events do not typically coincide with our Western holidays but we must make the accommodation to show respect.

Return Shipping

Zappos customer get **FAST, FREE SHIPPING** on every order with **NO** order minimums!

VIP customers—just **LOG IN** to access all your VIP perks, like **FREE** 1-Business day shipping and your **EXCLUSIVE** customer service phone number!

LOG IN »

If you are not 100% satisfied with your purchase for any reason, just go through our easy online return process, or call us 24/7 at (800) 927-7671 to print out **FREE** return label.

You have **365 DAYS TO RETURN** an item to us in its original condition.

A huge problem for any company in both consumer and commercial sales is dealing with return shipments.

- Determining the validity of the "return reason"
- Evaluating the *best customer service and most cost-effective* method for dealing with the return
- Making arrangements to manage the return

- In the case of a repair, managing the return, making the repair, and sending the shipment back to the customer
- Cost accounting the return expense in cost of time, resource, effort, and actual dollars

Make it an international shipment and each one of the areas outlined above is magnified.

A "return shipping policy" must be created proactively and as part of the overall sales and customer service program.

Those companies that have an excellent return policy will have satisfied clients, as mitigation well done can be a "value add."

International returns are dramatically heightened because of

- Customs issues
- Documentation problems
- Communication concerns with time, distance, and language
- Logistics nightmares
- Excessive costs
- Lack of trust between all parties

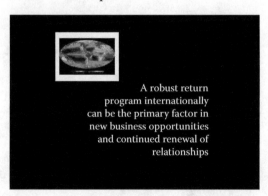

A robust return program internationally can be the primary factor in new business opportunities and continued renewal of relationships

These international concerns can differentiate supplier and vendor services dramatically when managed proactively, diligently, and with precision execution.

Return shipping internationally requires a high degree of coordination between a host of logistics providers, carriers, and internal operations.

Some companies may opt to place return facilities close to where their customers are located if this is monetarily feasible and makes business sense.

Creating a Robust Export Customer Service Capability: Ten Steps

In an export sales and customer service program that would be considered robust will take on 10 important characteristics:

1. Respect the customer's country and culture
2. Learn the economic factors in your customer's country
3. Make it easy for your customer to do business with you
4. Ease payment terms
5. Operate in their time frame
6. Visit and develop the very best of relationships
7. Have a robust "warranty" program
8. Provide effective INCOTerms
9. Create responsible documentation
10. Develop successful logistics

Some companies do business in over 100 countries. Think of how daunting the task is to manage the difference between all those cultures, languages, traditions, and business ideologies.

Respect the Customer's Country and Culture

Lose the arrogance, condescending approach, and "better than thou" attitude.

No matter how difficult our overseas clients can be and the numerous challenges they pose, we still need to set a balance and approach that is customer-service-focused.

The client may not always be right but they must not to be made to feel so badly or backed into a corner that it may jeopardize your working relationship.

The key to working with customers around the world is to

- Show "respect" by learning important basics of their history, culture, traditions, and what makes up who they are
- Learn some basic language skill sets to be able to say hello, thank you, goodbye, and other rudimentary local language word sets
- Learn how their culture does business and while it may be different and even sometimes viewed as "wrong" in our eyes, we still need to understand how it works and more importantly how best to navigate successfully through the challenges

Learn the Economic Factors in Your Customer's Country

Economic factors in a particular country will weigh heavily on your overall success in export sales, customer service, and business development in that country.

Concerns include

- Stability of their economy to impact favorable growth
- Currency inconvertibility risks with their foreign exchange
- Rates of exchange
- Likelihood of protracted default and bankruptcy caused by their overall economy
- Impact on how they represent your product or services in that country, particularly when selling through an agent or distributor

The economic cycles of the world continually grind in many directions but for certain have a major impact on export sales. This makes customer service such a key ingredient of business models and relationships that are integral in various cultures.

As economies go south and the potential for increased sales is diminished, making competition stiff, those sellers with robust and competitive customer service capabilities will have the best opportunity to maintain existing clients and grow when that potential is available.

Having some resource and intelligent capability for economic circumstances in the countries and regions you do business in is a good investment. This provides information flow so decisions and reactions can be done proactively and not just as a reaction after the fact.

Make It Easy for Your Customer to Do Business with You

Every time consulting organizations create surveys on customer service management there is a continual trend where it is identified that vendor/supplier choices are made based on the ease of doing business with a particular business partner.

In most of our own circumstances when we evaluate who we do business with we mirror those survey comments: "they are great" and "they are so easy to do business with."

This is a definite "truism" in business and rings solid in domestic and global trade as well.

Below is an outline of some questions to utilize in assessing how easy you are to do business with.

Above is an excellent approach to determining how best to determine how your customer service is doing and potentially identifying red flags. Any red flags will require

- Review
- Analysis
- Mitigation
- Resolve
- Follow-up

This analysis will lead to corrective action. Most responsible customers understand that problems will occur. It is how you mitigate the issues, resolve the problem, and communicate all of this internally and to the customer that is the "true test" of the strength of the client relationship.

CUSTOMER SERVICE QUESTIONS TO DETERMINE HOW EASY IT IS TO DO BUSINESS WITH YOUR ORGANIZATION

1. Do you survey your customers on how they feel about doing business with your company?
2. If yes, do you ask that question specifically?
3. Do you operate within the hours that your clients operate in, particularly taking in the time differences?
4. Do you have a policy for dealing with warranty, repair, and return issues that is working successfully?
5. How do you benchmark the rate of service and repair issues against other companies in your vertical?
6. Is there a consistency of problems that arise and cause staff serious or frustrating issues?
7. Are customers complaining?
8. Is there a decline in customer orders?

CREATE RESPONSIBLE DOCUMENTATION

Documentation is the engine of global trade and moves the freight from origin to destination.

There are many resources for determining guidelines for documentation. If the documentation is not completed correctly or timely the consequence is that the goods will not move successfully.

Some options for export documentation are the websites outlined in this book's appendix, freight forwarders and carriers, and government agencies and their websites such as trade.gov.

COMMON EXPORT DOCUMENTS

There are many documents that are commonly used in exporting, but specific requirements on documentation may vary by destination and type of product. Frequently documentation is divided into the following subsections: common export documents, transportation documents, export compliance documents, certificates of origin, other certificates for shipments of specific goods, other export-related documents, and temporary shipment documents.

Commercial Invoice

A commercial invoice is a bill for the goods from the seller to the buyer. These invoices are often used by governments to determine the true value of goods when assessing customs duties. Governments that use the commercial invoice to control imports will often specify its form, content, number of copies, language to be used, and other specific information to be included on the commercial invoice.

Export Packing List

Considerably more detailed and informative than a standard domestic packing list, an export packing list includes seller, buyer, shipper, invoice number, date of shipment, mode of transport, carrier, and itemizes quantity, description, the type of package, such as a box, crate, drum, or carton, the quantity of packages, total net and gross weight (in kilograms), package marks, and dimensions, if appropriate. A packing list is not a substitute for a commercial invoice. In addition, U.S. and foreign customs officials may use the export packing list to check the cargo.

Pro Forma Invoice

A pro forma invoice is an invoice prepared by the exporter before shipping the goods, informing the buyer of the goods to be sent, their value, and other key specifications. It also can be used as an offering of sale or price quotation.

TRANSPORTATION DOCUMENTS

Airway Bill

Airfreight shipments require airway bills. Airway bills are shipper-specific (i.e., USPS, FedEx, UPS, DHL).

Bill of Lading

A bill of lading is a contract of carriage between the owner of the goods and the carrier (as with domestic shipments). For vessels, there are two types: a straight bill of lading, which is nonnegotiable, and a negotiable or shipper's order bill of lading. The latter can be bought, sold, or traded while the goods are in transit. The customer usually needs an original as proof of ownership to take possession of the goods.

Electronic Export Information Filing (Formerly Known as the Shipper's Export Declaration)

Electronic export information (EEI) is the most common of all export control documents. It is required for shipments above $2500* and for shipments of any value requiring an export license. It has to be electronically filed via ACE online.

*Note: The EEI is required for shipments to Puerto Rico even though they are not considered exports (unless each "Schedule B" item contained in the shipment is valued under $2500).

Shipments to Canada do not require an EEI except in cases where an export license is required. (Shipments to third countries passing through Canada do need an EEI.)

EXPORT COMPLIANCE DOCUMENTS

Export Licenses

An export license is a government document that authorizes the export of specific goods in specific quantities to a particular destination and end user. This document may be required for most or all exports to some countries or for other countries only under special circumstances. Examples of export license certificates include those issued by the Department of Commerce's Bureau of Industry and Security (dual-use articles), the State Department's Directorate of Defense Trade Controls (defense articles), the Nuclear Regulatory Commission (nuclear materials), and the U.S. Drug Enforcement Administration (controlled substances and precursor chemicals).

Destination Control Statement

A Destination Control Statement (DCS) is required for exports from the United States for items on the commerce control list that are outside of EAR99 (products for which no license is required) or controlled under the International Traffic in Arms Regulations (ITAR). A DCS appears on the commercial invoice, ocean bill of lading, or airway bill to notify the carrier and all foreign parties that the item can be exported only to certain destinations.

CERTIFICATES OF ORIGIN

Generic Certificate of Origin

The certificate of origin (CO) is required by some countries for all or only certain products. In many cases, a statement of origin printed on company letterhead will suffice. The exporter should verify whether a CO is required with the buyer and/or an experienced freight forwarder.

Note: Some countries (i.e., numerous Middle Eastern countries) require that certificate of origin be notarized, certified by local chamber of commerce, and legalized by the commercial section of the consulate of the destination country.

For textile products, the importing country may require a certificate of origin issued by the manufacturer. The number of required copies and language may vary from country to country.

Certificate of Origin for Claiming Benefits under Free Trade Agreements

Special certificates may be required for countries with which the United States has free trade agreements (FTAs). Some certificates of origin, including those required by the North American Free Trade Agreement (NAFTA), and the FTAs with Israel and Jordan, are prepared by the exporter. Others, including those required by the FTAs with Australia, the Dominican Republic-Central America-United States Free Trade Agreement (CAFTA-DR) countries, Chile, and Morocco, are the importer's responsibility.

Specific documentation requirements for various countries' certificates can be found at trade.gov.

- Australia
- Bahrain CAFTA-DR (Costa Rica, Dominican Republic, El Salvador, Guatemala, Honduras)
- Chile
- Israel
- Jordan
- Morocco
- NAFTA
- Singapore: No certificate of origin is required. However, the importer is required to produce the necessary permits together with an invoice at the time of cargo clearance.
- Peru: There is no prescribed format. However, specific information is required.
- Korea: There is no prescribed format. However, specific information is required. See documenting origin guidance and required data elements for certification for Korea.
- Panama: there is no prescribed format; however, specific information is required.

Certificate of Analysis

A certificate of analysis may be required for seeds, grain, health foods, dietary supplements, fruits and vegetables, and pharmaceutical products.

Certificate of Free Sale

Certificate of free sale may be issued for biologics, food, drugs, medical devices, and veterinary medicine. More information is available from the Food and Drug Administration. Health authorities in some states as well as some trade associations also issue certificates of free sale.

Dangerous Goods Certificate

Exports submitted for handling by air carriers and air freight forwarders classified as dangerous goods need to be accompanied by the shipper's declaration for dangerous goods required by the International Air Transport Association (IATA). The exporter is responsible for accuracy of the form and ensuring that requirements related to packaging, marking, and other required information by IATA have been met.

For shipment of dangerous goods, it is critical to identify goods by proper name and comply with packaging and labeling requirements, which vary depending on the type of product shipper and the country to which the goods are being shipped. More information on labeling/regulations is available from the International Air Transportation Association or Department of Transportation—HAZMAT websites.

For ocean exports, hazardous material regulations are contained in the international maritime dangerous goods regulations.

Fisheries Certificate

The National Marine Fisheries Service conducts inspections and analyses of fishery commodities for export.

Fumigation Certificate

A fumigation certificate provides evidence of the fumigation of exported goods (especially agricultural products, used clothing, etc.). This form assists in the quarantine clearance of any goods of plant or animal origin. The seller is typically required to fumigate the commodity at their expense no earlier than 15 days prior to loading.

Halal Certificate

Required by most countries in the Middle East, this certificate states that the fresh or frozen meat or poultry products were slaughtered in accordance with Islamic law. Certification by an appropriate chamber and legalization by the consulate of the destination country is usually required.

Health Certificate

A health certificate is need for shipment of live animals and animal products (processed foodstuffs, poultry, meat, fish, seafood, dairy products, and eggs and egg products). Note that some countries require health certificates to be notarized or certified by a chamber and legalized by a consulate. Health certificates are issued by the U.S. Department of Agriculture's Animal and Plant Health Inspection Service (APHIS).

Ingredients Certificate

A certificate of ingredients may be requested for food products with labels that are inadequate or incomplete. The certificate may be issued by the manufacturer and must give a description of the product, contents, and percentage of each ingredient, chemical data, microbiological standards, storage instructions, shelf life, and date of manufacture. If animal fats are used, the certificate must state the type of fat used and that the product contains no pork, artificial pork flavor, or pork fat. All foodstuffs are subject to analysis by the Ministry of Health laboratories to establish their fitness for use.

Inspection Certificate

Weight and quality certificates should be provided in accordance with governing USDA/GIPSA regulations for loading at port and loading at source/mill site as appropriate. A certificate of origin certified by the local chamber of commerce at the load port and a phytosanitary certificate issued by APHIS/USDA and a fumigation certificate are to be provided to the buyer. Costs of all inspections, as well as certificates/documents at the load port, are usually the responsibility of the seller. Independent inspection certificates may be required in some instances.

Preshipment Inspections

The governments of a number of countries have contracted with international inspection companies to verify the quantity, quality, and price of shipments imported into their countries. The purpose of such inspections is to ensure that the price charged by the exporter reflects the true value of the goods to prevent substandard goods from entering the country and to deflect attempts to avoid payment of customs duties. Requirements for preshipment inspection are normally spelled out in letter-of-credit or other documentary requirements. Inspections companies include Bureau Veritas, SGS, and Intertek. Some countries require preshipment inspection certificates for shipments of used merchandise.

Insurance Certificate

Insurance certificates are used to assure the consignee that insurance will cover the loss of or damage to the cargo during transit. These can be obtained from your freight forwarder or publishing house. Note that an airway bill may serve as an insurance certificate for a shipment by air. Some countries may require certification or notification.

Phytosanitary Certificate

All shipments of fresh fruits and vegetables, seeds, nuts, flour, rice, grains, lumber, plants, and plant materials require a federal phytosanitary certificate. The certificate must verify that the product is free from specified epidemics and/or agricultural diseases. Additional information and forms are available from APHIS.

Radiation Certificate

Some counties including Saudi Arabia may require this certificate for some plant and animal imports. The certificate states that the products are not contaminated by radioactivity.

Other (Product-Specific) Certificates

Shaving brushes and articles made of raw hair must be accompanied by a recognized official certificate showing the consignment to be free from germs. Used clothing requires a disinfection certificate. Grain requires a fumigation certificate, and grain and seeds require a certificate of weight. Many countries in the Middle East require special certificates for imports of animal fodder additives, livestock, pets, and horses.

Weight Certificate

A certificate of weight is a document issued by customs, certifying gross weight of the exported goods.

OTHER EXPORT-RELATED DOCUMENTS

Consular Invoice

Required in some countries, a consular invoice describes the shipment of goods and shows information such as the consignor, consignee, and value of the shipment. If required, copies are available from the destination country's embassy or consulate in the United States. The cost for this documentation can be significant and should be discussed with the buyer.

Canadian Customs Invoice

Although not required by regulation, this customs invoice is a preferred document by Canadian Customs and customs brokers. It is issued in Canadian dollars for dutiable and taxable exports exceeding $1600 Canadian dollars. Detailed invoice requirements can be obtained at the Canadian Customs website.

Dock Receipt and Warehouse Receipt

A dock receipt and warehouse receipt are used to transfer accountability when the export item is moved by the domestic carrier to the port of embarkation and left with the ship line for export.

SHIPPER	SHIPPING INSTRUCTION **DOCK RECEIPT** Star-Concord Logistics.Co.,Ltd.		
CONSIGNEE			
NORTIFY PARTY	BOOKING NO.		
	CFS CUT :		
	ETD :		
PLACE OF RECEIPT	PRECARRIAGE BY	ETA :	
VESSEL & VOY.NO.	PORT OF LOADING		
PORT OF DISCHARGE	PLACE OF DELIVERY	FINAL DESTINATION(FOR THE MERCHANT'S REFERENCE ONLY)	

PARTICULARS FURNISHED BY THE MERCHANT

CONTAINER NO. AND SEAL NO. MARKS & NOS.	QUANTITY AND KIND OF PACKAGES	DESCRIPTION OF GOODS	MEASUREMENT (CBM) GROSS WEIGHT (KGS)
TOTAL NUMBER OF CONTAINER OR PACKAGES (IN WORDS)			

FREIGHT & CHARGES	REVENUE TONS	RATE	PREPAID	COLLECT
SERVICE TYPE	EXCHANGE RATE		PREPAID AT	PAYBLE AT

NUMBER OF ORIGINAL B(S)/L	PLACE OF B(S)/L ISSUE/DATE	

REMARK
この用紙は SHIPPING INSTRUCTION と DOCK RECEIPTを兼ねています。
ACTUAL SHIPPER名（貴社名）等、BLANKの箇所にご記入の上、CFSへ
ご提出願います。 H.B/Lは このINSTRUCTIONを基に作成致します。

搬入の際は、このDOCK RECEIPT 3部と許可証を
CFSへ 提出願います。

Import License

Import licenses are the responsibility of the importer and vary depending on destination and product. However, including a copy of an import license with the rest of your documentation may in some cases help avoid problems with customs in the destination country.

ISPM 15 (Wood Packaging) Marking

The International Standards for Phytosanitary Measures Guidelines for Regulating Wood Packaging Material in International Trade (ISPM 15) is one of several International Standards for Phytosanitary Measures adopted by the International Plant Protection Convention (IPPC). The IPPC is an international treaty to secure action to prevent the spread and introduction of pests of plants and plant products and to promote appropriate measures for their control. The American Lumber Standard Committee (ALSC) and the National Wooden Pallet and Container Association (NWPCA) provide phytosanitary certification for wood packaging materials (WPM). APHIS will issue a phytosanitary certificate for wood package materials only if WPM are the cargo.

Shipper's Letter of Instruction

The shipper's letter of instruction is issued by the exporter to the forwarding agent and includes shipping instructions for air or ocean shipment.

SHIPPERS LETTER OF INSTRUCTION

Addresses		References		
Exporter TPBO TPBO TPBO TPBO Seattle United States	**Ultimate Consignee** TPBO TPBO TPBO TPBO Seattle United States	**Shippers Reference**	**Consignee Reference**	**Booking Control** 517453101
		All References Trucker Bill of Lading-TBL ~ 1 Manifest-CGM ~ 1		
Pick Up Location TPBO TPBO TPBO TPBO Seattle United States	**Intermediate Consignee / Notify Party**			
Forwarder TPBO TPBO TPBO TPBO Seattle United States	**Other Booking Parties**			

Instructions	Documents	Attached / Prepare	Terms of Trade
Mode of Transport Air	Proforma Invoice	Booking Centre to	International Freight
Shipment Type	Packing List	Booking Centre to	Origin Freight
	Cargo Manifest	Booking Centre to	Terminal Handling
Containerized? NO	SED Shippers Export	Booking Centre to	Documents Customs Clearance
Dangerous Goods	NAFTA Certificate ~	Booking Centre to	Duty
	Certificate of Origin	Booking Centre to	Taxes
Insured Amount	Truck Bill of Lading	Booking Centre to	Domestic Freight
Declared Value for Carriage	Shipper's Decl. For	Booking Centre to	Destination Delivery Other
Declared Value for Customs			Handling Instructions
If Unable to Deliver			

Commodities and Packages						Currency	
D/F/M	**Description**	**Export HS** (Sched B)	**Export License**	**ECN**	**DG**	**Qantity**	**Total Value**
	65 Cartons, 3 x 2 x 5 MR, 1950 CBM, 22425 K						
	65 Crates, 2 x 1 x 2 MR, 260 CBM, 19500 K						
Total Quantity: 65	Gross weight: 22425 K (10180.95 LB) Volume: 1950 CBM (68728.22 CFT)						

Signature: Duly authorized officer or employee	Date

The above signature hereby authorizes the Forwarder named above to act as agent and attorney in fact with authority to perform any required by law, regulation of custom in connection with the exportation of the above referenced shipment.

TEMPORARY SHIPMENT DOCUMENTS

CARNET/Temporary Shipment Certificate

A carnet is a document that facilitates the temporary importation of products into foreign countries by eliminating tariffs and value-added taxes (VAT) or the posting of a security deposit normally required at the time of importation.

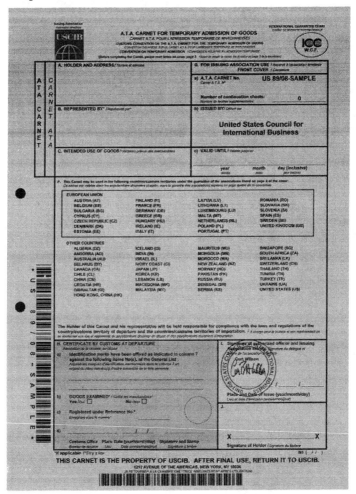

Customs Certificate of Registration

Customs Form 4455 may be used for goods that are leaving the United States on a temporary basis for alteration, repair, replacement, and processing.

Transporting Goods by Truck to Canada

An application to transact bonded carrier and forwarding operation, Form E370, is required to bring goods over the border to Canada when not already cleared through customs at the border.

Documentation and Customer Service

Documentation can make or break an export transaction and is often one of the most important responsibilities of the customer service team servicing foreign customers.

It can be a huge frustration for inexperienced customer service representatives who lack the skill sets and resources to get documentation done right.

Additional Documentation Concerns

1. Export requirements versus import requirements
2. Language
3. The number of copies required
4. Original versus copies versus electronic versions
5. Signature requirements and who has authority to sign
6. Color of paper
7. Legalization or consularization required
8. Power of attorney issues
9. Bills of lading, invoice or packing list requirements, specific language and details needed, product descriptions, pieces, weights, measurements (dims), and so on

DEVELOP SUCCESSFUL LOGISTICS

Moving the freight from A to B successfully requires intense knowledge in reducing risks and spend combined with meeting the requirements of all the parties in the supply chain.

Choice of transportation provider, freight forwarders, customhouse broker, mode of transit, carriers, and entry ports are all part of an equation that can move goods unsuccessfully or allow you to be the "hero." Experience, knowledge, resource development, and some good luck makes for better decision making.

Critical are the choices for partners who provide you with all the experience and resources to make sure your logistics initiatives are accomplished as required.

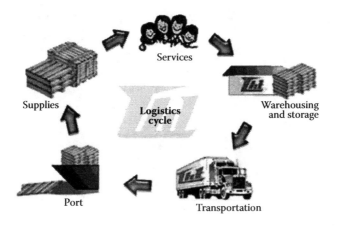

It is not the employer who pays the wages. Employers only handle the money. It is the customer who pays the wages.

Henry Ford
Founder Ford Motor Company

3

E-Commerce

Consumers all over the world are demanding products delivered to their door and now companies like Amazon are making it happen within hours.

Domestically e-commerce is a matured process. Internationally there are numerous challenges. This chapter focuses on identifying the challenges and creating solutions.

Almost every company is currently engaging or certainly ramping up for e-commerce sales on a global basis. This chapter serves as a great "primer" for e-commerce.

E-COMMERCE CHALLENGES

There is an array of issues confronting any company looking to move product or services to consumers globally through web portals.

In summary:

- International overview
- Assessing opportunity
- Market intelligence
- Marketing
- Managing web-based platforms
- Logistics
    - Shipping
    - Customs
    - Last mile delivery
- Getting paid
- Customer service
    - Managing returns
- E-commerce expansion

International Overview

We identified in Chapter 1 a host of risks, exposures, and challenges facing any exporter in managing foreign sales and customer service.

These risks also face companies engaged in e-commerce sales and are potentially magnified due to a lack of matured logistics and customs experience in this form of enterprise.

Geography, political, economic, language, time difference, and culture are but a few of the challenges you will face in e-commerce sales globally.

These risks are overcome by the opportunities. **You are obtaining access to 95% of the global population and that means significant potential that should not be missed.**

The keys to managing these risks are

- Obtaining the critical information to combat these challenges
- Obtaining the skill sets necessary to manage the e-commerce responsibilities
- Obtaining resources that can provide support
- Accessing government capabilities that can offer very valuable services that provide assistance

Assessing Opportunity

The theory is that almost any product or service offered through e-commerce in the United States has applicability in global markets. Maybe not in all markets because of local nuances but certainly in most! Options in assessing foreign opportunity:

- Department of Commerce resources
- Private consulting services
- Web-based search engines
- Trade shows located in the United States and abroad in your industry vertical

The Department of Commerce is one of the best resources in assisting companies and individuals not only with export sales but also specifically with e-commerce business development.

DEPARTMENT OF COMMERCE CASE STUDY: BASS PRO SHOPS

Six years ago, Bass Pro Shops, Inc., hired Shirley Drake to develop and direct its export-compliance program. The company—one of America's premier outdoor retailers, with retail stores across the United States and Canada and an online store at basspro.com—wanted to ensure that international sales from its website were fully compliant with U.S. export regulations.

Business Challenge

Bass Pro needed to ensure that its operations were as streamlined and efficient as possible. The company has over 90,000 SKUs and fills 800 to 1200 international orders per week, so the export-compliance process needed to be as automated as possible.

Approach

"The first thing we did was develop an internal IT program capable of storing the regulatory information about our products," Drake explained. The company modified its New Item Set-Up Form, adding fields for Export Control Classification Numbers (ECCNs), HS numbers, country of origin, and NAFTA eligibility so it could collect the required export information directly from its suppliers. (ECCNs are special numbers used for export licensing purposes which will be discussed in the Appendix.) "We now require each of our suppliers to provide harmonized codes and country of origin information when we order," Drake said. "Some suppliers are very sophisticated and we accept what they provide us, but with less experienced vendors, we review the information they supply to ensure it's accurate. In global commerce, you have to know how sophisticated your suppliers are."

The company ensures that its products comply with export regulations by stipulating that an item cannot be exported until it has been assigned a Schedule B code, an approved ECCN, and a corresponding country of origin, and that an export-compliance associate has approved this information.

If any of that information is missing, the order generates an error code and the products are ineligible for export until the requisite information has been entered or corrected. Also, Bass Pro's export-system software compares each product's ECCN to the destination's country code to determine whether the articles can be shipped to the destination country without an export license.

If all the information is present and correct, then the company's automated export system approves the articles for inclusion in an export order. Approved orders then appear on an Order Edit screen. At this time a member of the export-compliance team manually reviews the order to make sure that no errors were keyed into the system and that no items are destined for countries where export is prohibited by the United States.

Once the international order has been approved on the Order Edit screen, the items are processed for shipping.

Bass Pro has also developed a system to annually renew the country of origin for all products eligible for export. This allows them to take advantage of preferential tariff rates stipulated in trade agreements like the North American Free Trade Agreement (NAFTA). This annual renewal process requires Bass Pro to send a communication to suppliers to certify the country of origin of all products they supply. An employee then enters into the inventory management system the origin country and the expiration date of this certification (certifications are usually valid for 12 months).

Bass Pro uses this information to state the appropriate country of origin on the requisite export documentation. A physical certificate of origin is not included in shipments, but only when the customer asks for the certificate or if the item gets held up in customs.

"For shipments to NAFTA countries, low-value shipments (shipments valued at $1000 or less) don't require a certificate of origin in order to receive preferential tariff treatment. When Bass Pro exports certain items—its computer system tracks which SKUs are eligible for preferential treatment under NAFTA—a statement is added to the bottom of the commercial invoice noting that NAFTA treatment applies. Usually the statement is accepted in lieu of the certificate," Drake said.

Bass Pro does outsource some of its export-compliance tasks. All international shipments are processed in real time through a third-party online vendor in order to verify that the buyer is not on any U.S. government lists of parties to whom sales are prohibited.

Insights

When asked what advice she'd give to exporters looking to sell products globally, Drake said they should "get the full support of top management because selling internationally involves extra costs, and to be successful you need to spend some money on legal assistance, software changes, training, etc."

Also, every company should train a compliance associate, who will attend training on Export Administration Regulations and other export controls. It's essential to stay within the law. And, if your company sells products or technology that fall under International Traffic in Arms

Regulations (ITAR), as Bass Pro does, your compliance associate(s) must receive ITAR training.

Bass Pro and the U.S. Commercial Service

Shirley Drake and Bass Pro have worked with the U.S. Commercial Service on many exporting issues. Their relationship and the hard work of the entire team at Bass Pro have allowed them to take advantage of international sales opportunities.

The U.S. Commercial Service, recognizing Bass Pro's global efforts, presented the company with the "Export Achievement Certificate for Recent Accomplishments in the Global Marketplace."

MARKET INTELLIGENCE

Obtaining information on foreign markets is available through various options:

- Research and survey reports
- Department of Commerce
- Consultants
- Internet-based searches
- Trade shows in the United States and abroad in your industry vertical

As a starting point, the Department of Commerce (DOC.gov) can provide initial guidance along with specialized consultants, such as dragonfly-international.net.

Trade shows in your industry vertical will give you the best option for a concentrated approach where numerous companies gather globally that are looking to sell, buy, expand, and network mutual opportunities.

The amount of potential opportunity in one location over a 2–4-day period is enormous and is a typical way of accessing the forces that will impact the marketing circumstances you will face.

Trade shows allow sample and product showcasing that will readily determine your product viability.

MARKETING

Marketing internationally requires approaches that deal with macro branding and micro outreach that is designed for the nuances of that local market.

Language and culture will play a huge role in how you go about a specific marketing strategy.

External consultants who specialize in various industry verticals and specific regions and countries can be of great value here.

You ride on their experience, contacts, and networking.

Keep in mind that in certain cultures and countries a marketing approach successful in the United States may not necessarily work in foreign markets.

Some basic steps in foreign marketing:

1. Opportunity assessment
2. Product needs assessment

3. Mining for information and intelligence
4. Showcasing of product
5. Testing with samples and promotional initiatives
6. IPR issues and any legal requirements
7. Packing, marking, and labeling nuances
8. Delivery of customer service capabilities
9. Pricing and payment strategies
10. Logistics options and costs
11. Local distribution and last mile requirements

MANAGING WEB-BASED PLATFORMS

You will require IT support in determining how you approach both marketing and servicing your customers online.

A macro solution may handle most of the requirements, but in certain countries you will require "bolt-ons" and "tailored" technology solutions.

In the marketing assessment phase, you will determine what your IT approach should be.

An IT professional internally or outsourced will be necessary to make the "connectivity" work between you and your customers in the various foreign markets you sell to.

LOGISTICS

Logistics is managing the freight end of the supply chain, which has three primary responsibilities:

1. Move freight timely
2. Move freight safely
3. Move freight cost effectively

In e-commerce this becomes a difficult scenario because cost is a variable that must be minimized dramatically.

Commercially when you create a $375,000.00 sale of a container load of consumer products and the landed costs are 3%–4% of the value, that can be absorbed. But when you are selling an $80.00 single consumer item and the freight costs $30.00 or 35% of the value, that business model will not fly.

The goal is to bring the landed costs in to no more than 1% and less even works better!

In the United States in 2014–2017, most domestic e-commerce platforms incorporated the freight costs into the costs of goods sold.

This appeared to the consumer as "free shipping." Now we all know that shipping is not actually free. In reality shipping is a cost that is not "line-itemed" to the buyer.

What sellers have done is minimized the cost and the impact of shipping and incorporated this expense into the selling price. However, when looking at this from a "marketing perspective" it appears to be a value add to the customer.

In international e-commerce, which is still in the infant stages, this cost is visible to the buyer and can be a large part of their overall acquisition cost.

In fact, e-commerce is hampered by this cost. Shipping addresses this concern in the three areas detailed below.

Shipping

Finding less expensive modes of transit is the best option to lower freight costs. Ocean is 18 times less expensive than air freight.

Consolidations or the massing of small individual shipments and then shipping as larger orders lowers the unit cost dramatically.

Delaying the shipping by a few days or weeks can also allow time to accumulate larger shipments.

This makes "consolidations" a significant business process in e-commerce to lower the percentage of freight to the value of the goods.

CUSTOMS

Goods moving internationally must pass through customs in the arriving country.

In most countries customs has numerous tasks but always has two primary responsibilities:

- Security of goods and persons passing through the border
- Collection of duties and taxes

The clearance process adds risk, cost, and time.

If it is not done correctly, it can create a loss of goods and the potential for fines and penalties.

Typically, when goods pass through customs, the items are individually cleared by commercial invoice and consignee.

This adds a cost to the goods and merchandise either paid for by the seller or the buyer. If the seller assumes the cost, it will most likely be passed off in the costs of goods sold, directly or indirectly.

In e-commerce this cost can be a "deal breaker" as most sales would then be priced uncompetitively.

The better option is to find a carrier that can clear the merchandise under what is typically referred to as a "manifest clearance" where your goods along with all other goods within the shipment is cleared under one manifest entry document.

That process then shifts the overall cost of the product across all products in the entire shipment, lowering the cost dramatically to the individual order, keeping the sale competitive.

Most customs authorities in foreign markets have some forms of "manifest clearances," such as those utilized by the integrated carriers like UPS, FedEx, and DHL.

Additionally, in some countries like China, they have established flat duty and tax rates for e-commerce transactions on shipments moved directly to consumers, which are easier to deal with and lower then commercial sales.

The key is to find those carriers and service providers that can accommodate these manifest shipments and have access to these lower entry duty and tax rates.

LAST MILE DELIVERY

Once e-commerce shipments arrive in a country competitively shipped and cleared they have to be delivered to the final consumer.

Traditional shipping methods, such as by commercial truck, will not work, as on an individual basis the costs would be too high for the sale to absorb, making the sales uncompetitively priced.

Finding an inexpensive courier method will typically produce the most favored costing structure, where the individual home delivery is done at the least expensive option and thereby creating a "last mile" solution that maintains a competitively priced transaction from origin all the way through to the final consumer destination.

GETTING PAID

Getting paid in international sales has its challenges in all commercial transactions. In e-commerce this challenge is enhanced due to the newness of the marketplace and with the multitude of concerns in dealing with millions of consumers in multiple markets.

E-commerce payment options are maturing at a face pace in 2017.

Getting Paid Options:

1. Many companies market their e-commerce sales specifically through third-party sites, such as Amazon and Ali Baba, to transfer the payment challenge to that third party, at a cost.

2. There are numerous technology companies that provide software specifically designed to manage e-commerce payment solutions, such as PayPal, Shopify, Flagship, Cayan, and Bongo, to name a few.
3. The major credit card companies—American Express, Master Card, and Visa—all have options as well.
4. Mobile payment options also exist, such as Google Wallet, Dwolla, and V.me, to name a few.

Critical Concerns on E-Commerce Payment Risks

- Currency exchange
- Inconvertibility of funds
- Protracted default
- Problem resolution options
- Fraud
- Payment option costs cutting into margins
- Timing of payment funds availability
- Warranty or returned goods
- Trade compliance issues

All these risks and challenges can be managed successfully:

1. Build into costing model conservative costing estimates for payment issues, and build in higher reserves for nonpayments.
2. Utilize the services or established and proven third-party payment companies who can be a "partner" in your international e-commerce sales.
3. Be diligent in how you qualify customers and utilize reasonable care on how you process and screen overseas customers.
4. Government regulatory concerns follow e-commerce sales just as in any commercial sale; make sure you have trade compliance SOPs in place to manage these risks.

CUSTOMER SERVICE

There are several concerns in managing customer service issues in e-commerce:

- Small margins made up by volume sales
- Providing 24/7/365 services in a world consisting of different time zones

- Language concerns and website automation in local languages
- Local service representation
- Warranty and return issues
- Problem resolution strategies

If a company is going to succeed in their e-commerce international sales, they have to deal with all those above issues proactively and with a high degree of diligence.

In 2016/2017, many companies are still going through their learning curves and developing strategies in managing these issues.

The formula for dealing with these customer service issues are

- Recognize that you can establish an international customer service policy across the board, but it must allow "tailoring" solutions at a local level
- Be proactive in identifying issues and resolving first
- Invest in systems that can adapt to local nuances
- Train customer service personnel in regional and county-specific cultural issues
- Build regulatory and trade compliance SOPs into the business model
- Create a warranty and return policy that can work on a local level, and make sure these costs are accounted for in your overall business model

E-Commerce Expansion

The likely occurrence once you enter into e-commerce foreign sales is that as you are successful, you will want to expand globally and move into an array of new countries and cities.

We recommend the following steps in a global expansion strategy:

- Take it slowly; get one country up and running successfully before moving onto another country
- Mine for nuances aggressively, and apply this local information and intelligence to your in-country strategies
- Keep in mind that the differences in payment options, regulations, and cultural issues may be vast from one country to another

In e-commerce, your prices have to be better because the consumer has to take a leap of faith in your product.

Ashton Kutcher

4

Cargo Loss Control

Cargo must be adequately protected from all the physical transit risks that merchandise will face as it passes through all aspects of the global supply chain from origin through to the final destination. This chapter focuses on those risks and provides options on how to pack, mark, label and ship goods for international trade.

RISKS

The primary physical exposures to freight moving globally fall into several categories: water and handling damage; theft and pilferage; sinking; stranding; crashing of conveyances; war; strikes; and riots and civil commotions, along with acts of terrorism.

The pictures above depict damaged cargo moving by air, truck, and ocean vessel.

The reasons for loss and damage are varied. Most professionals will point out that at least 1% of all freight moving internationally will be lost or damaged.

Some industry professionals will bring this number up even higher to as much as 3%.

Whether 1% or 3%, the statistic is that 70% of all these losses are controllable.

Specifically, this means that steps in packing, marking, labeling, documentations, stowage, materials handling, and choice of service providers and carriers will all impact the outcome of cargo receipt favorably or unfavorably.

Customer service personnel typically will be involved in dealing with overseas customer dissatisfaction in loss and damage to arriving cargo.

This then requires customer service personnel to pay attention to this area of cargo loss control.

Some facts about global shipping that impact cargo outturn:

- The more times freight is handled, the greater the exposure to loss and damage
- Domestic packaging and stowage techniques are usually not sufficient for shipments moving internationally
- The extremes of weather, motion, handling, pressures, and people can increase exposures to loss and damage in international shipping by more than 10 times
- Delays in the shipment passing through the supply chains, such as in customs, creates an environment where there will be additional handling damage and theft and pilferage

- Specific product "branding and labeling," such as Samsung, Apple, General Motors, Coca-Cola, and Xbox is great to "market" your product to consumers, but has little value in the global supply chain during transit.

- **Packaging globally is typically inadequate to handle the extreme physical conditions that exist in international transportation**
- Some shippers believe that air freight provides less exposure than ocean freight. In some products and trade lanes that may have some truth, but in the clear majority of international shipping cases air freight can present significant exposures as well
- **Choice of freight forwarder, 3PL, customhouse broker, and carrier, along with mode of transit, will also impact freight outcome both adversely and positively, depending on the quality of its care, custody, and control loss control functions**

Here are some specific cargo loss control recommendations:

1. Make sure the documentation of the shipment is done correctly, accurately, and conforms with the regulations on both sides of the shipment—the export and the import.

    Bad documentation will misdirect freight to the wrong destination. It will delay freight moving through the supply chain. It will hold up freight at the border with customs.

    All those documentary issues expose the freight to theft, pilferage, and multiple handling.

2. An assessment needs to be made on all products, destinations, and modes of transit, along with the likely risks and challenges.

    This will then determine the packing, marking, labeling, stowage, and documentation requirements.

    This is best accomplished utilizing professional assistance; such as can be found with the consulting company bluetigerintl.com. Freight forwarders, marine cargo insurance companies, and various government agencies can also be good sources.

3. All freight should be handled mechanically when possible. This makes palletization and unitization a great option. The additional costs involved will be outweighed by the increase in favorable outturn results.

4. Carefully chose the service providers and carriers; those with loss prevention programs would best be suited for international freight.

    Ask for loss experience and their methods in cargo handling, routing, and shipping methods. Those that point to safe, conservative strategies would be better alternatives than those that don't.

5. Make sure freight moves quickly through the supply chain and avoid customs delays at all costs.

   Quality and responsible documentation will greatly assist with this initiative.

6. Stretch or shrink-wrap all cargoes to prevent water damage, which is a frequent cause of loss and damage.

Banding and securing of cargo is an excellent strategy.

7. Use strong pallets that allow forklift approach from both sides.

8. Remove any product identifiers. Blind marks and opaque wraps work well here.

9. Utilize dry lumber that is seasoned and pressure-treated. Utilize four-way corners and diagonals in crate construction that adds strength to the shipping process.

10. The following measures should be taken when dealing with freight shipped in ocean containers:

- Needs to be blocked and braced against the corners and the deck, not the sidewalls.
- Needs to be protected and be off the deck where moisture and contaminants will collect.
- Needs to be inspected before stowing cargo to make sure it is free from holes, odors, and any contaminants. Document the inspection process.
- Should not have heavy items loaded on top of lighter, more fragile units.
- Be sensitive about the types of freight mix in a container. An example of a "do not" would be loading food products with toxic chemicals or loading pharma with fertilizers.
- Be aware that condensation can play a large role in containers transiting from warmer, moist climates through to colder venues. Condensation impact can be devastating and costly. Make sure freight is protected from the potential of condensation damage. Overlaying sheets of plastic lining is an excellent method of protecting freight from condensation issues.
- Document all stowage of containers with photographs and make them part of the transaction file.

11. Freight shipped breakbulk will require another whole level of protection, primarily from potentially adverse handling or stowage. Crates and unitized loads are the preferable option. Shipping loose in breakbulk is a recipe for disaster.

12. Inspect freight immediately on arrival at all receiving stations. If the freight arrives in an ocean container, inspect the condition of the container as well.

    Document the findings.

13. Utilize the resources available from your insurance broker and underwriter who may have defined expertise in cargo loss prevention, making their professionals available to assist you and your team.

Sample of a Container Inspection Report:

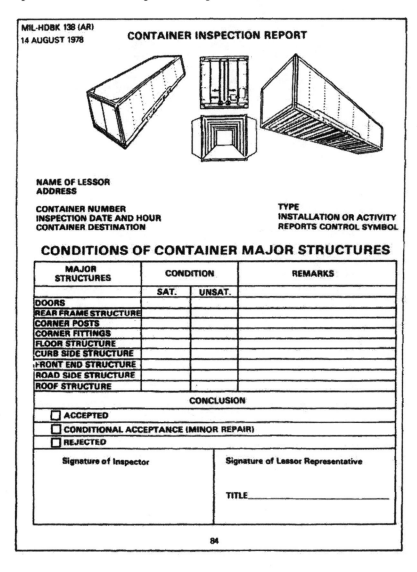

MIL-HDBK 138 (AR)
14 AUGUST 1978

CONTAINER INSPECTION REPORT

NAME OF LESSOR
ADDRESS

CONTAINER NUMBER
INSPECTION DATE AND HOUR
CONTAINER DESTINATION

TYPE
INSTALLATION OR ACTIVITY
REPORTS CONTROL SYMBOL

CONDITIONS OF CONTAINER MAJOR STRUCTURES

MAJOR STRUCTURES	CONDITION		REMARKS
	SAT.	UNSAT.	
DOORS			
REAR FRAME STRUCTURE			
CORNER POSTS			
CORNER FITTINGS			
FLOOR STRUCTURE			
CURB SIDE STRUCTURE			
FRONT END STRUCTURE			
ROAD SIDE STRUCTURE			
ROOF STRUCTURE			
CONCLUSION			
☐ ACCEPTED			
☐ CONDITIONAL ACCEPTANCE (MINOR REPAIR)			
☐ REJECTED			

Signature of Inspector

Signature of Lessor Representative

TITLE_____

84

The National Cargo Bureau, which is an excellent resource for cargo loss prevention, provides an outline on how best to load an ocean freight container:

10 STEPS TO LOAD, STOW, AND SECURE
A FREIGHT CONTAINER

THE GOALS

The safe shipment of cargoes is a primary objective, of course. This is especially important when hazardous cargoes are carried. A related goal is the delivery of the cargo in complete, clean, and undamaged condition.

The following are 10 steps and issues to be aware of when loading, stowing, and securing (stuffing) a freight container.

1. The Key Person Is the Shipper and/or the Person Responsible for Loading (Packing/Stuffing) the Container

   The right container for the job should be selected. Does the cargo need refrigeration, ventilation, special handling equipment, securing devices, or special dunnaging in the container?

Is it for exclusive use? If in doubt, consult your ocean carrier or container leasing firm.

2. Container Condition

Check your container when it arrives. Is it the type you ordered? Examine it for

- Cleanliness. Is it odor-free? Is it weatherproof? If it happened to be raining (or there is melting snow on top), that's a good time to check for leaks. Otherwise a visual check can be made by inspecting the freight container from within. If any light enters, then water will. (If in doubt, spray it with a hose.) Take particular note of the door gaskets and how well the doors close. This is often a vulnerable point.
- If it is fitted with cargo restraint devices, are they in good condition and in sufficient supply?
- Examine the container carefully for its physical condition just as if you were buying it. (You are, in a sense—even if only for one trip.) Has it been repaired? If so, does the repair quality restore the original strength and weatherproof integrity?
- Look at the sides. Examine them carefully to see if there are any holes or fractured welds. Is the container racked (twisted) or out of line? If so, it has been misused and will probably be inadequate for the safe carriage of your cargo. (Distorted containers are unlikely to fit properly with chassis and handling equipment that must lock into all corner fittings.) Have all placards and markings applicable to previous hazardous cargoes, precautions, or destinations been removed from sides and doors?

If it doesn't pass these tests, call for another container. Remember, if you do not give your cargo the right start, it has little chance of arriving in good condition.

3. About Stowing and "Stuffing"

In a sense, the shipper is now stowing the ship because a container ship is loaded with hundreds of small portable cargo "compartments" (i.e., freight containers) offered by numerous shippers of many containerized cargoes.

"Stuffing" has become a commonly used term for the loading of cargo into freight containers. The International Maritime

Organization refers to that operation as "packing." To "stow" is to place or arrange compactly and put safely in place. This is a traditional seafaring word meaning to make things ready for sea—to prepare and place cargo and equipment properly for the sea voyage. "Load," as used by the railroad and trucking industries, is generally synonymous with "stow."

Whatever you call it, "stow" your cargo properly in the correct freight container and secure it well. (Note that "stow" and "secure" are two distinct operations.)

4. Weight Distribution and Space Utilization

IMPORTANT: Preplan the stowage of the cargo in container. The weight should be spread evenly over the entire length and width of the floor of the container.

For example, if you have a 40-foot container with a cargo capacity of 55,000 pounds and a cubic capacity of 2090 cubic feet, and your cargo weighs 55,000 pounds but measures only 1000 cubic feet, it should be stowed about half the height of the container over the entire floor, rather than to the top for one-half the length.

If you are stowing cargoes of uniform density (other than heavily concentrated packages), then a proper, even weight distribution is not a problem. Cargoes of various densities are more of a problem.

5. Compatibility of Cargoes

If the container is loaded with packages of various commodities, give careful attention to their proper segregation and stowage. The commodities' physical characteristics (such as weight, size, and density) must be considered, as well as whether they are liquids or solids.

Cargo can be of high density, hard-to-damage commodities such as galvanized metal sheets, or low-density but also hard-to-damage goods. Cargoes can be high-density, easily damaged electronic components or low-density items such as lampshades. There are numerous possibilities.

A shipper should be aware of previous commodities stuffed in the container, especially if foodstuffs are to be included.

6. Improper Stowage Can Cause Damage to Any Cargo, Including So-Called Hard-to-Damage Commodities

Each commodity must be considered on the basis of its characteristics and properties when planning its packaging and stowage in containers for shipment. The commodity's compatibility with other cargo in the same container must always be considered.

To achieve the proper cube utilization, a compatible configuration of cargo packaging units is also essential. Exposure to damage by chafing, crushing, odor or fume taint, and wetting by condensed moisture or leakage also must be avoided.

Segregation of hazardous materials/dangerous goods within the same or adjacent containers is regulated. Compatibility with other hazardous commodities (and certain nonregulated cargoes) must be in compliance with general and sometimes also specific segregation requirements.

7. Hazardous Cargoes

U.S. regulations applicable to the transportation of packaged hazardous materials are contained in Title 49 of the Code of Federal Regulations, Parts 100-178. Those regulations apply to all modes.

The international recommendations for such shipments, but as applicable only to the water mode, are published in the International Maritime Dangerous Goods Code. That IMDG Code takes on the force of regulations in each of the countries that have adopted the code into their own laws. Therefore, it should be regarded as a set of international "regulations."

The above-referenced U.S. regulations, usually referred to as "49CFR," apply to packaged hazardous materials for all modes of transportation. Regulations specifically applicable to "Carriage by Vessel" are contained in Part 176 of 49CFR, Parts 100–177.

Both the 49CFR and IMDG Code specify the regulatory requirements for packaged hazardous materials (the U.S. term) and dangerous goods (the international term).

8. Stowage of Wet and Dry; Heavy and Light Cargo

Wet and Dry Cargo

When the container is to be stowed with both packaged wet and dry cargo, the wet goods should never be stowed above the cargo that is liable to damage from moisture or leakage, or in an adjacent position where leakage might spread along the floor. The dry goods should either be stowed over the wet, or if on the same level, raised off the floor by an extra layer of dunnage. Leakage is most likely to occur in cargoes of barreled or drummed goods. Due care must always be given to proper stowage and securing of drums to prevent movement within the container.

Heavy and Light Cargo

Improper stowage of heavy and light cargo together causes crushing and damage to contents. Heavy packages, such as cases of machinery parts and heavy, loose, or skidded pieces, should always be stowed on the bottom or floor of the container with lighter goods on top.

Each tier should be kept as level as possible. Lateral crushing should be avoided by carrying the stow out to the sides and ends of the container and filling void spaces with dunnage or an adequate substitute.

If packages are stowed loosely, chafing damage is likely to occur due to the motion or vibration of the truck, train, or ocean vessel. They can rub against each other and against boundaries of the container unless secured from movement. Cargo with little or no covering is especially susceptible to chafing damage. A cushioning material should be used to protect against this type of damage.

9. Stowage of Heavy Concentrated Weight

When planning the stowage of heavy concentrated weights, careful consideration must be given to the maximum permissible weight and the floor loads allowed in the container. The bedding required to properly spread the weight should be arranged with weight distribution factors in mind.

This bedding should consist of lumber of sufficient thickness that will not deflect under the planned load, with the bottom bearers placed longitudinally in the container. The cargo piece or pieces should be bolted to cross members resting on the longitudinal. The cross members must be adequately bolted or fastened to the bottom pieces with backup cleats placed where necessary.

10. Securing

Fill it or secure it. Use dunnage. Block it out. Leave no void spaces or loose packages on top. Smooth metal-to-metal contact should be avoided as this causes a slippery surface. The slogan "pack it tight to ride right" is a good one. Remember, typical trucking and railroad cargo securing guides stress stowing to prevent the longitudinal movement in the container. For ocean transport, however, the same rules should be applied to prevent additional sideways movement.

Avoid direct pressure on doors and use a proper fence or gate to fill any void space.

When stowing or loading the cargo in the container, you have a regulatory responsibility to do it correctly. The securing techniques and materials used should be more than just "adequate" when ocean shipments are involved.

Check that package hazard labels and container placards, if required, have been applied.

Finally, secure the doors, lock and seal them, and note the seal numbers for insertion on the bill of lading.

www.natcargo.org

Initiatives in loss prevention have cost, resource depletion, and utilization of personnel times.

These issues are very much outweighed by the enormous benefits of

- More satisfied customers
- Reduced internal costs in dealing with claims
- Lower insurance rates
- Lower costs in freight where goods are unitized, palletized, or shipped in larger consolidated loads

Build "loss prevention" into your global supply chain, as you would a "sprinkler system" in one of your warehouses. The payback will be grand.

The business risk in international sales is significantly increased when companies do not pay attention to packing, marking, labeling, documentation, and shipping concerns.

Those companies that pay attention to this critical area of detail easily grow their export sales, earn larger margins, and have more satisfied customers.

Kelly Raia
Dragonfly Global

5

Regulatory and Trade Compliance Concerns in International Trade

This chapter delves into import and export trade compliance with a focus on a comprehensive regulatory review so the reader is provided a sound foundation to build security, compliance, and best practices in their global customer services.

COMPLIANCE OVERVIEW

In every organization that is engaged in global trade there will always be some point person or division that has responsibility for trade compliance management. In many organizations this falls on the personnel responsible for customer service.

If it falls outside customer service, it is still critical that customer service personnel have a good understanding and comprehension of trade compliance, import and export regulations, and all related areas of governance, as it will impact how they handle their overseas sales and business relationships.

The events of 9/11 set off a frenzy of trade compliance concerns that have now continued to develop in 2016/2017 and beyond. The Department of Homeland Security, Customs and Border Protection, and other government agencies have tweaked their approach to security and compliance with companies that import and export from the United States and all over the world.

This process will continue to develop as authorities find new ways to combat the growing threats of terrorism and the disruptions we face in managing global trade day to day.

Technology, communications, and comprehensive initiatives will continue to expand into how we buy, sell, and ship freight all over the globe.

The balance of this chapter peers into all the areas that customer service personnel must begin to grasp and information flow and skill set development that they need to "master" to some extent.

Knowledge is gold, and understanding all you need to know about import and export regulations is valuable knowledge to someone who moves, sells, and buys freight internationally.

Customs and Border Protection (CBP), which has a primary responsibility in global security, began a layered approach to global security almost 10 years ago that starts with the foreign port of loading, encompassing the transmission of cargo manifest data, advanced security filing, and partnering with foreign governments and other U.S. government agencies. Recent developments include the advancement of mutual recognition of foreign security programs such as Authorized Economic Operator (AEO), Business Alliance for Secure Commerce (BASC), and the inclusion of exporters in the Customs-Trade Partnership against Terrorism (C-TPAT) program.

At the same time, trade compliance continues to be a technical and integral part of the global supply chain and now includes global security as regulations have been enacted to ensure compliance with security measures. Technology continues to integrate itself into the supply chain and the U.S. government is keeping up with those changes. In 2015, we saw the initial implementation of U.S. Customs and Border Protection (CBP) unveiling of the Automated Commercial Environment (ACE) as its operating platform. For example, the International Trade Data System (ITDS) incorporates the single window concept to allow businesses to submit import and export data required by Customs and Border Protection (CBP) and Partner Government Agencies (PGAs).

The government has many goals in managing security and compliance concerns. While these measures overall create a single window for businesses, this same window will provide the government with the capability of streamlining data received from many government agencies and compare that data for consistency and accurate reporting, leading to safer shipments and raising the compliance bar for importers.

GLOBAL SUPPLY CHAIN SECURITY FOR IMPORTS

Trade compliance, security, and risk assessment have become key words in the vocabulary of every logistics, purchasing, import, and export and transportation management professional in the United States as well as their global trading partners, vendors, and service providers. U.S. Customs and Border Protection (CBP) continues to manage and develop strategies to secure U.S. borders and protect the supply chain from terrorist and other aggressive threats.

Container Security Initiative

The events of 9/11 caused authorities to push out our borders to deter the risk for terrorism in the supply chain. The Container Security Initiative (CSI) was established and stations U.S. CBP officers in foreign locations to work with their foreign government counterparts in identifying and inspecting containers in foreign ports that pose a potential risk for terrorism. This is done through the use of intelligence information. These containers are evaluated and prescreened prior to shipment. This is usually done at the port of departure through the use of large scale x-ray machines and radiation detectors.

CSI is currently operating in 58 ports around the world and accounts for the prescreening of over 80% of all ocean containerized cargo imported into the United States. This program demonstrates the successful collaboration and partnership outlook of supply chain security of the United States and its foreign partner governments.

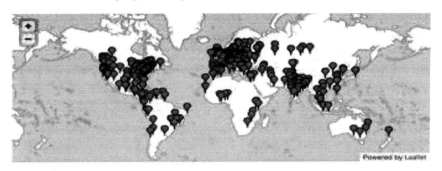

Advanced Manifest Regulations

Advanced manifest regulations are relevant to freight inbound from overseas. Actual carriers create a manifest listing of the goods loaded on the vessel, truck, rail, or plane by bill of lading number. The manifest lists the details of the goods including the shipper, consignee, pieces, weights, description, and whether dangerous or not.

The Bureau of Customs and Border Protection (CBP) requires carriers to provide information on cargo entering the United States prior to arrival. This enables CBP to target shipments for security examination. This information is required to be filed electronically through the automated manifest system. While the required information to be filed is based on the mode of transportation, the information includes at minimum origin port/airport, destination port/airport, shipper, consignee, manifest quantity, and weights and measures. The time frames for transmitting this information varies by mode of transport, as reflected in the regulation which utilize charts to assist imports.

Electronic information for air cargo is required in advance of arrival and must be received from the inbound air carrier, and if applicable, an approved party. Failure to provide this information in a timely manner will result in a penalty of $5000.

While CBP has established its time frame for receiving the advanced manifest information, the carriers establish shorter time frames for transmitting this information to ensure they are in compliance with CBP regulations and avoid penalties.

Timing of inbound reporting to Customs Border and Protection

	Inbound: Transmission Received by CBP in AMS
Vessel	24 hours (before loading at foreign port) for nonbulk shipments
	24 hours before arrival for bulk shipments
Air	4 hours before "Wheels up" from NAFTA (Canada and Mexico) and Central and South America above the equator
Rail	2 hours before arrival in the United States
Truck	1 hour before arrival for non-Free and Secure Trade (FAST) participants
	30 minutes before arrival for FAST participants

CUSTOMS-TRADE PARTNERSHIP AGAINST TERRORISM PROGRAM

One of the more aggressive voluntary programs emanating from CBP following the events of 9/11 was the Customs-Trade Partnership against Terrorism program (C-TPAT), which seeks to safeguard the world's vibrant trade industry from terrorists, maintaining the economic health of the United States and its neighbors.

Today there are approximately 10,678 certified partners that have been accepted into the program. These include U.S. importers, U.S. and Canadian highway carriers, rail and sea carriers, U.S. Customs brokers, marine port authority/terminal operators, freight consolidators, ocean transportation intermediaries and nonoperating common carriers, and Mexican and Canadian manufacturers. These companies account for over 54% by value of what is imported into the United States.

Other countries, such as, but not limited to, Japan, members of European Union, and Canada have also begun programs similar to C-TPAT.

By extending the United States' zone of security to the point of origin, C-TPAT allows for better risk assessment and targeting, freeing CBP to allocate its inspection resources to more questionable shipments. C-TPAT members are considered low-risk and are therefore less likely to be examined. This designation is based on a company's past compliance history, security profile, and the validation of a sample international supply chain.

CBP has numerous Mutual Recognition Arrangements with other countries. The goal of these arrangements is to link the various international industry partnership programs so that together they create a unified and sustainable security posture that can assist in securing and facilitating global cargo trade.

The goal of aligning partnership programs is to create a system whereby all participants in an international trade transaction are approved by the customs function as observing specified standards in the secure handling of goods and relevant information. C-TPAT signed its first Mutual Recognition Arrangement with New Zealand in June 2007 and since that time has signed similar arrangements with South Korea, Japan, Jordan, Canada, the EU, Taiwan, Israel, Mexico, and Singapore.

In 2015, the C-TPAT program was expanded to include exporters. In 2016/2017, authorities have exporters following much of the same requirements for importers in documenting how they do business with their foreign customers, choose their service providers, and monitor shipments. For many exporters, participation in the C-TPAT program has become a significant marketing strategy for doing business, particularly with those partners located in countries that are participating in a Mutual Recognition Arrangement with the United States.

The benefits of C-TPAT participation include the following:

- Reduced compliance exams and reduced number of inspections.
- Reduce waiting time for cargo to be examined.
- If cargo is selected for exam, it will receive priority and is moved to the front of the exam line.
- Decreased transportation times.
- Assignment of a CBP supply chain security specialist.
- Raising the bar of general security within your company's locations and supply chain overall.

- Access to Free and Secure Trade (FAST) lanes at Mexican and Canadian borders.
- Invitation to participate in C-TPAT training seminars offered by CBP.
- Incorporation of security practices into existing logistical management methods.
- Greater supply chain integrity.
- Reduced freight surcharges such as exam fees and demurrage.
- Ability to comply with C-TPAT customer requirements.
- Reduces risk and insurance costs.
- Reduce theft/loss and damage of inventory.
- Mutual recognition as CBP has signed Mutual Recognition Arrangements with its top trading partners including China, Canada, Mexico, Japan, and the European Union. This allows freight exported to move more quickly through participating countries customs.
- When an event occurs that closes the borders, C-TPAT member shipments will be prioritized when the borders reopen.
- Participation in the C-TPAT program provides mitigation of fines and penalties.
- Five to eight times fewer exams than non-C-TPAT importers.

C-TPAT FOR EXPORTERS

In 2015, U.S. Customs and Border Protection began accepting applications from exporters for participation in the Customs-Trade Partnership Against Terrorism (C-TPAT) program. Prior to 2015, the program focused on those involved in the United States import supply chain. The inclusion of exporters follows the objectives of the National Export Initiative (NEI) to facilitate and expand U.S. exports.

Benefits for exporters include

- Reduced examinations and prioritized examinations at ports of export
- Increased clearance facilitation from foreign partner countries participating in a Mutual Recognition Arrangement with the United States

- Ability to market shipments as more secure and to meet customer security requirements
- Business resumption and ability to maintain communication and coordination with C-TPAT partners during shipping disruptions

Under C-TPAT, the exporter is defined as the principal party in interest in the export transaction that has the power and responsibility for determining and controlling the sending of the items out of the United States. In addition to meeting this definition of an exporter, a company must be an active U.S. exporter out of the United States, have an office staffed in the United States, be an active U.S. exporter with a documentable employer identification number or Dun and Bradstreet number, have a documented security program, have a designated C-TPAT program point of contact, commit to the supply chain security criteria, and meet, maintain, and enhance internal policy to meet the C-TPAT exporter criteria and have an acceptable level of export compliance reporting with U.S. government agencies such as the Department of Commerce, Department of State, and Department of Treasury.

EXPORTER MINIMUM SECURITY CRITERIA

C-TPAT recognizes the complexity of international supply chains and endorses the application and implementation of security measures based on risk analysis by exporters. Therefore, the program allows for flexibility and the customization of security plans based on the member's business model. Appropriate security measures, as listed throughout this document, must be implemented and maintained throughout the above C-TPAT export participants' supply chains. Exporters must conduct a comprehensive risk assessment of their international supply chain based on the following C-TPAT security criteria. Where an exporter outsources or contracts elements of its supply chain, such as to a warehouse, logistics provider, carrier, or other export supply chain element, the exporter must work with these business partners to ensure that effective security measures are in place and adhered to throughout the entire supply chain.

BUSINESS PARTNER REQUIREMENTS

Exporters must have written and verifiable processes for the screening and selection of business partners including service providers, manufacturers, product suppliers, and vendors. Where applicable, these processes must include checks against the Department of Commerce/ Bureau of Industry and Security (BIS), Department of State/Directorate of Defense Trade Controls (DDTC), and Department of Treasury/Office of Foreign Assets Control (OFAC) lists. Entities on prohibited lists should be reported to the SCSS and relevant authority within 24 hours prior to departure.

SECURITY PROCEDURES

Written procedures must exist for screening business partners that identify specific factors or practices, the presence of which would trigger additional scrutiny by the exporter.

For those business partners eligible for C-TPAT certification (importers, carriers, ports, terminals, brokers, consolidators, etc.) the exporter must have documentation (e.g., SVI number) indicating whether these business partners are or are not C-TPAT certified and/or participating in a reciprocal Authorized Economic Operator (AEO) program (e.g., AEO certificate).

For those business partners not eligible for C-TPAT certification or participation in an AEO program, exporters must require their business partners to demonstrate that they are meeting C-TPAT security criteria via written/electronic confirmation (e.g., contractual obligations, via a letter from a senior business partner officer attesting to compliance, a written statement from the business partner demonstrating their compliance with C-TPAT security criteria or an equivalent AEO security program administered by a foreign customs authority, or by providing a completed exporter security questionnaire). Based on a documented risk assessment process, non-C-TPAT eligible business partners must be subject to verification of compliance with C-TPAT security criteria by the exporter.

Risk assessments of the company's export program must be completed on an annual basis.

POINT OF ORIGIN

Exporters must inform business partners of security processes and procedures that are consistent with the C-TPAT security criteria to enhance the integrity of the shipment at point of export.

Periodic reviews of business partners' processes and facilities should be conducted based on risk to maintain the security standards required by the exporter.

PARTICIPATION/CERTIFICATION IN FOREIGN CUSTOMS ADMINISTRATIONS SUPPLY CHAIN SECURITY PROGRAMS

Current or prospective business partners who have obtained a certification in a supply chain security program being administered by foreign Customs Administration should be required to indicate their status of participation to the exporter.

OTHER INTERNAL CRITERIA FOR SELECTION

Internal requirements, such as financial soundness, capability of meeting contractual security requirements, and the ability to identify and correct security deficiencies as needed should be addressed by the exporter.

Internal requirements should be assessed by management utilizing a risk-based document.

CONTAINER SECURITY

Container integrity must be maintained to protect against the introduction of unauthorized material and/or persons.

At point of stuffing, written procedures must be in place to properly seal and maintain the integrity of the shipping containers.

CONTAINER INSPECTION

Procedures must be in place to verify the physical integrity of the container structure prior to stuffing to include the reliability of the locking mechanisms of the doors. A seven-point inspection process is recommended for all containers:

- **Front wall**
- **Left side**
- **Right side**
- **Floor**
- **Ceiling/roof**
- **Inside/outside doors, door hardware, and fasteners**
- **Outside/undercarriage**

CONTAINER SEALS

The sealing of export containers to include continuous seal integrity are crucial elements of a secure supply chain, and remains a critical part of an exporter's commitment to C-TPAT.

A high-security seal must be affixed to all loaded containers destined for export from the United States. All seals must meet or exceed the current ISO 17712 standards for high-security seals.

Written procedures must stipulate how seals are to be controlled and affixed to loaded export containers to include procedures for recognizing and reporting compromised seals and/or containers to CBP or the appropriate foreign authority.

Only designated employees should distribute seals for integrity purposes.

CONTAINER STORAGE

Containers must be stored in a secure area to prevent unauthorized access and/or manipulation and to ensure container integrity is being maintained, especially to protect against the introduction of unauthorized material.

A container ready for loading

Procedures must be in place for reporting and neutralizing unauthorized entry into containers or container storage areas and any structural changes, such as a hidden compartment, discovered in containers destined for export. Notification should be made within 24 hours of discovery to the assigned supply chain security specialist (SCSS).

CONVEYANCE TRACKING AND MONITORING PROCEDURES

Exporters should ensure that their transportation providers adhere to the following tracking and monitoring procedures.

Conveyance and container integrity is maintained while the conveyance is en route transporting cargo to the point of export. Utilizing a tracking and monitoring activity log or equivalent technology is required. If driver logs are utilized, they should reflect that trailer/container integrity was verified.

Predetermined routes should be identified by the transportation provider for the exporter and these procedures should consist of random route checks by the transportation provider along with documenting and verifying the length of time between the loading point/trailer pickup, the export point, and/or the delivery destinations, during peak and nonpeak times.

Drivers should notify the dispatcher of any route delays due to weather, traffic, and/or rerouting.

Transportation provider management must perform a documented, periodic, and unannounced verification process to ensure the logs are maintained and conveyance tracking and monitoring procedures are being followed and enforced.

Drivers must report and should document any anomalies or unusual structural modifications found on the conveyance or container.

PHYSICAL ACCESS CONTROLS

Access controls prevent unauthorized entry to cargo facilities, maintain control of employees and visitors, and protect company assets. Access controls must include the positive identification of all employees, visitors, service providers, and vendors at all points of entry. Employees and service providers should only have access to those areas of a facility where they have legitimate business.

Ocean container ready to be loaded onboard a vessel

Employees: An employee identification system must be in place for positive identification and access control purposes. Employees should only be given access to those secure areas needed for the performance of their duties. Company management or security personnel must adequately control the issuance and removal of employee, visitor, and vendor identification badges. Procedures for the issuance, removal, and changing of access devices (e.g., keys and key cards) must be documented.

Visitors/vendors/service providers: Visitors must present photo identification for documentation purposes on arrival. All visitors should be escorted and provided temporary identification that must be visibly displayed on their person.

Challenging and removing unauthorized persons: Procedures must be in place to identify, challenge, and address unauthorized/unidentified persons.

Deliveries (including mail):

Proper ID and/or photo identification must be presented for documentation purposes on arrival by transportation providers. Arriving packages and mail should be periodically screened before being disseminated.

PERSONNEL SECURITY

Processes must be in place to screen prospective employees and to periodically check current employees.

Preemployment verification: Application information, such as employment history and references, must be verified prior to employment.

Background checks/investigations: Consistent with federal, state, and local regulations, background checks and investigations should be conducted for prospective employees. Once employed, periodic checks and reinvestigations should be performed based on cause and/or the sensitivity of the employee's position.

Personnel termination procedures: Companies must have procedures in place to remove identification, facility, and system access for terminated employees.

PROCEDURAL SECURITY

Security measures must be in place to ensure the integrity and security of processes relevant to the transportation, handling, and storage of cargo in the supply chain.

Security procedures should be implemented that restrict access to the export shipment. The procedures should prevent the lading of contraband while en route from facilities in domestic locations prior to export from the United States.

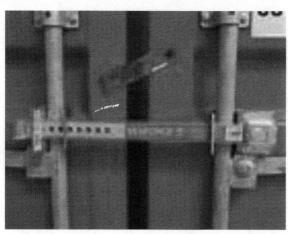

Container security seals locked in place provide a high level of security from theft and pilferage along with unwarranted container access.

Cargo discrepancies: All shortages, overages, and other significant discrepancies or anomalies must be resolved and/or investigated appropriately.

Customs, the assigned supply chain security specialist, and/or other appropriate law enforcement agencies must be notified if illegal or suspicious activities are detected, as appropriate.

Documentation processing: Procedures must be in place to ensure that all information used in the preparation of merchandise/cargo for export (EEI or other required export form) is legible, complete, accurate, and protected against the exchange, loss, or introduction of erroneous information. Documentation control must include safeguarding computer access and information.

Bill of lading/airway bill/manifesting procedures: To help ensure the integrity of cargo being exported, procedures must be in place to ensure that information transmitted/received to/from business partners is reported accurately and timely.

Shipping: The export cargo should be accurately described and the weights, labels, marks, and piece count indicated and verified. Departing cargo should be verified against purchase or delivery orders. Drivers delivering or receiving cargo must be positively identified before cargo is received or released.

Screening for prohibited or restricted parties: Documentable procedures and processes must exist to identify any party on lists from State/DDTC, Commerce/BIS, or Treasury/OFAC denied persons and who are involved in an export transaction with the exporter. Entities on prohibited lists should be reported to the SCSS and relevant authority within 24 hours prior to departure.

PHYSICAL SECURITY

Procedures must be in place to prevent, detect, or deter undocumented material and unauthorized personnel from gaining access to conveyance, including concealment in containers.

Cargo handling and storage facilities in domestic locations should have physical barriers and deterrents that guard against unauthorized access. Exporters should, according to their business models, incorporate the following C-TPAT physical security criteria throughout their supply chains as practical and appropriate.

Fencing: Perimeter fencing should enclose the areas around cargo handling and storage facilities. Interior fencing within a cargo handling structure should be used to segregate domestic, international, high-value, and hazardous cargo. All fencing must be regularly inspected for integrity and damage.

Secured container yard fencing gates and gate houses: Gates through which vehicles and/or personnel enter or exit must be manned and/or monitored. The number of gates should be kept to the minimum necessary for proper access and safety.

Parking: Private passenger vehicles should be prohibited from parking in or adjacent to cargo handling and storage areas.

Building structure: Buildings must be constructed of materials that resist unlawful entry. The integrity of structures must be maintained by periodic inspection and repair.

Locking devices and key controls: All external and internal windows, gates, and fences must be secured with locking devices. Management or security personnel must control the issuance of all locks and keys.

Lighting: Adequate lighting must be provided inside and outside the facility including the following areas: entrances and exits, cargo handling and storage areas, and fence lines and parking areas.

Alarm systems and video surveillance cameras: Alarm systems and video surveillance cameras should be utilized to monitor premises and prevent unauthorized access to cargo handling and storage areas.

EXPORT TRAINING AND THREAT AWARENESS

A C-TPAT exporter must have a documented export security program as well as a designated officer or manager who will act as the C-TPAT program point of contact. This program should have support throughout the corporate structure of the company displayed in correspondence to personnel.

A threat awareness program should be established and maintained to recognize and foster awareness of the threat posed by illegal activities at each point in the supply chain to include final point of export. There should be documented procedures on how the export security officer or manager receives information about changes in regulations or procedures.

Employees must be made aware of the procedures the company has in place to address a security incident or suspicion thereof and how to report it.

Additional training should be provided to employees in vital export areas such as the shipping and receiving areas, as well as those receiving and opening mail.

Additionally, specific training should be offered to assist employees in maintaining cargo integrity, recognizing internal conspiracies, protecting access controls, and enhancing physical security.

Security training includes firearms and tactics.

These programs should offer incentives for active employee participation.

INFORMATION TECHNOLOGY SECURITY

Password protection: Automated systems must use individually assigned accounts that require a periodic change of password. IT security policies, procedures, and standards must be in place and provided to employees in the form of training.

Accountability: A system must be in place to identify the abuse of IT including improper access and tampering or the altering of business data. All system violators must be subject to appropriate disciplinary actions for abuse.

Free and secure trade

To help expedite the movement of goods between the United States, Canada, and Mexico, the FASTprogram was developed.

The Free and Secure Trade program (FAST) is a commercial clearance program for known low-risk shipments entering the United States from Canada and Mexico. Participation in FAST requires that every link in the supply chain, from manufacturer to carrier to driver to importer, is certified in the Customs-Trade Partnership Against Terrorism program. The key benefits of FAST enrollment are

- Access to dedicated lanes for greater speed and efficiency in processing transborder shipments

- Reduced number of inspections resulting in reduced delays at the border
- Priority, front-of-the-line processing for CBP inspections

Customs Governance in Compliance and Security with Importers: Five-Step Risk Assessment:

1. **Map cargo flow and identify business partners**
2. **Conduct a threat assessment**
3. **Conduct a vulnerability assessment**
4. **Prepare an action plan**
5. **Document how the risk assessment was conducted**

In the evolution of the C-TPAT program, as supply chain security specialists (SCSSs) performed on-site validations in the United States and overseas, it was recognized that many importers were not maintaining their initial high level of enthusiasm and management of their security program. An analysis by CBP in 2013 indicated 22% of importers did not have a risk assessment process that effectively addressed their international supply chains.

CBP introduced the Five-Step Risk Assessment Guideline to assist companies in developing their own risk assessment process.

1. Map Cargo Flow and Identify Business Partners

Mapping out the entire supply chain allows the importer to highlight when and where cargo is most vulnerable so they can take action. It is important to analyze all parties involved in a shipment from the point of origin to final destination in order to verify that none have been overlooked, such as foreign inland drayage providers or other agents handling paperwork.

2. Conduct a Threat Assessment

The Threat Assessment is an evaluation of all possible threats to the supply chain and must be based on quantitative evidence. Evidence from trusted open-sourced websites and local, state, and federal authorities can be a great resource to identify regional threats. The Threat Assessment should be conducted for all regions in the supply chain and should focus on these key items: terrorism, contraband smuggling, human smuggling, organized crime, and any other conditions in a country or region that may foster such threats. Not all countries and regions pose the same threat, and as a result, it might be determined that low-risk countries do not require analysis under steps 3 and 4.

3. Conduct a Vulnerability Assessment

The Vulnerability Assessment should be of all business partners and service providers throughout the supply chain. Vulnerability should be rated as high, medium, or low. When warranted by medium- or high-level threats, a Vulnerability Assessment is a further evaluation of suppliers' compliance with the C-TPAT minimum security criteria. Such criteria include the following categories: business partner requirements, securing instruments of international traffic, procedural security, physical security, physical access controls, personnel security, security and threat awareness training, and information technology security. Examples of ways in which a Vulnerability Assessment can be conducted include a security questionnaire, an on-site assessment, a review of cycle times with transit points, or an annual business review.

Action plan

4. Prepare an Action Plan

When deficiencies or vulnerabilities are discovered in any part of the supply chain, a corrective action plan must be established with service providers to identify the areas of improvement. The next steps are to prioritize the deficiencies, nominate who is responsible, and establish documentation for dates of completion and verification.

5. **Document How the Risk Assessment Was Conducted**

Written procedures must reflect the policies and processes in place for international risk assessments. Ownership within the company must be assigned for responsibility of duties. Other things that need to be documented are dates and frequency of assessments as well as training and follow-up procedures. The Five-Step Risk Assessment is not inclusive of every scenario or threat that exists. However, it is intended to show the level of planning and effort that is needed to adequately address threats and vulnerabilities.

IMPORTER SECURITY FILING

In 2010, CBP introduced the Importer Security Filing (ISF) rule. ISF requires the importer to electronically submit advance cargo information to CBP no later than 24 hours prior to the loading of ocean freight aboard a vessel destined to the United States. The importer or their agent, such as a customs broker or freight forwarder, is required to file the following data elements:

- Seller
- Buyer
- Ship to party
- Importer of record number/Foreign Trade Zone (FTZ) applicant identification number
- Consignee numbers
- Manufacturer (or supplier)
- Country of origin
- Harmonized tariff number
- Container stuffing location (required 24 hours prior to ship's arrival at a U.S. port)
- Consolidator (required 24 hours prior to ship's arrival at a U.S. port)

The penalty for inaccurate, incomplete, or untimely filing of information is $5000 with a maximum of $10,000 per shipment. In addition to the penalty, importers may find themselves subject to additional inspections and subsequent delays if the ISF is not properly filed. Additionally, noncompliant cargo could be subject to "do not load" orders at origin. Through the ACE web portal, importers can access their ISF report card to monitor and manage their ISF compliance.

Air Cargo Advanced Screening

Similar to the ISF for ocean freight, CBP has been developing a similar program for airfreight shipments. The Air Cargo Advanced Screening (ACAS) program would require the transmission of advance electronic information for air cargo. This information would be required to be filed 4 hours prior to arrival in the United States and/or no later than the time of departure of the aircraft, depending on the location.

As of this writing, ACAS is currently in test mode with voluntarily participants working with U.S. Customs to pilot the program and determine the best way to effectively target, identify, and mitigate risk in the air cargo environment. The ACAS program will probably see fruition by 2017 as it will be a slow integration into the supply chain.

Prior Notice FDA

In 2002, Congress passed the Bioterrorism Act (BTA) as part of its ongoing effort to combat terrorism and to prevent contamination of foods imported into the United States. Twenty percent of imports into the United States are food and food products. BTA requires that the Food and Drug Administration (FDA) receive prior notice before all food, for humans and animals, is imported into the United States, allowing the FDA to effectively target shipments for import inspections. Prior notice is filed electronically.

Consumer Product Safety Commission

The Consumer Product Safety Commission (CPSC) has regulatory authority over consumer products and those products manufactured for children. Importers for these types of products must be aware of the regulatory requirements prior to import to ensure the goods will be allowed entry into the United States as well as to prevent the costs and bad publicity of a public recall. Manufacturers and importers of general-use products and children's products for which consumer product safety rules apply must certify that their products comply with all applicable rules.

In some instances, third-party testing laboratories may be required. Due to the wide range of products that fall under the scope of CPSC, manufacturers and importers should consult the CPSC website for requirements specific to their product.

Consolidated Screening List for Denied Parties

A frequent area missed by most companies and their customer service and supply chain personnel are the regulations concerning the checking and reviewing of the various government lists outlining those parties we cannot deal with.

There is no escaping the importance of exercising due diligence in the supply chain. Knowing our supply chain partners, whether manufacturers, suppliers, agents, consolidators, truckers, and so on is key to demonstrating reasonable care and working toward a secure supply chain.

The Bureau of Industry and Security (BIS) maintains a listing of companies and individuals who have been found to have violated export regulations, Treasury regulations and State regulations. Prior to entering into business agreements with any supply chain partner, companies should screen their business partners through these lists. Any match should be investigated further to ensure the supply chain partner is not a party who is considered a bad actor. The specific lists to be screened may be found further along in this chapter under "Export Compliance."

IMPORT MANAGEMENT OVERVIEW

Americans import more than twice what they export. Therefore, any company that engages in exports has typical import issues as well and knowledge of the regulations is an important aspect of "best practice."

All companies in the United States are required to comply with government agencies regulating their businesses, whether they are on the federal level such as the Department of Transportation, Occupational Safety and Health Administration or the Internal Revenue Service or local authorities. Those companies that import and export must also comply with the various U.S. government agencies regulating the inbound/outbound supply chain.

In order to successfully manage compliance in the supply chain, importers and exporters must develop expertise and understand their regulatory responsibilities. Noncompliance with import and export regulations will likely result in clearance delays and additional charges such as demurrage and may even include government seizure and penalties.

Importer of Record

Customs and Border Protection (CBP) is a revenue-generating agency. CBP was always part of the Department of Treasury along with the Internal Revenue Service. When the Department of Homeland Security was formed, CBP as an agency moved from one department to the other. CBP is charged with protecting the revenue of the United States. This is an important concept for importers to understand so they act responsibly and prudently in their import activity.

The importer of record is the party responsible for the statements and affirmations provided to customs in the entry process. While many importers use a third-party licensed customs broker to actually process the customs entry, the importer remains the responsible party. The entry declarations made minimally include the description, tariff classification, values, and country of origin and statements of use.

Many importers also fail to realize the release of goods from customs and receipt of delivery of goods is not the end of the clearance process. Following customs clearance, CBP has 314 days to review all entry declarations made during the entry process. This time frame is called the liquidation period. During the liquidation period CBP may ask for additional information regarding the imported items to ascertain the correctness of the information provided at the time of entry.

CBP does not permit the importer to distance itself from the import process by expecting the customs broker to respond to any requests for information. In fact, CBP requires the customs broker to act in a compliant manner in the import process as well. In the event CBP finds that the importer and the customs broker did not act in a compliant manner, CBP may fine both parties.

It is the legal requirement of an importer to know CBP rules and regulations and to supervise and control their customs broker.

Reasonable Care

Reasonable care is a degree of care that an ordinary person would exercise in the normal course of business. For importers, it is the degree of care that an importer or their agent uses in the process of entering merchandise into the commerce of the United States. The ability of an importer to demonstrate that they exercised reasonable care in the case of a violation will serve as a mitigating factor and likely not result in liquidated damages being assessed but only the loss of revenue (if any) plus interest.

Importers must be able to demonstrate supervision and control and exercising reasonable care and due diligence over the import process. The import process must be strategically set up to include these additional elements in the import process and not just get the goods from overseas point A to domestic point B as soon as possible and as cheaply as possible. Failure to include due diligence will certainly result in supply chain issues.

The following guidelines must be applied to assist in meeting reasonable care:

- Consult with qualified experts, such as customs brokers, consultants, and attorneys specializing in CBP law.
- Seek guidance from CBP through the formal binding ruling program.
- If using a broker, provide the broker with full and complete information sufficient for the broker to make proper entry (import declaration) or provide advice on how to make entry.
- Obtain analysis from accredited laboratories to determine the technical qualities of imported merchandise.
- Use in-house employees who have experience and knowledge of CBP regulations and procedures.
- Follow binding rulings received from CBP.
- Ensure that products are legally marked with the country of origin to indicate to the ultimate purchaser the origin of imported products.
- Do not classify or value identical merchandise in different ways.
- Notify CBP when receiving different treatment for the same goods at different entries or different ports.
- Examine entries (Import Declaration CF 3461) prepared by the broker to determine the accuracy in classification and valuation.

Ultimate Consignee

Contact First Name	Ultimate Consignee Contact First Name not allowed if To Be Sold en Route Indicator is Y.	If consignee name is SOLD EN ROUTE and there is a first name
	Ultimate Consignee Contact First Name contains more than 13 characters.	If its length is more than 13 (X12: Ultimate Consignee Contact First Name will be truncated if the length is more than 13)
	Ultimate Consignee Contact First Name contains invalid character(s).	If it doesn't contain ALPHABETIC chars (X12 & AESTIR: All non ALPHABETIC chars will be removed)
	Ultimate Consignee Contact First Name contains leading spaces.	If it starts with spaces
	Ultimate Consignee Contact First Name ineligible.	If name is one of the ineligible strings
	Ultimate Consignee Contact Last Name required if Ultimate Consignee First Name is reported.	If there is a first name and no last name

On most import transactions, the importer of record and the ultimate consignee are the same. The opinion of CBP is that the ultimate consignee caused the import to occur and is one of the responsible parties to the import transaction. Therefore, the ultimate consignee can be held accountable for regulatory requirements even if they are not the importer of record.

An example of this is when a foreign manufacturer uses Federal Express to deliver a shipment door to door with all charges being billed to the FedEx account of the foreign manufacturer. In this instance, CBP recognizes that Federal Express is not the actual purchaser and did not cause the import.

CBP requires that if a buyer causes the import, the buyer must have the usual records required to import. This includes the bill of lading, entry documents, purchase order, and invoice.

Power of Attorney

The customs broker is required to have a power of attorney in order to handle the import on behalf of the importer. One way of managing the import process and exercising supervision and control over the import process is for the importer to manage the number of customs brokers that are conducting customs business on their behalf.

Importers should exercise control using the power of attorney to include the time frame for which the power of attorney is valid and not leave it open-ended. Importers may even add that any changes or subbing out of customs broker activities are not permitted without the written consent of the importer.

The power of attorney is established for the protection of the importer of record to control brokers and this is an important compliance tool that also enables an importer to demonstrate how they control the import process.

All powers of attorney should be dated with a date of expiration not to exceed an initial period of 30 days for renewal, pending proven performance. Once the importer is satisfied with the broker's performance, powers of attorney should not be issued for a period that exceeds 1 year.

Importers should perform extensive reviews of all brokerage services to critique the internal expertise being applied to each entry. Broker reviews should be done minimally on a yearly basis, if not more often, as a way to manage the performance of customs brokers. Any broker who falls below the importer's standards of compliance should have their power of attorney revoked by a letter of revocation sent to the CBP port director at the port of entry by the importer.

Here are some ways the broker can validate a power of attorney:

- To the greatest extent possible, have powers of attorney (POAs) completed in person so the grantor's personal identification (driver's license, passport, etc.) can be reviewed.
- Check applicable websites to verify the POA grantor's business and registration with state authorities.
- If the principal uses a trade or fictitious name in doing business, confirm that the name appears on the POA.

- Verify that the importer's name, importer number, and Employer Identification Number (also known as the Federal Tax Identification Number) on the POA match what is in ACS.
  - Check whether the POA grantor is named as a sanctioned or restricted person or entity by the U.S. Government. See the Bureau of Industry and Security's Export Enforcement.

COMMERCIAL INVOICES

Invoices must be in English and must include the following:

a. Probable port of entry
b. Name and address of importer of record
c. Name and address of ultimate consignee if known at the time of import and if different from the importer of record
d. Name and address of the manufacturer and shipper
e. Description of merchandise, including the name each item is known as
f. Unit price of the merchandise
g. Currency of sale
h. Country of origin for each item
i. Statement of use in the United States (if applicable)
j. Discounts from price and rebates offered between buyer and seller
k. Values of assists including tools, molds, dies, and engineering work (performed outside the United States) and provided to the manufacturer to assist in product the imported items
l. Packing list
m. Endorsed by the person who prepared the invoice

The acquiring company should request a sample entry package and purchase order as well as copies of the correspondence on a typical import shipment to review whether invoices appear to be in line with the transaction prior to performing a full import review.

RECORDKEEPING

Recordkeeping is a significant area of scrutiny in CBP audits and can lead to serious fines and penalties when recordkeeping requirements are not followed correctly. Recordkeeping may be as simple as maintaining folders in a secure and comprehensive manner. It is very important for importers to be aware of all records they are required to maintain. Records that must be kept include any that substantiate the facts in the entry declaration, including payments to foreign vendors, and contracts and agreements.

For importers whose products are subject to other government agency clearances, those government agency recordkeeping requirements must also be followed.

Many importers rely on their customs broker to maintain their records.

However, the legal requirement is for the importer to keep their own records. Additionally, the customs broker may not have certain records such as payments to a foreign vendor in their files. Another reason not to rely on the customs broker to maintain documents is if the relationship between the importer and the customs broker is terminated through a change in corporate management, broker error, or the broker goes out of business, the importer will not have access to those records. Records are required to be kept by the importer and establishing a recordkeeping system and auditing those records on a periodic basis is a demonstration of reasonable care in the import process.

Documentation requirements are as follows:

- Purchase inquiries
- Purchase verifications

- Purchase negotiations between the buyer and seller of importer merchandise
- Purchase order communications
- Commercial invoices
- Packing list information
- Special customs declarations and certifications
- Customs Import Declaration (CBP 3461)
- Customs Entry Summary (CBP 7501)
- All communication records between the customs broker and import compliance and traffic department in reference to each import transaction
- Supervisory communication detailing supervision and control of import decisions between the importer and broker, freight forwarder, consultants, and attorneys
- All records of communication received from CBP
- All records of communication relating to any statements or acts made by CBP
- Notice of liquidations communication records
- Communication records detailing receipt of merchandise into the importer's establishments or designated receiving stations
- Communication records detailing the disposition of the merchandise after receipt and distribution
- Records indicating actual proof of purchase of imported goods
- Records indicating contract of carriage agreements, airway bills, and bills of lading
- Records indicating the exact amount of prepaid international freight and/or insurance contained in the import sales transaction

TRANSACTIONAL VALUATION

It is the importer's responsibility to ensure the proper values are fully disclosed to CBP.

Many importers make the common practice error of relying on the commercial invoice as the value for the goods. However, the commercial invoice may not represent the true price paid or payable for an import shipment. Incorrect valuation determinations may lead to fines and penalties against the importer of record.

For CBP purposes, the value of the goods is based on the price paid or payable to bring the goods to the foreign port/airport of loading overseas, what is commonly called the FOB/FCA foreign port value.

Keeping in mind that because CBP has the period of liquidation to review any value declarations, the importer must exercise reasonable care that the value stated at the time of entry is the correct value. The customs broker does not have knowledge of all facts associated with the import and unless the customs broker is asking additional questions regarding the commercial invoice the importer must make certain they are controlling the value declarations made to CBP.

ASSISTS

The import valuation declaration process has many components that require specific attention to purchasing and sourcing details that are included within the scope of proper value reporting practices. Many importers are not aware of these specific responsibilities of compliant reporting through the formal declaration process of imported articles. An example of a common practice error in the valuation declaration process is the omission of proper reporting of assist values. Assists are defined as any materials such as dies, molds, tools, and machinery provided from the buyer of imported merchandise to the seller of imported merchandise at a reduced cost or free of charge.

Import shipments that contain an assist must be accompanied by a proper commercial invoice that itemizes the value and existence of an assist as an invoice requirement. There are some exemptions from an assist declaration include design work, engineering work, and research and development fees undertaken in the United States that will not be treated as an assist.

DRAWBACK

Drawback is a privilege granted by CBP that allows an importer to collect 99% of duties previously paid by exporting the merchandise from the United States or destroying the imported goods under CBP supervision.

There are three types of drawback:

- *Unused merchandise drawback*: a 99% refund of duties paid on imported merchandise that is exported in the same condition as when imported and remains unused in the United States. The importer may submit a drawback claim within 3 years from the date of importation.
- *Rejected merchandise drawback*: a 99% refund on imported merchandise that does not conform to the importer's standards of approval or the standards of any government agency. The importer may submit a drawback claim for 3 years from the date of importation.
- *Manufacturing drawback*: a 99% refund of duties paid on imported merchandise that is further processed or manufactured in the United States and subsequently exported. CBP will allow a 99% refund of duties paid on the imported merchandise for up to 5 years from the date of importation.

Unless a company is given prior permission otherwise, all merchandise must be examined by CBP before export to qualify for the drawback privilege. A filer notifies CBP of the intent to file a drawback claim in reference to an export by filing a Notice of Intent. The importer must allow at least five working days before the export of the merchandise. CBP will notify the drawback claimant of the intent to examine or waive the examination.

HARMONIZED TARIFF CLASSIFICATION

All merchandise entering the United States must be properly identified through the assignation of a Harmonized Tariff Classification number. CBP requires that all merchandise be identified by a commodity classification number referenced in the Harmonized Tariff Schedule of the United States (HTSUS). Merchandise entering the commerce of the United States requires specific identification to afford CBP and other government agencies an opportunity to make the proper affirmation of release into the commerce of the United States utilizing commodity-specific controls.

Many importers rely on their customs brokers to determine the HTS codes on their behalf. This practice is noncompliant and may result in penalties to the importer for lack of reasonable care. The HTS should be determined by the importer and the importer may ask the customs broker for assistance with the classification since the customs broker is considered a customs expert. However, the HTS determination is ultimately the responsibility of the importer. The importer should manage the tariff classification process through training its employees on the general rules of interpretation and proper classification principles.

Importers should create a classification database for their products. The HTS number can then be added to the purchase order and be used from the beginning of the import transaction to be included on the commercial invoice created by the supplier and be carried through the import process. This practice will demonstrate reasonable care in the import process.

HOW TO CLASSIFY

The code is divided into 97 sections. Each section is divided into chapters, each chapter into numerical headings, and each heading into subheadings.

The goal is to drill down or further clarify and identify the product in more detail in order to narrow down the definition to more completely identify your product.

Let's say you are exporting a "large telescopic poolside umbrella, which you can open to 8 feet coverage."

Following this path:

Section
Chapter
Heading
Subheading

We would first identify "umbrellas" in Section XII:

"Footwear, Headgear, Umbrellas, Sun Umbrellas, Walking Sticks, Seat-Sticks, Whips, Riding-Crops and Parts Thereof; Prepared Feathers and Articles Made Therewith; Artificial Flowers; Articles of Human Hair."

COUNTRY OF ORIGIN MARKING

It is an import requirement that goods are marked with the country of origin in order to indicate to the ultimate purchaser the specific country of origin of the product. The criteria for country of origin may also play a role in the applicability of preferential tariff treatment and corresponding rates of duty.

Country of origin is also seen to be of importance in global security. This is crucial in assessing risk should an alert be issued on products from a particular place of origin. Goods not properly marked are subject to delays and marking duties.

The inclusion of marking instructions in a purchase agreement demonstrates reasonable care in the import entry process.

PAYMENT OF DUTIES AND TAXES

Customs collects duties and taxes as goods pass through the border.

Many importers use customs brokers to pay their duties and taxes. This is a very common practice. It should be noted that while the importer may pay the broker the monies to submit to CBP on their behalf, if the broker does not pay CBP the importer will still be held liable for payment of duties.

Every importer is required to have a bond in order to clear customs. The first condition of a bond is to pay duties, fees, and taxes on a timely basis. Payment may be made directly by the importer or the broker via check or electronic payment (Automated Clearing House [ACH]).

In a CBP audit, the importer will be asked how they manage the duty payment process. It is unacceptable to simply state that the broker pays the duty. A system of accountability must be implemented to ensure timely payment, and the importer must understand how payment is being managed. Copies of the final ACH statement as well as a copy of the check will serve as proof of payment.

ITDS

Importing and exporting involves over 48 different government agencies that require nearly 200 different forms in order to process a shipment. The prior system requires a lot of paper and information to be entered in multiple electronic systems. The International Trade Data System (ITDS) will eliminate redundancy, operational costs, and facilitate more efficient processing of imports and exports. As of this writing, the implementation for other government agencies participating in ITDS is staggered over 2016.

ACE

The Automated Commercial Environment (ACE) is the system through which the single window of International Trade Data System will be realized. It is the primary system used by the international trade community to submit import and export data and communicate with CBP and other participating government agencies (PGA). ACE will be used by CBP and PGAs to collect, track, and process required trade information to determine the admissibility of shipments.

As of this writing, U.S. Customs and Border Protection (CBP) is transitioning its cargo release and entry summary processing to a paperless environment. Through use of the Document Image System (DIS) filers can submit supporting documentation to the government during the import process and for export manifests. This process allows for timely receipt of documentation as opposed to hard copy paper.

Supporting documentation for Participating Government Agencies (PGA), CBP, RLF documents, and CBP forms 28, 29 and 4647 may all be submitted through DIS and ACE.

For exporters, ACE will allow the exporter to obtain their own filer reports directly through the ACE system as opposed to submitting a formal written request to Census. This will enable exporters to better supervise their export activity on a timelier basis.

CENTERS OF EXCELLENCE AND EXPERTISE

CBP has established the Centers of Excellence and Expertise (CEE) to operate as an organizational structure for postrelease trade activities. These centers operate within an industry sector and from a national perspective. Some of these trade functions include entry summary processing; decisions and activities regarding packing, country of origin marking, merchandise sampling, trademarks, classification, appraisement, and rules of origin; and processing of liquidations, protests, and petitions.

CBP has 10 centers operating in a virtual environment, strategically managed as follows:

- Agriculture and Prepared Products: Miami
- Apparel, Footwear and Textiles: San Francisco
- Automotive and Aerospace: Detroit
- Base Metals: Chicago
- Consumer Products and Mass Merchandising: Atlanta
- Electronics: Los Angeles
- Industrial and Manufacturing Materials: Buffalo
- Machinery: Laredo
- Petroleum, Natural Gas and Minerals: Houston
- Pharmaceuticals, Health and Chemicals: New York

**U.S. Customs and
Border Protection**

Centers serve as a centralized source for trade inquiries for resolving issues. While centers are industry-focused they are also account-based, meaning once an importer has been assigned to a center that center will handle postrelease trade activity for all imports regardless of the tariff classification.

GLOBALLY HARMONIZED SYSTEM OF CLASSIFICATION AND LABELING OF CHEMICALS

The Globally Harmonized System of Classification and Labeling of Chemicals (GHS) became effective in 2015. This rule requires all manufacturers and importers to comply with new label requirements and Safety Data Sheets formats. The Occupational Safety and Health Administration (OSHA) revised its Hazard Communication Standard in 2012 to require employers to adhere to elements of the Globally Harmonized System for the Classification and Labeling of Chemicals, setting deadlines for worker training and for the labels and SDSs; along with new requirements for information, the labels must include signal words, hazard statements, pictograms, and more.

CUSTOMER SERVICE RESPONSIBILITIES IN EXPORT COMPLIANCE

The four standards in export trade compliance are

- Due diligence
- Reasonable care
- Supervision and control
- Proactive engagement

These standards are how a company and personnel need to develop in demonstrating a secure and trade-compliant supply chain.

Every country controls exports and imports. In the United States, there are several government agencies involved in the export process. Within the Department of Commerce there is the Bureau of Industry and Security (BIS) and the Bureau of Census. The Office of Foreign Assets Control (OFAC) is part of the Department of Treasury. Companies that deal with items on the United States Munitions List (USML) will also fall under the jurisdiction of the Department of State Office of Defense Trade Controls (DTC). Homeland Security's Bureau of Customs and Border Protection (CBP) is also involved in the enforcement of export regulations.

The Export Administration Regulations (EAR) are the rules by which the BIS regulates and controls the export of goods from the United States. The EAR also controls certain activities such as the transfer of information to foreign nationals or engaging in restrictive trade boycotts not sanctioned by the United States. Companies that export from the United States are required to comply with these regulations and must have a process for managing their exports and international activities such as an Export Management Compliance Program. The Export Management Compliance Program becomes the game plan for staying compliant and avoiding export violations.

ELECTRONIC EXPORT INFORMATION

The Bureau of Census is the agency responsible for the collection of export data. The Electronic Export Information (EEI) is required for export shipments that have a value above $2500 per HTS line item. For licensed items, the EEI is required regardless of the value of the shipment.

The Foreign Trade Regulations outline the requirements for filing the EEI including exceptions to filing. For example, the EEI is not required for exports to Canada.

The information required to be filed as part of the Electronic Export Information include

- U.S. Principal Party in Interest Name and Identification Number
- Date of export
- Ultimate consignee

- U.S. state of origin
- Country of ultimate destination
- Method of transportation
- Conveyance/carrier name
- Carrier identification code
- Port of export
- Related party indicator
- Domestic or foreign origin indicator
- Commodity classification number
- Commodity description
- Shipping weight
- Value
- Export information code
- Shipment reference number
- Hazardous material indicator
- Routed export transaction indicator
- Conditional data elements as required

Incorrect data transmitted on the EEI can lead to potential delays if the information does not appear valid or CBP holds the shipment because the incorrect HTS/Schedule B number is transmitted.

There are two types of export transactions, standard export transactions and routed export transactions. Compliance with the Foreign Trade Regulations depends on the type of export transaction and the roles of the players within those transactions.

In a standard export transaction, the U.S. Principal Party in Interest (USPPI) is the party in the United States who is responsible for compliance with export regulations and the correct filing of the EEI. The USPPI will choose their own freight forwarder and supervise the export process. The EEI may be filed by the USPPI or their freight forwarder. The freight forwarder must have written authorization from the U.S. Principal Party in Interest to file the EEI on their behalf. The U.S. Principal Party in Interest must provide the freight forwarder with the information needed to file the EEI timely and accurately.

In a routed export transaction, the Foreign Principal Party in Interest (FPPI) chooses the freight forwarder. The USPPI and FPPI have specific requirements under the Foreign Trade Regulations that they must follow.

The USPPI must provide the customer's (FPPI's) freight forwarder with the data elements necessary for the freight forwarder to file the EEI. The freight forwarder must obtain written authorization from the FPPI to file the EEI on their behalf. The interesting part of this is that the USPPI is still listed on the EEI but the authorization for the filing the EEI on a routed export comes from the FPPI.

Upon request by the USPPI, the freight forwarder must provide the USPPI with a copy of the FPPI's written authorization and a copy of the filed EEI data elements provided by the USPPI in a routed export transaction.

If the USPPI wants to file the EEI in a routed export, the USPPI must obtain written authorization to file the EEI from the FPPI.

In either a standard export transaction or a routed export transaction, the USPPI must maintain records for 5 years from the date of export.

Bureau of Industry and Security

The Bureau of Industry and Security (BIS) administers the Export Administration Regulations (EAR) and regulates exports from the United States of most commercial items. These items are referred to as dual-use items. Items that are controlled for export may require authorization from the BIS prior to export.

Items that are controlled for export are listed on the Commerce Control List (CCL). The specific products described on the Commerce Control List are designated by an Export Control Classification Number (ECCN). The ECCN is broken down into 10 categories as follows:

- Nuclear materials, facilities, and equipment
- Materials, chemicals, microorganisms, and toxins
- Materials processing
- Electronics
- Computers

- Telecommunications and information security
- Sensors and lasers
- Navigation and avionics
- Marine
- Propulsion systems, space vehicles, and related equipment

Proper classification of the item to be exported is essential to determine licensing requirements under the EAR. In many cases, the assistance of company product designers and engineers is required because the information used to ascertain the correct classification is specific and technical. If exporters have difficulty classifying a product, they can turn to outside sources such as consultants or the BIS.

In the classification process, a product will be found to be either on the list or not. In the case of an item found on the list, the exporter must review the destination country to determine whether a license is required to ship to the country. The Commerce Country Chart is a matrix of reasons for control tied to the destination country and is contained within the EAR. If, after review of the Commerce Country Chart, a license is found to be necessary, the exporter must review the transaction to determine if a license exception is available. A license exception may be used in lieu of a license, provided the exporter performs the balance of the due diligence in the export transaction. This information is reported to the Census Bureau and BIS on export as part of the EEI transmission.

If, after review of the Commerce Country Chart and review of the transaction a license is found to be required before export, the exporter can apply for a license. This can be done electronically through the BIS website via the Simplified Network Application Process (SNAP).

If, after review of the Commerce Control List a product is not found to be on the list, the product may be shipped under no license required (NLR) status, provided the exporter has performed other required responsibilities before export.

DENIED PARTY SCREENING

Companies engaged in exporting and importing must exercise various levels of due diligence. They must be aware of who the end user of the product is and who the parties to the transaction are. This requires screening of all the parties in the transaction. In the event an exporter is uncomfortable with an export transaction or cannot ascertain answers to the end user and end use questions, the exporter should not move ahead with the export as the transaction may be detrimental to national security.

All parties to the export transaction should be screened through the following lists:

Department of Commerce: Bureau of Industry and Security

Denied Persons List: Individuals and entities that have been denied export privileges. Any dealings with a party on this list that would violate the terms of its denial order are prohibited.

Unverified List: End users who BIS has been unable to verify in prior transactions. The presence of a party on this list in a transaction is a "Red Flag" that should be resolved before proceeding with the transaction.

Entity List: Parties whose presence in a transaction can trigger a license requirement supplemental to those elsewhere in the Export Administration Regulations (EAR). The list specifies the license requirements and policy that apply to each listed party.

Department of State: Bureau of International Security and Nonproliferation

Nonproliferation sanctions: Parties that have been sanctioned under various statutes. The linked webpage is updated as appropriate, but the Federal Register is the only official and complete listing of nonproliferation sanctions determinations.

Department of State: Directorate of Defense Trade Controls

AECA Debarred List: Entities and individuals prohibited from participating directly or indirectly in the export of defense articles, including technical data and defense services. Pursuant to the Arms Export Control Act (AECA) and the International Traffic in Arms Regulations (ITAR), the AECA Debarred List includes persons convicted in court of violating or conspiring to violate the AECA and subject to "statutory debarment" or persons established to have violated the AECA in an administrative proceeding and subject to "administrative debarment."

Department of the Treasury: Office of Foreign Assets Control

Specially Designated Nationals List: Parties who may be prohibited from export transactions based on OFAC's regulations. The EAR require a license for exports or reexports to any party in any entry on this list that contains any of the suffixes SDGT, SDT, FTO, IRAQ2, or NPWMD.

Foreign Sanctions Evaders List: Foreign individuals and entities determined to have violated, attempted to violate, conspired to violate, or caused a violation of U.S. sanctions on Syria or Iran, as well as foreign persons who have facilitated deceptive transactions for or on behalf of persons subject to U.S. Sanctions. Transactions by U.S. persons or within the United States involving Foreign Sanctions Evaders (FSEs) are prohibited.

Sectoral Sanctions Identifications (SSI) List: Individuals operating in sectors of the Russian economy with whom U.S. persons are prohibited from transacting in, providing financing for, or dealing in debt with a maturity of longer than 90 days.

Palestinian Legislative Council (PLC) List: Individuals of the PLC who were elected on the party slate of Hamas, or any other Foreign Terrorist Organization (FTO), Specially Designed Terrorist (SDT), or Specially Designated Global Terrorist (SDGT).

The List of Foreign Financial Institutions Subject to Part 561 (the Part 561 List): The Part 561 List includes the names of foreign financial institutions that are subject to sanctions, certain prohibitions, or strict conditions before a U.S. company may do business with them.

Non-SDN Iranian Sanctions Act List (NS-ISA): The ISA List includes persons determined to have made certain investments in Iran's energy sector or to have engaged in certain activities relating to Iran's refined petroleum sector. Their names do not appear on the Specially Designated Nationals or Blocked Persons (SDN) List, and their property and/or interests in property are not blocked, pursuant to this action.

COMPLIANCE WITH ANTIBOYCOTT REGULATIONS

Antiboycott regulations prohibit U.S. companies from participating in foreign boycotts that the United States does not sanction. The effect of these regulations is to prevent U.S. companies from being used to implement foreign policies of other countries that run counter to U.S. policy.

The antiboycott regulations of the EAR apply to all U.S. persons, defined to include individuals and companies located in the United States and their foreign affiliates. These regulations pertain to exports, imports, financing, forwarding, shipping, and other transactions that may occur offshore.

Antiboycott regulations prohibit

- Agreements to refuse or actual refusal to do business with Israel or blacklisted companies
- Agreements to discriminate against other persons based on race, religion, sex, national origin, or nationality
- Agreements to furnish information about business relations with Israel or blacklisted companies
- Agreements to furnish information about the race, religion, gender, or national origin of another person
- Implementing letters of credit containing prohibited boycott terms or conditions

If a company receives a purchase order or document containing boycott language, they need to consider if the language in the document is prohibited and reportable. Prohibited language will require the company to obtain a clean document with the boycott language removed. Reporting is required and can be done electronically.

OFFICE OF FOREIGN ASSETS CONTROL

Within the Department of the Treasury is the Office of Foreign Assets Control (OFAC), which administers and enforces economic and trade sanctions based on U.S. foreign policy and national security goals. These sanctions are targeted against foreign countries, terrorists, international narcotics traffickers, and those engaged in activities related to the proliferation of weapons of mass destruction. Many of these sanctions are based on United Nations and other international mandates, are multilateral in scope, and involve close cooperation with allied governments.

Under these sanctions, U.S. companies are prohibited from trading or engaging in financial transactions with individuals, companies, and countries on the sanctions list unless the company has received specific authorization to engage in the transaction.

All U.S. persons must comply with OFAC regulations, including all U.S. citizens and permanent resident aliens, regardless of where they are located, all persons and entities within the United States, and all U.S. incorporated entities and their foreign subsidiaries.

OFAC Enforcement Examples:

International Traffic in Arms Regulations (ITAR)

The Department of State manages export control over military items through the Arms Export Control Act (AECA). This act authorizes the president to control the export and import of defense articles and defense services. License or approval may be granted only to U.S. companies who are registered with Defense Trade Controls for export of such items.

Through Export Control Reform the ITAR has been significantly overhauled. Many items have moved from the U.S. Munitions List (USML) to the Commerce Control List (CCL). The USML has moved to a positive list and is much more specific than it was previously. As of this writing there are still a few categories remaining that have not undergone overhaul but are pending review.

IMPORT/EXPORT COMPLIANCE MANAGEMENT

Due diligence, reasonable care, and supervision and control are critical deliverables of export compliance. The core elements of an effective compliance management are the same for all companies regardless of the commodities and services they are shipping and providing. There may be additional steps that must be taken for those companies who are engaged in commodities that are controlled for export due to the type of commodity or fall under another government agency requirement for imports.

The basic elements of any company's compliance management must include the following elements in order to be effective:

- Compliance awareness
- Senior management commitment
- Identification of risks based on commodities and types of transactions
- Formal written manual
- Training and awareness
- Knowledge of valuation concepts
- Screening of business partners, customers, financial institutions, and supply chain partners
- Recordkeeping requirements
- Periodic auditing and monitoring
- System for reporting violations and handling compliance issues
- System for implementing corrective actions where a compliance issue is indicated
- Partnering with knowledgeable and compliant service providers

TRADE COMPLIANCE AND INTERNALIZED AUDITING

Importers and exporters should perform internal audits based on the risks within their supply chain. CBP and the BIS both offer guidance on managing internal audits. The documents outlined in the appendix can be the start of creating a template for managing the internal audit process.

Audits are designed to assure that a company is acting with due diligence, reasonable care, and with supervision and control.

Companies are different in every country, but true politeness is everywhere the same.

Oliver Goldsmith

6

Utilizing Service Providers and Other Useful Third Parties to Enhance Your Customer Service Capabilities

Managing the global supply chain for most companies requires partners. These partners are freight forwarders, customhouse brokers, third party logistics (3PLs), and the carriers (ocean, air, rail, and truck).

In some instances, the warehousing and distribution systems located both in the United States and abroad in all the countries we sell to and service would be included in this mix as well.

This chapter provides a perspective into that world and outlines how best to work with these partners and obtain the most favored results of well-managed vendor relationships.

The favorable utilization of these third parties will "make or break" how well your supply chain operates!

OVERVIEW OF SERVICE PROVIDERS

Service providers are third-party companies that handle your logistics needs. Although easily stated, the reality is that moving freight internationally is both a convoluted and arduous process requiring highly skilled professionals with tenured experienced.

The mantra of this book series is "Global Warrior." Quality service providers would be considered true "global warriors" under any standard or microscope? .

The primary responsibility of service providers is to act as an intermediary between the shippers and receivers of international freight and the various parties, carriers, and government agencies that are also engaged in that process.

There is no requirement or legal necessity to utilize service providers. A company can move its own freight. It can even customs-clear its own freight.

But having said that, there is a clear majority of companies that utilize the services of third-party service providers.

Typically, the rationale is

- They have defined expertise not existing with the principal shipper, importer, or exporter

- They have depth and manpower within their organizations that the principal shipper can access
- They have a global network of offices and agents
- They have technology capabilities that we can access
- They understand how best to deal with government regulatory agencies, such as Customs (CBP) and the FDA
- They grant access to their freight contacts, which can provide competitive options
- They have access to warehouses and distribution systems to assist with storage, fulfillment, and cargo handling requirements

- They provide expertise to reduce risk and spend out of the global supply chain in all the areas as depicted in the image on the left
- They assist with trade compliance management responsibilities
- They can assist with overseas collections of monies as well as letters of credit and other financial instruments
- Through their international connections can sometimes be of value in making introductions for business value
- They have expertise in documentation, record-keeping, HTS/Classifications, and other foreign sales processing responsibilities
- They can access foreign trade zones, bonded warehouses, and other similar services to help our global supply chains gain competitive advantage
- They can handle deferred, regular, and expedited freight needs

Service providers go under many names and banners, but primarily they are referred to as

- Freight forwarders
- Customhouse brokers
- 3PLs
- Carriers
- Warehousing, fulfillment, and distribution

SERVICE PORTFOLIOS AND EXPECTATIONS

The basic forwarder varies greatly from their competition.
They all provide the basic services:

- Provide shipping expertise
- Book actual shipments pickups and deliveries
- Create necessary export and import documentation
- Track and trace shipping activity
- Customs clearance services

These five areas are the most frequently utilized areas of third-party expertise that principal companies utilize freight service providers for.

This is the basic "value add" that these providers offer. There is no magic here. A shipper could handle these responsibilities.

PUTTING ALL YOUR "EGGS" IN ONE BASKET

The theory in service provider utilization up until 2008 was to diversify your portfolio so as not to be too dependent on one company.

While this theory still has some merit, as the recession grew in 2009, companies leveraged their spending by concentrating business into singular entities.

This practice created the most "leverage" to reduce costs.

The business process then required intense management of that "basket" if you placed all your "eggs" in it!

MANAGING FREIGHT RFPs

Freight RFPs are an excellent method to

- Identify potential supply chain partners
- Benchmark services and costs
- Weed out bad players
- Bring in better players
- Determine who your partners will be

The RFP process is designed to allow a comprehensive, fair, and responsible process for selecting companies to provide services to your organization. The RFP process includes the following:

- RFP Internal Committee selection process
- Assessment of needs
- Assessment of incumbent's performance and place in the RFP
- Potential RFP participants

- Creation of RFP Module
- Timing and execution of the RFP process
- Evaluation of RFP presentations in writing and in person
- Selection process
- Implementation
- Business review

Working through all those steps will maximize the opportunity for the most favorable results in selecting service providers, carriers, and actually most companies competing for your business.

Great customer service ... makes for your best sales person.

Thomas A. Cook
Founder, Blue Tiger International

7

Negotiating Skill Sets in Global Trade

This chapter outlines the necessary skill sets to negotiate with leverage, advantage, and with success. Customer service is not an easy responsibility but can be made manageable when an individual understands what is necessary to do to negotiate better.

Negotiation is both an art and a science. Master both aspects and succeed more times!

Thomas A. Cook

THE WINNING PREMISE OF NEGOTIATION

While we all want to win in every negotiation we enter, the likelihood is that is not probable.

Nor should it be a desired goal. We need to enter into our global customer service responsibilities with a mind-set of getting the job done.

Our primary responsibility in customer service is to manage our company's relationship successfully with our overseas clients and vendors.

Negotiation prowess is a tool to help us accomplish that goal. Winning may not necessarily be the direct result.

Winning is achieving our goal, which may include various levels of compromise and sacrifice to get where we want to be:

1. Obtain new customers
2. Grow with existing customers
3. Sustain relations with existing customers
4. Successfully working out the day-to-day issues and finding good problem resolution
5. Eliminating as much difficulty, frustration, and angst as possible

In global trade, successful negotiation gets us to where we are achieving our goals 1–5, as outlined above.

This is a highly "emotionally intelligent" perspective that winning is not the critical goal—achieving results in the areas outlined above is!

Negotiation is therefore a skill set that helps us achieve those desired results.

AN EXAMPLE BASED ON TRUE EVENTS

You are the customer service manager (Marie) for a tool manufacturer in Ohio who exports to over 19 countries. Your European salesman (Nigel) has opened a new account in Germany.

The terms of the first sale were delivered duty paid (DDP). This meant that you the seller/exporter are required to ship the goods to final destination in Frankfurt and pay for all the expenses inclusive of the customs clearance process, duties, and taxes (VAT).

It was a small kind of test order, with only four pieces of equipment valued at $21,300. The additional costs added another $1100 to the transaction, totaling $22,400.

The shipment left the Ohio plant on schedule on Tuesday afternoon, and was being shipped by airfreight and was scheduled to arrive and be delivered by Friday morning.

The exporter utilized an integrated carrier to handle the shipment. That carrier's office needed information from the buyer (Ultimate Consignee) enabling customs clearance. That office waited too late and only requested the information on Friday morning.

By the time it received the necessary information, it was too late and they missed delivering on Friday morning. It was delivered on Monday morning.

At that point, the client was not very happy as they needed the equipment for tooling that was going to occur on Friday and over the weekend.

The client found another solution on Friday with a local tool company that was a "Band-Aid" fix, which was more costly and not exactly what they required or wanted.

The terms of payment were 30 days and now the customer was making a case about not paying in their anger.

The salesperson was also unhappy at how this was handled and was all over Marie, the customer service manager, to resolve the issue and the dissatisfaction with the shipping problem.

The resolution is in structuring a strategy that is fact-based. When we discuss key elements later in this chapter, mining for information is a strategy and tactic. Creating a plan is also part of the negotiation process.

It can work as follows:

- Part of problem resolution is negotiating a favorable outcome.
- The outcome needed by the seller is to not lose the new client.
- The outcome from the clients' perspective is not known at this time and must be found out. The mistake that Marie could make is by assuming she knows what the resolution is, rather than investigate what they need to bring back favor.
- The German culture favors honoring commitments tightly, delivering as scheduled and being on time!
- At some point the salesperson won the confidence over from the buyer. He has the best relationship, at this point.
- The responsibility for the problem lays clearly with the seller in Ohio and possibly Marie herself.

Let me explain:

The shipment had a very specific delivery schedule. The freight arrived on Thursday morning in Frankfurt for customs clearance and last mile delivery.

Marie's office alerted the shipping agent in Frankfurt of the shipment and all the important documentation and delivery instructions. The customer service department followed up; when they arrived at 0900 EST, the time was 2 PM in Frankfurt.

By the time the customer provided the necessary information for customs clearance, it was after 5 PM local time in Frankfurt—passing the time frame for customs clearance.

Marie's office should have had their integrated carrier's local agent in Frankfurt obtain the necessary information from the customer a few days before the needed delivery date, proactively obtaining the required information. Then Marie's office should have established a follow-up procedure on Thursday to make sure that had been accomplished.

This would have reduced the opportunity for service failure dramatically and may have prevented any customer dissatisfaction to begin with.

NEGOTIATION OR PROBLEM RESOLUTION STRATEGY

Have the salesperson visit with the customer on Monday morning or soon thereafter. Nigel will get Marie on the phone while he is present in the customer's office.

Remember the goal is to keep the client for the long term and mitigate the current problem.

When the call begins, Marie takes the lead. She apologizes for the problem, takes ownership of the problem, makes no excuses and explains that her office failed to follow up proactively with the clearance and delivery agent in Frankfurt.

Marie advises that there will be no charge for the freight portion and will reissue a discounted invoice. She also advises that within the next two orders, delivery will be made for free.

Marie also advised that her staff will proactively follow up on all their shipments to make sure delivery occurs as committed and she will personally supervise that responsibility.

The offer works and the customer places another order. A year later the relationship is good and is growing well.

The customer witnessed Marie's commitments being honored and she stayed on top of all the shipping from that day forward. Marie and the client developed a relationship based on commitment and promises made, and trust was now established.

The goal of the negotiation was to keep the customer and this was achieved.

The negotiation accomplished the following:

- Accepted responsibility and faced the problem "head-on" without making excuses
- Created a mitigation in cost for the immediate problem and continued mitigation on the next two shipments
- Offered commitments for preventive measures
- Created a relationship between Marie and the customer that was based on "trust"
- Created a "win-win" for both parties

There could have been another ending to that story for the company in Ohio. But Marie had taken a class with the National Institute for World Trade (niwt.org) and learned about how to problem resolve and negotiate solutions—the best $375 she ever spent!

Negotiation is a tool, a process, and an action to obtain a favorable result.

Negotiation can be utilized to

- Change behavior
- Influence a different outcome
- Overcome unwillingness
- Gain a more favorable decision

Negotiation is best accomplished by individuals who understand the psychology of human behavior and can apply that understanding to a reasonable thought process of communication and action to achieve desired results, as outlined in the above four outcomes.

CULTURAL ISSUES IN NEGOTIATION

The premise of "Negotiation" is the same everywhere in the world. But the strategy on execution will change based on the cultures we are working with.

In many cultures:

- Relationship is more important than the product or service
- Time is not as important as it is in the United States or in other Western countries such as Germany or Switzerland
- Confrontation can be viewed as very offensive
- Price can be a huge factor outweighing any other aspect
- Contracts don't have the same meaning as in the West
- Looking into someone's eyes can be seen as offensive and confrontational
- Women are held in less regard
- Religion may play a big part of relationship and attitude
- Detail may have less importance
- Short-term considerations seriously outweigh any long-term benefits
- Certain mannerisms of people will be considered strange, rude, or hard to comprehend
- Politics may be "verboten" to discuss or be a major point of interest
- Compliance will have little meaning

RELATIONSHIP IS MORE IMPORTANT THAN THE PRODUCT OR SERVICE

In the countries that border the Mediterranean and certain Latin American cultures, relationship is the driving factor of building business opportunity.

While "relationship" is critical in all cultures, in a place like Italy or Venezuela, you will need to work on creating a "bond" with your prospective customer or vendor before any opportunity will mature in your favor.

Time and effort need to be put forth to develop relationships with overseas buyers and vendors. The financial side needs to be budgeted and the effort needs to be expended.

TIME IS NOT AS IMPORTANT AS IT IS IN THE UNITED STATES OR IN OTHER WESTERN COUNTRIES SUCH AS GERMANY OR SWITZERLAND

Americans run on schedules and are generally responsible about being on time, but nowhere as diligent as the Germans and the Swiss, who are fanatics about being on time.

In contrast, the Latin culture is 180 degrees the opposite, who from a time perspective treat it very liberally.

It is not a right or wrong matter, it is just different and we need to be sensitive to that fact!

CONFRONTATION CAN BE VIEWED AS VERY OFFENSIVE

Most Americans are pretty direct and very willing to speak their minds. In some cultures, this can be viewed as "confrontational."

Asians would be offended if we "stared" them down or were "in their face" in the midst of a discussion or meeting.

On the other hand, if you were in Australia or England, a straightforward, no-nonsense approach would be welcome.

Again, we need to be sensitive to our approach and handle discussions and meetings accordingly.

PRICE CAN BE A HUGE FACTOR OUTWEIGHING ANY OTHER ASPECT

In most Western cultures proposal and business development contain a balance of service, value add, and price.

In China, as an example, price rules in business and outweighs most other factors. It sometimes becomes frustrating when dealing with China on the balance that needs to take place in a negotiation between cost and quality or price and value.

In making a best effort to manage this concern

- Clear, concise, and detailed expectations are helpful
- Financial consequences for service or quality failures
- Being extremely diligent, demanding, and always "squeaking the wheels"

CONTRACTS DON'T HAVE THE SAME MEANING AS IN THE WEST

In the West, a "contract" is a conclusionary event at the end of a negotiation. In the East, the contract is that final event, but it is also a starting point of continued negotiations.

To be "frank," the Asian community does not feel as committed to a contract to the same extent as Americans do in the West. This is not a being-honorable issue, it is a difference in viewpoint on the basis of how Americans view a contract and how Asian culture views a contract.

Again, this is not a right or wrong issue, it is just a different approach.

Unfortunately, the consequences of this difference in how contracts are viewed does raise some serious issues in customer and vendor relationships and in how legal matters become handled or resolved.

The utilization of qualified counsel with local representation in the countries you do business in is valuable in mitigating this concern.

LOOKING INTO SOMEONE'S EYES CAN BE SEEN AS OFFENSIVE AND CONFRONTATIONAL

As mentioned previously, conformation can be a liability. But behaviors in the West that are not offensive can be construed as offensive in the East.

An example of this is "eye contact." In the West we expect eye contact in a serious discussion. In the East, eye contact is minimized and viewed as an aggressive behavior.

This is even more so with women.

This point validates the need to learn the cultures of the people we are doing business with. The last thing we want to do is to start a relationship off by being offensive even though that is not our intent.

Sometimes we are called the "Ugly American." One of the reasons for that is our general lack of sensitivity to the cultural differences that exists in the world. Eye contact is one of them.

In the Middle East a good business rapport between men will have them holding hands like a "couple" would.

In most of the world, this would be viewed as homosexuality or a feminine behavior. In Saudi, this is a sign of business confidence and a relationship mannerism acceptable in that world.

WOMEN ARE HELD IN LESS REGARD

Women have risen to serious levels of leadership in Western businesses. This is not true in a number of countries throughout the world.

Factors influencing this behavior and pattern are tied into politics, religion, and traditions in those societies.

I have a number of women executives as clients who operate globally and in some Western cultures have no problem navigating their responsibilities. But in countries dominated by Islamic culture, they struggle. In some circumstances they are not even accepted.

In other cultures, women are still considered to be the matriarch of their family and have little or no place in the world of business.

The clothes women wear, whether they are allowed to drive, vote, hold public office, or own assets are all challenges in many countries. This then creates some issues when we do business in cultures where women have less relevance.

We have to modify our behavior to work successfully in these arenas that keep women down and out.

RELIGION MAY PLAY A BIG PART IN RELATIONSHIP AND ATTITUDE

There are over 100 religions or sects in the world.

As reported by Project World Impact, on average, eight in 10 people in the world currently align themselves with a religious group.

A recent religious demographic study shows that 2.2 billion, or 32%, of the world follows Christianity, 1.6 billion, or 23%, are Muslims, 15% are Hindus, 7% are Buddhists, and 0.2% of the world is Jewish.

Additionally, 400 million people are affiliated with indigenous, folk, or other traditional religions, and 58 million people are religiously affiliated with smaller-scale/lesser known religions such as Zoroastrianism, Wicca, and Sikhism. Christianity is currently the most evenly distributed religion with roughly equal amounts of Christians residing on the various continents. Muslims, Hindus, and Christians all tend to live in countries in which they are the majority.

People who claim to be religiously unaffiliated are beginning to grow in number and are the majority groups in China, the Czech Republic, Estonia, Hong Kong, Japan, and North Korea.

At the beginning of 2014, organizations noted that religious conflicts had reached a new high from observations taken over the past 6 years.

In 2012, nearly one-third of all countries in the world recorded religiously motivated conflicts. For example, Middle Eastern countries are still rebounding from the impact of the Arab Spring uprisings.

China has recently seen an increase in the amount of religious conflict in the Asia-Pacific region. Additionally, nearly 29% of the world's nations had high levels of government-sanctioned religious restrictions for their citizens.

The most common form of religious discrimination over the past year has been the abuse of citizens who are members of religious minorities.

Around 47% of countries reported that this was the type of persecution that they face.

Religiously motivated terrorist activities have also increased in frequency over the past 2 years. Sectarian violence, especially in Syria, has increased in nearly one-fifth of the world.

Sectarian strife has created strain on neighboring countries since violence has caused entire groups of people to seek asylum in other countries.

Religious relationships between clergy and governments impact business relationships and how businesspeople react in business situations.

Understanding the role religion plays in business and culture can be another important factor in terms of how we proceed in managing our sales and customer service responsibilities in global trade.

DETAIL MAY HAVE LESS IMPORTANCE

Attention to detail and its incorporation into business relationships are important in most cultures around the world.

But there are individuals in certain cultures that believe "detail" is not as critical a factor in the decision-making process as is "relationship." In the Middle East and North Africa you sometimes witness this circumstance.

They weigh the relationship to their business partner so heavily that the details are not so important. The big picture will take care of the little picture, or in other words, if the important relationship and confidence level is in place, the details will take care of themselves.

This becomes a much more relaxed way of doing business and carries a lot more trust into the equation of negotiating for favorable results.

SHORT-TERM CONSIDERATIONS SERIOUSLY OUTWEIGH ANY LONG-TERM BENEFITS

A consequence of a majority of companies around the world having to go "lean and mean" as a result of the 2008 recession has them looking at short-term results at the expense of longer-term benefits.

Most of this mind-set was considered a "survival strategy" that has continued on into 2017 and beyond.

In certain places in the world, economic malady continues, and those cultures still foster a spirit for short-term benefit.

We need to make sure that we understand who these buyers are and respond in our customer service strategies accordingly.

CERTAIN MANNERISMS OF PEOPLE WILL BE CONSIDERED STRANGE, RUDE, OR HARD TO COMPREHEND

In the Middle East, "burp" after a meal and you just congratulated the chef. Burp in the middle of a Manhattan restaurant and you might be thrown out onto the street.

In India, the right hand is always offered and the left hand is not, because that is the one we do "potty" with.

In rural China, it ok for children to defecate in the streets as part of their learning process. Clothing is slotted to accommodate that occurrence.

In the United Kingdom, roundabouts replace most stoplights.

In Chile and Ecuador, it is fashionable to show up to 30–60 minutes late for an appointment.

In Russia, which has a serious rate of alcoholism, you can never put a glass back on to the table after a toast with any liquor left in the glass.

Children in Greece place their lost teeth up on the roof and not under their pillow.

In Japan, the practice of Bushido teaches strength, integrity, and loyalty and is incorporated into their business practice.

In Brazil, "showers" are often taken by people several times a day and are often discussed as a daily topic among Brazilians at meetings.

In Taiwan, handing a business card over to another person is done as if it was a sacred document.

In Egypt, regularly driving in traffic in the opposite direction is acceptable as a means to get where you need to go.

Above are a few of the thousands of customs around the world that we have to be aware of and be sensitive to when we operate in those countries and deal with their people.

The more we understand and are reasonable about, the better our negotiations and outcomes.

POLITICS MAY BE "VERBOTEN" TO DISCUSS OR BE A MAJOR POINT OF INTEREST

Early in my career I learned quickly to leave politics behind in my conversations with clients, vendors, prospects, and business relationships.

It served no real value and it was a lose-lose proposition.

In European and Middle Eastern cultures there is a deep passion about politics and the role America has played in the years 2009–2017 under the Obama Administration.

Discussing politics will lead to arguments and a less-than-desirable outcome.

Leave it to the dignitaries to politicize.

COMPLIANCE WILL HAVE LITTLE MEANING

The entire world views the United States as being too compliant in almost every area of governance, such as but not limited to

- OSHA
- Labor laws
- Trade Compliance
- Sarbanes–Oxley
- Internal Revenue Service
- Securities and Exchange Commission
- Federal Aviation Administration
- Transportation Safety Administration

Compliance creates cost, infrastructure, and personnel standards greater than most countries have around the globe. Many foreign business managers look with disdain and uncertainty at the amount of regulation and compliance issues when doing trade with America.

Pundits would argue that regulation and compliance make for a safer and more secure world. Adversaries say the United States goes too far.

On either side of the issue, compliance is an area of concern when trading with the United States and must be navigated diligently to be successful in global trade.

Key words to live by in compliance are

- Due diligence
- Reasonable care
- Supervisor and control
- Proactive engagement

KEY ELEMENTS IN GLOBAL NEGOTIATION

Why study negotiation?

WHY STUDY NEGOTIATION?

Studying negotiation will help you achieve the following:

- More responsible and favored results
- Lead people to make better, more favored decisions
- Protect you and your company
- In supply chain/purchasing/domestic/international business, a critical skill to define success!

And personally translates to big benefits, as well!

Transaction by transaction and long term that provides sustainable results!

NEGOTIATION

The KEY ISSUES in negotiation that show favorable results are

- Change
- Behavior modification
- Influencing decision making
- Leading in various directions

When you negotiate you are creating a "win-win" scenario for all parties involved.

We are not processing a "zero-sum" conclusion where only one party wins and the other loses.

International business requires a certain degree of détente in order to be successful.

Trust! Here only one party wins ...

What Are Our Primary Responsibilities in Negotiation Management?

- Create a win-win scenario for all parties
- Obtain favorable outcomes
- Have everyone walk away feeling comfortable with the results

What Are Our Primary Responsibilities?

If we "Negotiate" better, we increase our chance of successful business management in every area of responsibility, and personally, as well!

Trump, The Art of the Deal: Everything is Negotiable! Is it?

Donald Trump, successful businessman, author,
and leading presidential candidate

Most senior and experienced executives in global trade will prefer to say that everything can be discussed and all matters are up for change, or put in other words: Everything is negotiable!

Negotiation ...

is it innate or can it be learned?

There is a continued debate on whether negotiation skill sets are innate or can be learned.

The author has concluded the following:

There are people who have an internal strength for negotiating better than others. There are some people who cannot negotiate anything well.

In either situation, some people "got it" and some people "don't."

In either situation, though, there are negotiation skill sets that can be learned, developed, and honed.

The key is obtaining education, training, and hands-on experience from those that can negotiate well and teach others to do so.

MASLOW AND NEGOTIATION

The author believes that the better one understands human behavior, the better one can negotiate.

Maslow* wanted to understand what motivates people. He believed that people possess a set of motivation systems unrelated to rewards or unconscious desires.

---

* Abraham Harold Maslow was an American psychologist who was best known for creating Maslow's hierarchy of needs, a theory of psychological health predicated on fulfilling innate human needs in priority, culminating in self-actualization.

Maslow (1943) stated that people are motivated to achieve certain needs. When one need is fulfilled a person seeks to fulfill the next one, and so on.

The earliest and most widespread version of Maslow's (1943, 1954) *hierarchy of needs* includes five motivational needs, often depicted as hierarchical levels within a pyramid.

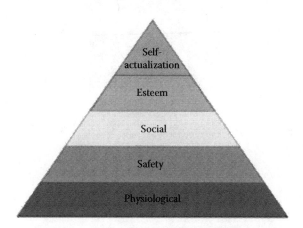

Maslow's pyramid of people's behaviors and motivations

This five-stage model can be divided into basic (or deficiency) needs (e.g., physiological, safety, love, and esteem) and growth needs (self-actualization).

The deficiency or basic needs are said to motivate people when they are unmet. Also, the need to fulfill such needs will become stronger the longer they are denied. For example, the longer a person goes without food the hungrier they will become.

One must satisfy lower-level basic needs before progressing on to meet higher-level growth needs. Once these needs have been reasonably satisfied, one may be able to reach the highest level called self-actualization.

Every person is capable and has the desire to move up the hierarchy toward a level of self-actualization. Unfortunately, progress is often disrupted by failure to meet lower-level needs. Life experiences, including divorce and loss of job, may cause an individual to fluctuate between levels of the hierarchy.

Maslow noted only one in a hundred people become fully self-actualized because our society rewards motivation primarily based on esteem, love, and other social needs.

In business, motivation for individuals is usually linked to three key areas:

Career–Security–Money

Business motivation comes in the three forms above for most people everywhere in the world. Some might add "patriotism" as a motivator, which might be true in some cases for military, government, and career politicians, but that would be a serious exception.

Knowing these motivators in business will help us in how we approach a negotiation when people are driven by these factors.

INTERNATIONAL BUSINESS

International business requires a differentiation of methodology incorporating political, economic, and cultural allowances.

International negotiation incorporates all the skills we have outlined above combined with the nuances of culture and the variables unique to those people and countries they represent.

The better we understand these cultural issues, the better our outcomes will be in moving forward in our negotiations.

Global Negotiation is managed by:

- General negotiation skill sets
- Negotiating domestically versus internationally

The biggest differences between domestic versus international negotiation are

- Consequences when a mistake is made
- Cultural issues
- Mind-set of a "contract or an agreement"
- Commitment to mine and exercise patience

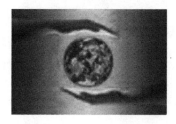

Basic strategy

- Win–win negotiation theory
- Outcome for both sides or numerous parties and benefits
- Internationally is maybe just more complex

Basic Strategy
The Psychology of Negotiation in Business:

- Change behavior
- Impact decision making
- Persuade
- Change mind-set
- Move in a different direction
- Convince
- Create

On a "softer" note, we refer to it as "Influence"
Basic Strategy
The psychology of negotiation in business:

- Win-win-win
- Compromise
- Timing … Process
- Lifespan
- In steps … timing?
- Pieces
- Short-term versus long-term
- Patience is a virtue
- Potential consequences of winning or losing?

Basic Strategy
The psychology of negotiation in business:
Which "animal" are you ... and which one are they?

Some theorists believe that the majority of people can be grouped into four categories of personality style: the owl, the eagle, the dove, and the rooster.

The owl is the thinker, is conservative, and is a knowledge seeker.

The eagle is driven by a greater goal and does not get lost in minutiae. They are A+ personality types and quick and decisive.

The dove is a "social butterfly," is relationship-driven, approaches things cautiously, and is very trusting.

The rooster is aggressive, outspoken, opinionated, social, and clearly the loud one at the party.

Knowing these traits would then allow us to create the best approach and negotiation strategy.

Basic Strategy

The psychology of negotiation in business:

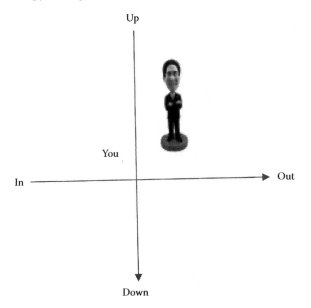

Remember that negotiation has to occur internally as well. The pictorial above depicts the scenario where one has to negotiate in four directions: Bosses above. Reports below. Colleagues laterally along with vendors, suppliers, and customers.

Some negotiation thoughts:

- Quantify price anticipation
- Determine other issues or benefits/value added
- Send "tests"
- Don't get "lost" in the detail or minutiae
- Determine decision makers and meet if possible
- As an example, longer-term commitments, bundling, and purchasing options may add to price-lowering opportunity
- Importance of knowledge, wherewithal, and specific awareness of the issues
- Bring to closure; example as it relates to a RFP!

Some additional thoughts…
What are some of the things we regularly negotiate for?

- Price
- Business process improvements
- Terms
- Contracts/statements of works (SOWs)/master service agremeents (MSAs)
- Risks

Strategy versus tactics.

Goals ... Strategies ... Tactics ... Action Plans ... Accountability and Responsibility Systems

Table Tennis
One Year Action Plan: April 2009 – March 2010

1. Communication
Objective
To improve the structure of communication within Table Tennis in Hampshire

Planned Action	How	Target	Where	Who	When	Resources	
						Unit Cost	Total
1. COMMUNICATION							
1.1 Provide Communication and improve the structure of Table Tennis across Hampshire and IOW	Align Key objectives of Hampshire County Table Tennis Association and Schools Table Tennis through representation of all providers of Table Tennis on the SAG, including competition structures.	Hold quarterly meetings for the SAG group.	HSSF SAG HCTTA	CDO/ CM / CSP / HSSF/ HCTTA	Quarterly	No Cost	
1.2 Develop communication with schools	Distribute information through PDM's and CM's to deliver to schools within each SSP. Develop a Schools Competition booklet to circulate to CM's outlining table tennis activity in schools.	To have clear communication with schools	All SSP's in Hants and IOW	CDO/ CM / PDM's / HCTTA		No Cost	
1.3 Ensure Clubs and Leagues on CSP database	Send out Contact Detail Forms to Clubs and Leagues. Can return or update themselves	All Clubs and Leagues in Hants	CSP	CDO & CSP	On Going	No Cost	

Step one: Set goals
Goal Setting

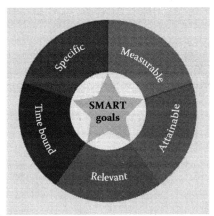

S: specific
M: measurable
A: attainable
R: relevant
T: timely and trackable (also "timebound")

Goals that utilize SMART characteristics have the best chance to succeed and are good "markers" to determine just what goals you want to achieve.

In a negotiation goals are determined for both or the multiple sides involved.

Twelve steps in successful negotiation:

1. Understanding what you are looking to accomplish (goals!)
2. Gaining senior management support
3. Creating a team approach
4. Mining
5. Setting the stage
6. Executing initial strategy
7. Outline what will be necessary to earn an agreement
8. Tactics/execution/problem resolution
9. Closing the deal
10. Implementation
11. In ongoing negotiations that will repeat, evaluate and set the stage for next year
12. Follow-up (win or lose)

Take the 12 steps and create a path to a successful negotiation

Understanding what you are looking to accomplish

1. What you have determined
2. What others have determined

3. If goals, are they SMART?
4. Parameters and timing
5. This effort will be successful if we accomplish ….?
6. Emotional intelligence reigns supreme!

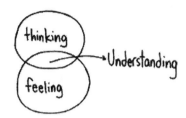

Gaining senior management support

- Why?
- How to obtain?
- How to utilize?
- Risks and Rewards … take notice!
- Keep them appraised
- Leadership to help get the deal done!

Mining:

Knowledge can be the most critical element of any negotiation.

- Resources
- Spending and investing time … every day!
- Building a "Rolodex"
- See vendor options

- Internet
- Networking; trade shows, industry events

Setting the stage:
Bringing a plan together, first in your head, second with your management, and then with a written outline.

- Relationship building
- Initial information gathering
- Determine decision makers

Executing initial strategy:

- Short-term goals versus long-term goals
- Meetings; business and social
- Establishing relationship and "trust"
- Qualifying
- Commit ... then honor!
- Ask questions ... probing ... "strengths, weaknesses, opportunities and threats (SWOT) analysis"
- Time frames are potentially established
- Next steps: intellectual confrontation on what to expect ... action plan is created
- Prioritize issues, needs, and wants ("must haves vs maybes")

Outline what will be necessary to earn an agreement:

- Ask, ask again and again, and be creative in your approach
- Obtain an understanding and maybe even an agreement
- Establish actions and next steps
- Set up next meeting or action time frame
- Beginning of the "close"
- The close

The framework or foundation is established, which everything will rest upon, in the negotiation initiative!

Tactics/execution/problem resolution:

- Straightforward … no nonsense
- Make sure you are heard
- Persistence, pushy, aggressive, forward
- Set stage for close; the close should happen naturally!

Closing the deal:

- Should happen "naturally" and without asking
- Closing questions … indirect approach
- Direct approach
- Prior agreements in writing
- Action plan; creating comfort level and continued sensibility that a correct decision was made

Implementation

Creating an implementation strategy is important to bring closure to a negotiation and helps allowing for a smooth transition if a change will be occurring.

Ongoing Negotiations

In some circumstances, a final negotiation may not come to a finality at one particular point in time. It may take several mini-negotiations to bring an entire successful conclusion.

Follow-up

Follow-up is a necessary element of making sure the "I's" are dotted and the "t's" are crossed in bringing a favorable closure.

Making sure all parties are satisfied with the closure and the results shows character, diligence, and a good business acumen.

RELATIONSHIP BUILDING

We tend to accomplish more with good relationships.

Good relationships translate better with quality, honesty, and transparency.

Good relationships also get you through the difficult times.

Allow more honesty in the relationship that will help the negotiation be more successful.

The SWOT analysis can be an integral part of the negotiation process that allows you to assess the opponents and come up with a more successful strategy.

S trengths
W eaknesses
O pportunities
T hreats

Some thoughts:

S: Price, valued added
W: Incumbent may have relationship
O: Capture business
T: One-time chance, do you know what you need to do, how you are perceived, current strength of existing relationships (change issue)

Good SWOT analysis leads to strategies, then tactics, to specific actions, which drive results.

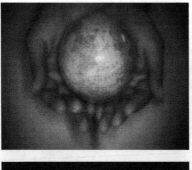

In international contracts, export sales, and import purchase orders, some of the areas we can negotiate to create a better deal for both parties are

- Terms of sale
- Terms of payment
- Freight
- Insurance
- Title
- Revenue recognition
- Marking, packing, and labeling
- Permits and registrations
- IPR
- Disputes

NEGOTIATION CHARACTER TRAITS

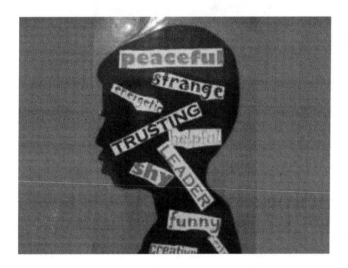

Twenty negotiation character traits that will help a person more successfully close deals:

1. Honesty
2. Sincerity
3. Caring
4. Product and industry knowledge
5. Problem solver
6. Responsive
7. Quality communicator

8. Leadership
9. Charisma
10. Serious, but not too much so
11. Funny, but not too much so (sense of humor)
12. Make them feel good
13. Cater to their ego, needs, and wishes
14. Learn how they listen and learn
15. Think on your feet
16. Credible
17. Authority figure
18. Do what you say you will
19. Be persistent
20. Be responsible

NEGOTIATION QUESTIONS

Ten questions you can ask to obtain a sense of where a prospect is at without being offensive or too obtrusive.

Negotiation questions:

1. In a perfect world, what would make you 100% satisfied with your supplier/vendor?
2. What things do you like best about your current supplier/vendor?
3. What things would you change if you could?
4. What would motivate you to change suppliers?
5. You have seen our proposal…what is attractive about it? Where does it fall short?
6. Who else is involved in the decision-making process? Is there an opportunity to dialogue with them directly?
7. In your RFP/RFQ, what are the deliverables you are specifically looking for that would cause a vendor to receive a favorable result?
8. Will there be an opportunity to revise our proposal once the dialogue and the purchasing process are moved along?
9. Is price your only issue?
10. When are you looking to make a final decision?

Some additional thoughts on negotiations in regard to global supply chains and servicing customers worldwide:

- SWOT analysis on all serious competitors
- Get past nonnegotiation issues ... how?
- Build offering and sales process to make it as difficult as possible to say no; negotiate with "leverage"
- Short-term considerations for longer-term benefits; market share versus margins
- Landed cost analysis can produce assessments that will help negotiate with leverage

Some additional thoughts on landed cost analysis:

- List of all the costs involved in a domestic or import/export trade.
- How can we impact these costs?
- Develop strategy to implement negotiations to make impact happen!

Excellent firms don't believe in excellence—only in constant improvement and constant change.

Tom Peters

8

Best Practices in Sales, Business Development, and Customer Service

Companies that chose to become "World Class" and lead in their vertical must establish a "Best Practices" approach to managing customer service in their international sales. This is a complicated process that has been outlined in this book. This chapter summarizes the book and creates a comprehensive thought process and strategy for implementation.

Best practices can best be viewed in a 14-step outline:

1. Senior management mind-set
2. Assessment
3. Goal setting
4. Establishing point person and committee
5. Creating tactics and an action plan
6. Creating reasonable goals and time frames
7. Establishing SOPs
8. Training
9. Technology

10. Work-in-process
11. Intelligent marketing strategy
12. Aggressive sales and customer service management
13. Structure a security and terrorism strategy
14. Manage RFPs responsibly

SENIOR MANAGEMENT MIND-SET

The best opportunity for any initiative to be successful in the corporate culture is to have the "buy-in and support" from senior management.

Customer service responsibilities typically interface with every silo in a company: manufacturing, distribution, sales, finance, logistics, legal, and so on.

If the bar is going to be raised to a "World Class" level, it will take a team effort. The team is more likely to support the necessary changes and actions when they know that senior management is actively in support of the initiative.

Senior management support allows the customer service team to cross into other company silos in their interface with greater ease and fewer "turf wars" being raised.

Keep in mind that most people are resistant to change, particularly when they are asked to do more, not less!

Helping any initiative to influence people to change will be the power in senior management throwing their weight into the quay and forcing results when required.

Senior management will also provide leadership influence to set the stage for personnel following and participating in a "Best Practice" initiative.

Additionally, disputes on how matters need to progress will occur. Senior management becomes a "backstop" for resolution when the middle management team is struggling to move forward.

Assessment

Benchmarking is an excellent method to determine "where your company is at" so you can eventually create a strategy to get where you are planning to go.

Benchmarking assists you in identifying market trends and contemporary scenarios.

Benchmarking is an important assessment tool in learning where your deficiencies are and what is possible.

Benchmarking leads into an assessment process. Many corporate executives utilize a SWOT analysis:

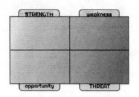

S ... Strengths, identifying where your company has advantages

W ... Weaknesses, identifying where your company has disadvantages

O ... Opportunities, identifying where your company can create opportunity

T ... Threats, identifying where your company has potential exposures

The SWOT process formalizes to some extent an evaluation process where you evaluate the basic advantages and disadvantages your company has in the area being assessed.

It also brings into the equation the potential opportunities and benefits when compared with the risks and threats in the circumstance being assessed.

The SWOT process sets the stage for then creating a strategy to deal with the issue, problem, or initiative. The SWOT process allows you to think through the issue with a logical path of utilizing your experiences, skill sets, and emotional intelligence.

The SWOT analysis then provides you the best opportunity to make a more favorable decision.

Goal Setting

The goals need to be developed. This guides you to where you want to be, what the expectations and deliverables are, and how they align with the overall mission and objectives of the company.

Goals need to be SMART.

SMART is a logical approach to creating goals that have the best opportunity to succeed.

Specific: the goal cannot be a generality; it must be very specific, such as a unit of measure (e.g., we need to increase sales versus we need to grow sales by 8%; our plan is to increase efficiency by a lot; we need to better efficiency by 3%).

Specific versus general or rhetorical … specific is better!

Measurable: is the idea that whatever we decide the goal to be, we need to be in a position to make sure we get to where we want to be by having some unit of measure or distinction.

Achievable: is the concept that a goal be set at a level that is achievable or attainable based on the initial assessment and strategy you have laid out.

Realistic: will only occur when common sense is combined with metrics to come up with a goal or goals that have a reality to their being achieved. This makes goals relevant and contemporary.

Unrealistic goals generally do not produce favorable results.

Having lofty or aggressive goals is ok, but not to such an extent that they become unrealistic.

This will create a disappointing outcome and no one will be very happy.

Realistic also includes a "time frame" of completion that is doable in agreed parameters.

Trackable: are goals that can be followed to make sure they are working successfully.

Tracking also allows when the "train comes off the track" to be rectified and brought back in line.

Tracking is also attached to the concept of "measurement" outlined above.

It creates an affirmation that the goal is moving in the direction of achievement. If not, it then allows mitigation to occur or necessary changes to get the initiative back on track.

Tracking also creates "accountability and responsibility" of the initiative so personnel are held to a standard of achievement.

This all ties into "Best Practice" and attaining the highest levels of success in a corporation.

Establishing Point Person and Committee

A single person needs to take "ownership" of the "Best Practice Initiative in Customer Service."

That person strives to take a leadership position to move a "team" who will provide support in the overall strategy and at tactical level in action and implementation.

The point person in charge is responsible and accountable to senior management in making the goals and deliverables happen.

Additionally:

- They move the day-to-day responsibilities along
- They keep senior management advised of status
- They communicate status to all the stakeholders and interested parties

- Assign tasks
- Maintain the action plan
- Tweak the strategy and tactics to mitigate potential issues
- Proactively reach out to vested interests to solicit input and counsel

CREATING TACTICS AND AN ACTION PLAN

The key ingredient to making "Best Practice" happen as strategically designed is to create tactics leading into an action plan.

Tactics

An action or strategy carefully planned to achieve a specific end and/or the art of disposing armed forces in order of battle and of organizing operations, especially during contact with an enemy.

Action Plan

An **action plan** is a detailed plan outlining actions needed to reach one or more goals.

Tactics are a result of coming up with steps that will align with the strategy. The process is as follows:

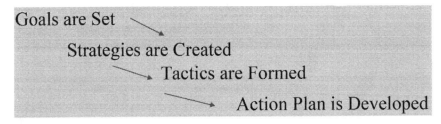

Goals are Set
Strategies are Created
Tactics are Formed
Action Plan is Developed

When these four steps are followed the company obtains the best opportunity to be making sure it has success in achieving their goals.

The ultimate tool is the action plan. This places everything agreed on into motion and sets up the basis for

- Who does what
- Where everyone stands
- Next steps
- Time frames
- Additional needs and steps identified

An example is below:

Tom Cook Action Plan	Growth Strategy for 2017	15-Feb-17		
Action	**Status**	**Person Responsible**	**Close Date**	**Next Steps**
Update prospect database	Waiting for IT to acquire new technology	Travis	1-Feb	f/u with Angela in IT
Send out new mailing piece	Completed	James	1-Jan	James is evaluating responses to the mailing and will advise sales team by 3/1
Create new Customer Service capability for tracking and tracing projects	First testing taking place next week	Kelly and Ben	6-Jun	Ben will advise by setting conference call for sales team next week and advise of first testing results
Attend new trade show on Purchasing management in Austin, TX	Registration opens 4/1	Travis and Matt	2-Apr	Travis has diary for 4/1 to register

The action plan above depicts a typical action plan outlined in an Excel format. There are a number of project software available to help manage and track projects and action plans.

The best Action Plans contain the following areas of importance:

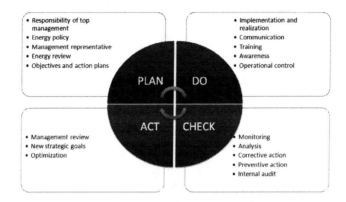

- The date of the update
- Who is in charge of the action plan
- Key line item areas of
  - Action
  - Status
  - Person responsible
  - Close date (date looking to bring closure to that topic)
  - Next steps

Action Plans:

- Need to be updated regularly
- Need to be communicated to all vested interests and stakeholders
- Need to be clear, concise, and easy to comprehend (keep in mind you may not know who will be reading the document)
- Need to be reviewed and checked again before distribution
- Need to be shown to senior management
- Need to be decisive on next steps and clear what needs to be done
- Need to be clear about who on the team has ownership
- Do not leave areas open without a next step to bring closure
- Need to honor dates outlined

CREATING REASONABLE GOALS AND TIME FRAMES

Many plans fail because the goals and expectations are unrealistic, or the plan is good, but the time frame to make it work is not doable.

Both areas must be aligned with one another.

> *Goals must tie into a time frame and both must be reasonable and attainable!*

In prior chapters I discussed that in planning there is one central and focal point: SWOT analysis!

- Strengths
- Weaknesses
- Opportunities
- Threats

As well, I outline how goals should be SMART:

- Specific
- Measurable
- Attainable or achievable
- Relevant or realistic
- Trackable

It is a critical aspect and a "Best Practice" to carefully think out your goals, expectations, and your wish list of needs and wants.

Tied directly into this factor is the time frame required to make these goals happen. Often the goals can be sound but the time frame is unrealistic.

Or the time frame works but not for the right goals. The two areas need to be synched with one another and well thought out as part of the overall strategy in global customer service when making the changes necessary to compete effectively and expand your business into new markets.

ESTABLISHING SOPs

A cornerstone of any well-run company in customer service is in the creation of protocols, business processes, and standard operating procedures (SOPs).

The importance of SOPs are as follows:

- Brings everyone in the company onto the same page
- Creates a written record of operating guidelines for business personnel to follow legal, human resources, and senior management acceptance
- (For public companies, this would be important for SOX, Sarbanes–Oxley requirements)
- Allows for a consistent application of business process within an organization and provides an internal reference for staff and management to determine answers to questions and process requirements

- Evidences compliance to government regulatory agencies who may be looking for a company to act with
  - Due diligence
  - Reasonable care
  - Supervision and control
  - Proactive engagement

SOPs create a blueprint and foundation on how a company operates. Matured organizations usually have too many SOPs or ones that have become antiquated.

Therefore, SOPs need to be updated and made contemporary on an ongoing basis. Additionally, SOPs require a simplified approach. The easier they are to comprehend and work within, the more successful they will be.

SOP Template

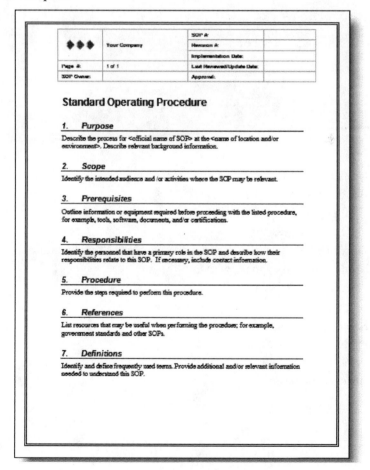

TRAINING

The big question to ask in corporate governance over customer service is where do they learn the necessary skillsets and capabilities to deliver "World Class" customer service?

Tough question to answer, unless a company has established a proactive, aggressive, and comprehensive training program to educate and train all of their sales and customer service staff and management team.

Areas to train in:

- Cultural basics in international business
- Language capabilities
- Challenges of global trade
- Logistics in foreign sales
- Documentation, operations, and procedures in shipping internationally
- Trade compliance management
- Negotiation skill sets
- Management
- Sales and business development
- Problem resolution
- Project management
- Accounting basics

Training is accomplished in a number of ways:

- Internally through mentoring and coaching
- Internally through corporate in-house training programs
- Externally in-person or web-based professional training programs
- Through formal higher educational institutions, colleges, universities, etc.

The options for training are numerous. Two excellent professional training organizations are **NIWT.org** and **AMANET.org**, both managed out of New York with a global footprint.

At the end of the day it does not matter how the training occurs. What is important is that training is ingrained into the culture of a company.

Training needs:

- To happen continually and at levels within an organization
- To be contemporary, comprehensive, and expedient
- To be customized to specific nuances of your company
- To be both basic and advanced
- To be managing supply chain and logistics issues in international customer service with a focus on doing business in foreign cultures

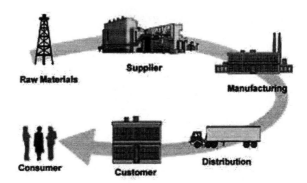

Customer Service Training follows the responsibilities in the global supply chain. The graphic above has six or probably over a dozen areas that impact customer service personnel who operate internationally.

These areas require expertise in every step of the process. That expertise is learned on the job and enhanced through formal professional training programs.

The very best of companies who operate "World Class" business models have "training" as part of their culture, their internal DNA, and their management responsibilities.

They recognize that international business requires a strong and competent customer service team. For that team to perform with "excellence" requires skill set training in all aspects of global business acumen.

TECHNOLOGY

Technology in 2016/2017 is moving at a pace almost near impossible to keep up with. I grew up in business with the telex, typing pools, rotary phones, and fax machines. Seems like yesterday, but that was 40 years ago. From 1977 until now, a huge leap has developed in how the world operates.

Today technology is so critical a factor in business that without it, a company cannot survive.

Those companies that engage technology are prospering. Those that are not are struggling.

Those companies that structure technology into their customer service—not to replace human activity, but to enhance human capability—have the best opportunity to prosper internationally.

Technology can play into several areas in international customer service, as follows:

1. Affords EDI interface for the placement of orders. In some circles, this is referred to as a PO Management System or Export Order Entry System.

   It allows the efficient transfer of orders from buyer to manufacturer or distributor, including all those involved in the supply chain.

2. Creates an efficient use of information transfer, handling, and storage, utilizing less of personnel's time and effort and freeing them up for more important customer service tasks.

3. Assists companies be more trade-compliant.

4. Ties in all sorts of data, communications, and messaging between all the parties of the supply chain, including third-party or government agencies.

5. Makes international transactions paperless.

6. Can be utilized as a "record-keeping" system under certain conditions.

7. Can be utilized as a tool in rating performance of all the parties involved in a global transaction.

8. Can be utilized as a "customer service" enhancement providing leverage, differentiation, and competitive advantage.

Technology is now a necessary evil that should really be viewed… as a necessary tool to gain competitive advantage!

Thomas A. Cook

Technology is a serious commitment that has cost, resource deprivation, and reoccurring issues to maintain "state-of-the-art" capabilities.

It must be budgeted successfully and the cost factored into "cost of goods sold" so its burden is covered in sales and business development activity.

In the new millennium, it is important from a customer service perspective that we recognize its value, not as replacement for personnel, but a tool and an advantage to support sales, business development, and customer service in our foreign sales and operations.

Technology allows manpower to focus on delivering effective and robust customer service and not waste time in dealing with the minutiae of administrative details.

INTELLIGENT MARKETING STRATEGY

The marketing executive of the new millennium must find solutions utilizing vast creative skills. In global commerce the differences from one country to another, one culture to another, and one demographic to another are so varied that only a highly intelligent approach will provide differentiation and have growth and expansion of sales.

The marketing officer and team approaching global commerce have to have a broad range of skill sets and expertise centered around intelligence, creativity, and cultural prowess.

When traveling overseas I always pay attention to the marketing approach of U.S.-based businesses operating in foreign markets. I always compare their approaches from their business models here in the United States and from the various countries in which they operate.

Only those that market to the nuances and differences of the countries they sell to do very well.

You can see the creative juices in their strategy and execution. It requires persistence, drive, and most of all a very intelligent process.

MARKETING GUIDELINES FOR FOREIGN SALES

Research and mining is always a critical factor in any marketing initiative, but in export sales, it becomes very important, particularly in developing information, to make decisions that prove to be of value to your overseas sales.

The more work that you do at creating a basic marketing strategy will go a long way in developing successful and robust export sales.

One resource is **BizMove**, which creates electronic guides on an array of business subjects including export marketing **(Bizmove.com)**.

Research, information, and data collection are critical first steps so that you can make better marketing and business development decisions. Marketing is an expense you want to control and keep in balance to the other expenses associated with overseas sales.

You will look into a number of areas:

- Competitive advantages with your product
- Historical sales in foreign markets (if any available)
- The largest markets for its product
- Markets with higher margin potentials
- Markets with growth potential
- Trends and conditions in markets that would impact your decision making
- Cultural issues impacting marketing strategies
- Whether there are competitors and knowing what their strengths are... conduct a SWOT analysis

Methods of Export Research

Choices exist for marketing initiatives:

- Internal expertise, if available
- Develop internal expertise
- Utilization of PR and marketing companies
- Utilization of consultants

All four are good options. What needs to be considered is the internal expertise and the cost of outside resource and support.

Many times, external support can offer

- Immediate access to qualified personnel
- Immediate expertise in the markets you are looking to develop
- Greater access to information and resources
- Better awareness of competitive pressures
- Office network in foreign markets providing local expertise

Because of the expense of primary market research, most firms rely on secondary data sources. Secondary market research is conducted in three basic ways:

1. By keeping abreast of world events that influence the international marketplace, watching for announcements of specific projects, or simply visiting likely markets. For example, a thawing of political hostilities often leads to the opening of economic channels between countries.
2. By analyzing trade and economic statistics. Trade statistics are generally compiled by product category and by country. These statistics provide the firm with information concerning shipments of products over specified periods of time. Demographic and general economic statistics such as population size and makeup, per capita income, and production levels by industry can be important indicators of the market potential for a company's products.
3. By obtaining the advice of experts. There are several ways of obtaining expert advice:

- Contacting experts at government agencies.
- Attending seminars, workshops, and international trade shows.
- Hiring an international trade and marketing consultant.
- Talking with successful exporters of similar products.
- Contacting trade and industry association staff.
- Gathering and evaluating secondary market research can be complex and tedious. However, several publications are available that can help simplify the process.

Market Research

Research can be accomplished in various stages:

- Preliminary interviews with stakeholders
- Product and market assessment

- External resource development
- Government material availability
- Initial assessment
- Testing of marketing options
- Tweaking of marketing options
- Reassessment
- Final marketing strategy

BizMove Outlines Sources of General Information Provided by the Department of Commerce (doc.gov)

- *Business America.* This biweekly publication of the U.S. Department of Commerce contains country-by-country marketing reports, incisive economic analyses, worldwide trade leads, advance notice of planned exhibitions of U.S. products worldwide, and success stories of export marketing. Annual subscriptions cost $49 (GPO:703-011-00000-4). Contact Superintendent of Documents, U.S. Government Printing Office, Washington, DC 20402; telephone 202-783-3238.

- *Commerce Business Daily (CBD).* Published daily, Monday through Friday (except holidays), by the U.S. Department of Commerce, CBD lists government procurement invitations, contract awards, subcontracting leads, sales of surplus property, and foreign business opportunities as well as certain foreign government procurements. It is available by subscription and online (electronically). A first-class mail subscription is $260 per year or $130 for six months; second-class, $208 per year or $104 for six months (GPO:703-013-00000-7.) Contact Superintendent of Documents, U.S. Government Printing Office, Washington, DC 20402; telephone 202-783-3238.

- *International Financial Statistics (IFS).* Published by the International Monetary Fund, IFS presents statistics on exchange rates, money and banking, production, government finance, interest rates, and other subjects. It is available by monthly subscription for $188 yearly (yearbook, $50 alone, included in the price); single copy, $20. Contact *International Financial Statistics*, Publication Services, Room C100, 700 19th Street, N.W., Washington, DC 20431; telephone 202-623-7430.

- *UN Statistical Yearbook.* Published by the United Nations (UN), this yearbook is one of the most complete statistical reference books available. It provides international trade information on products, including information on importing countries useful in assessing import competition. The yearbook contains data for 220 countries and territories on economic and social subjects including population, agriculture, manufacturing, commodity, export–import trade, and many other areas. The latest edition available is about 900 pages and costs $100. Contact United Nations Publications, Room DC2-0853, New York, NY 10017; telephone 212-963-8302.

- *World Bank Atlas.* The *World Bank Atlas* provides demographics, gross domestic product, and average growth rates for every country. Contact World Bank Publications, 1818 H Street, N.W., Washington, DC 20433; telephone 202-473-1154.
- *World Factbook.* Produced annually by the CIA, this publication provides country-by-country data on demographics, economy, communications, and defense. The cost is $23 (GPO:041-015-00169-8). Contact Superintendent of Documents, U.S. Government Printing Office, Washington, DC 20402; telephone 202-783-3238.
- *Worldcasts.* This eight-volume annual series presents 60,000 abstracted forecasts for products and markets for 150 countries. Forecasts are arranged by modified standard industrial classification (SIC) codes and are typically one-line entries providing short- and long-range projections for consumption, employment, production, and capacity. A product volume and a regional volume are published each quarter. The complete annual set of four product volumes and four regional volumes costs $1,300; the product set and the regional set, $900 each; single volumes, $450 each. Contact Predicasts, 11001 Cedar Avenue, Cleveland, OH 44106; telephone 800-321-6388 or 216-795-3000.

GENERAL INDUSTRY INFORMATION

- *National Institute for World Trade* (NIWT; niwt.org) is a nonprofit organization with a global reach into world markets and a great resource for companies engaged in global trade. They have intense connections into both government and private resources and a staff of 20 year+ experienced executives to assist you in your overseas business development.

- *Exporters Encyclopedia.* This extensive handbook on exporting is updated annually and contains exhaustive, in-depth shipping and marketing information. More than 220 world markets are covered country by country. Topics include country profile, communications, trade regulations, documentation, marketing data, health and safety regulations, transportation, and business travel. The annual price is $535. Contact Dun's Marketing Services, 3 Sylvan Way, Parsippany, NJ 07054-3896; telephone 800-526-0651 or 201-605-6749.
- *Organization for Economic Cooperation and Development (OECD) surveys.* These economic development surveys produced by OECD cover each of the 24-member OECD countries individually. Each survey presents a detailed analysis of recent developments in market demand, production, employment, and prices and wages. Short-term forecasts and analyses of medium-term problems relevant to economic policies are provided. The surveys are shipped from France. The complete set costs $180 ($203, airmail); a single copy, $13. Contact Organization for Economic Cooperation and Development, Publications and Information Center, 2001 L Street, Suite 700, Washington, DC 20076; telephone 202-785-6323.
- *OECD Publications.* OECD publishes widely on a broad range of social and economic issues, concerns, and developments, including reports on international market information country by country, such as import data useful in assessing import competition. The chartered mission of OECD is to promote within and among its 24-member countries policies designed to support high economic growth, employment, and standard of living and to contribute to sound economic expansion in development and in trade. For information and prices on these publications, contact Organization of Economic Cooperation and Development, Publications and Information Center, 2001 L Street, Suite 700, Washington, DC 20076; telephone 202-785-6323.

The Department of Commerce

The DOC has a very robust export program with USEACs in every major city. It employs trade specialists who have access to significant resources of data here in the United States and most of the markets you would sell to internationally.

The primary purpose is to serve companies looking to export globally.

U.S. Domestic Offices

Anchorage, AK	Greensboro, NC	Missoula, MT	Salt Lake City, UT
Atlanta, GA	Greenville, SC	Monterey, CA	San Antonio, TX
Austin, TX	Harlem, NY	Montpelier, VT	San Diego, CA
Bakersfield, CA	Harrisburg, PA	Nashville, TN	San Francisco, CA
Baltimore, MD	Honolulu, HI	New Hampshire, NH	San Jose, CA
Birmingham, AL	Houston, TX	New Orleans, LA	San Juan, PR
Boise, ID	Indianapolis, IN	New York, NY	San Rafael, CA
Boston, MA	Indio, CA	Newport Beach, CA	Savannah, GA
Buffalo, NY	Jackson, MS	Northern New Jersey, NJ	Seattle, WA
Charleston, SC	Jacksonville, FL	Oakland, CA	Shreveport, LA
Charleston, WV	Kansas City, MO	Oklahoma City, OK	Sioux Falls, SD
Charlotte, NC	Knoxville, TN	Omaha, NE	Spokane, WA
Chicago, IL	Las Vegas, NV	Ontario, CA	St. Louis, MO
Cincinnati, OH	Lexington, KY	Orlando, FL	Tacoma, WA
Clearwater, FL	Libertyville, IL	Peoria, IL	Tallahassee, FL
Cleveland, OH	Little Rock, AR	Philadelphia, PA	Toledo, OH
Columbia, SC	Long Island, NY	Phoenix, AZ	Trenton, NJ
Columbus, OH	Los Angeles, CA	Pittsburgh, PA	Tucson, AZ
Denver, CO	Los Angeles	Pontiac, MI	Tulsa, OK
Des Moines, IA	(West), CA	Portland, ME	Ventura, CA
Detroit, MI	Louisville, KY	Portland, OR	Virginia
El Paso, TX	McAllen, TX	Providence, RI	(Northern), VA
Fargo, ND	Memphis, TN	Raleigh, NC	Washington, DC
Fort Lauderdale, FL	Miami, FL	Reno, NV	Wheeling, WV
Fort Worth, TX	Middletown, CT	Richmond, VA	White Plains, NY
Fresno, CA	Midland, TX	Rochester, NY	Wichita, KS
Grand Rapids, MI	Milwaukee, WI	Rockford, IL	Ypsilanti, MI
Grapevine, TX	Minneapolis, MN	Sacramento, CA	

Foreign Offices

Albania	Gambia	New Zealand
Algeria	Georgia	Nicaragua
Argentina	Germany	Nigeria
Angola	Ghana	Norway
Australia	Greece	Oman
Austria	Guatemala	Pakistan
Azerbaijan	Guinea	Panama
Bahamas	Haiti	Paraguay
Bahrain	Honduras	Peru

(Continued)

Foreign Offices

Bangladesh	Hong Kong	Philippines
Barbados	Hungary	Poland
Belgium	Iceland	Portugal
Belize	India	Qatar
Benin	Indonesia	Romania
Bosnia and Herzegovina	Iraq	Russia
Botswana	Ireland	Rwanda
Brazil	Israel	Saudi Arabia
Brunei	Italy	Senegal
Bulgaria	Jamaica	Serbia
Burkina Faso	Japan	Singapore
Cambodia	Jordan	Slovakia
Cameroon	Kazakhstan	Slovenia
Canada	Kenya	South Africa
Chile	Kuwait	South Korea
China	Latvia	Spain
Colombia	Lebanon	Sri Lanka
Congo - Kinshasa	Lesotho	Swaziland
Costa Rica	Liberia	Sweden
Cote d'Ivoire	Libya	Tanzania
Croatia	Lithuania	Taiwan
Cyprus	Macedonia	Thailand
Czech Republic	Madagascar	Trinidad and Tobago
Denmark	Malawi	Tunisia
Dominican Republic	Malaysia	Turkey
Ecuador	Malta	Turkmenistan
Egypt	Mali	Uganda
El Salvador	Mauritius	Ukraine
Estonia	Mexico	United Arab Emirates
Ethiopia	Mongolia	United Kingdom
European Union	Montenegro	Uruguay
Fiji	Morocco	Uzbekistan
Finland	Mozambique	Vietnam
France	Namibia	West Bank
Gabon	Netherlands	Zambia

The personnel that staff these offices can be reached by going to the website: http://www.export.gov/worldwide_us/index.asp.

Each city and country has a listing that looks like this:

Taiwan
Contact Us

The American Institute in Taiwan Commercial Section maintains offices in Taipei and Kaohsiung.

Taipei 臺北
American Institute in Taiwan Commercial Section
Suite 3207, 333 Keelung Road Section 1
Taipei, Taiwan
Telephone from the United States: 011-886-2-2720-1550 Ext. 382 or 345
Telephone from within Taiwan: (02) 2720-1550 Ext. 382 or 345
Fax from the United States: 011-886-2-2757-7162
Fax from within Taiwan: (02) 2757-7162
E-mail for general inquiries: Office.Taipei@trade.gov

Kaohsiung 高雄
American Institute in Taiwan Commercial Section
5F, 88 Chenggong 2nd Road
Kaohsiung 806, Taiwan
Telephone from the United States: 011-886-7-335-5006
Telephone from within Taiwan: (07) 335-5006
Fax from the United States: 011-886-7-338-0551
Fax from within Taiwan: (07) 338-0551

New York
Staff Directory for New York

Name: Carmela Mammas, USEAC Director
Phone: 212-809-2676
Fax: 212-809-2687
Email: Carmela.Mammas@trade.gov
Industries: Audio/Visual Eq., Books/Periodicals, Cosmetics/Toiletries, Dental Eq., Education/Training Services, Films/Videos, Management Consulting Services, Musical Instruments

Name: Susan Hettleman, Commercial Officer
Phone: 212-471-0060
Fax: 212-809-2687
Email: Susan.Hettleman@trade.gov
Industries: Architectural/Constr./Engineering SVC, Books/Periodicals, Management Consulting Services

Name: Peter Sexton, Senior International Trade Specialist
Phone: 212-809-2647
Fax: 212-809-2687
Email: Peter.Sexton@trade.gov

Name: Anastasia Xenias, Senior International Trade Specialist
Phone: 212-809-2685
Fax: 212-809-2687
Email: Anastasia.Xenias@trade.gov
Industries: Apparel, General Consumer Goods, Jewelry, Textile Fabrics, Textile Machinery/Eq., Transportation Serv. (other than Aviation), Travel and Tourism Industries

Name: Toni Corsini, Financial Management Analyst
Phone: 212-809-2645
Fax: 212-809-2687
Email: Toni.Corsini@trade.gov

Name: Melissa Hill, International Trade Specialist
Phone: 212-471-0062
Fax: 212-809-2687
Email: Melissa.Hill@trade.gov
Industries: Cosmetics/Toiletries, Dental Eq., Drugs/Pharmaceuticals, Health Care Services, Medical Eq.

Name: Ashish Vaid, International Trade Specialist
Phone: 212-809-2644
Fax: 212-809-2687
Email: Ashish.Vaid@trade.gov
Industries: Air Conditioning/Refrigeration Eq., Aircraft/Aircraft Parts, Airport/Ground Support Eq., Automobile/Light Truck/Vans, Automotive Parts/Services Eq., Aviation Services, Biotechnology,

Building Products, Chemical Production Machinery, Commercial Vessel/Eq. (Non-Fisheries), Composite Materials, Computer Services, Computer Software, Computers/Peripherals, Consumer Electronics, Defense Industry Eq., Electronic Components, Furniture, General Consumer Goods, Household Consumer Goods, Industrial Chemicals, Machine Tools/Metalworking Eq., Non-Ferrous Metals, Packaging Eq., Paper/Paperboard, Plastics Materials/Resins, Plastics Production Machinery, Pleasure Boats/Accessories, Port/Shipbuilding Eq., Railroad Eq., Security/Safety Eq., Sporting Goods/Recreational Eq., Telecommunications Eq., Telecommunications Services, Tools—Hand/Power, Trucks/Trailers/Buses, Used/Reconditioned Eq.

Office Information For: New York U.S. Export Assistance Center

AGGRESSIVE SALES AND CUSTOMER SERVICE MANAGEMENT

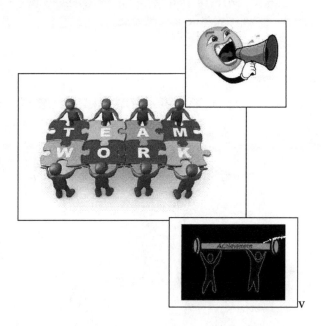

There will be a very defined need to take an aggressive posture to grow internationally.

Internationally, the challenges are vast and daunting as outlined in every preceding chapter in this book.

A weak, soft, or limp approach will not work.

We suggest the following:

- Your top sales people sell internationally
- Provide effective leadership consistently
- Build excess costs to make sure your sales campaigns are done correctly
- Raise the bars on performance and hold personnel to higher standards
- Set up intense lines of accountability and responsibility
- Make it a "team" effort and make sure everyone is on the same page
- Sync marketing to sales to customer service
- Create "best practices" and "world class" into all aspects to you managing customer relationships globally
- Master local cultural and language capabilities
- Invest in relationships with vendors, suppliers, and customers that are "partnerships"
- Develop "enterprise" solutions versus only "transactional" ones
- Communicate often, articulately, and comprehensively
- Be innovative, creative, and assertive

STRUCTURE A SECURITY AND TERRORISM STRATEGY

Threats to your company and personnel security along with terrorism can be very disruptive to your international outreach and customer service operations.

Create a step-by-step plan at attacking security and terrorism threats to your foreign customer service and business development strategy. Outlined in eight steps are our recommendations:

The eight-step best practices for managing risks of terrorism

1. Awareness

    Supply chain executives must become aware of what all the issues are and how they might affect the specific import and export supply chain for which they are responsible. Being reactive after the fact will cause delays, potential fines and penalties, and extra costs, typically not anticipated or budgeted for. Awareness means having a consistent inbound flow of information and developing resources to know what the issues are, the most recent modifications, and ultimately what options of response are available.

2. Information inflow

    Information inflow is as important a skill set as knowing how to get goods cleared by customs in China or dealing with the FDA in the United States if we bring in food, pharmaceuticals, or related merchandise. An enterprise needs to be able to drill down deep enough into its global supply chain to be able to identify lower-tier suppliers, all of whom can have an effect on the security of the flow.

3. Senior management support

    Compliance, security, and terrorism issues cross all the boundaries of a corporation. Finance, legal, customer service, operations, logistics, traffic management, inventory, purchasing, manufacturing, and even marketing have a stake in securing the supply chain.

    The nature of most organizations is to resist change, even when such a vital issue is at stake. Thus it is imperative that senior management sponsor and support security initiatives to break down internal resistance. Simply stated, those supply chain initiatives that carry senior management support will have a much more likely opportunity for successful implementation than those that do not.

4. Analysis and review

    The process to determine actual conditions and exposure is to conduct a facilities review, detailed analysis and mock audit of your supply chain and operations. Typically, this is best accomplished by engaging an independent consultant—an objective third-party analysis without specific internal agendas is most likely to generate valid "benchmarks" for where your company is. A facilities review can also access the relationships to vendors, providers, carriers, forwarders and brokers.

In conjunction with this review is the development of a "blueprint" for actions to be taken. The review and scrutiny also satisfies the government's requirement of exercising due diligence, reasonable care, and supervision and control.

5. Individual and team responsibility

Irrespective of the size of the corporation or the complexity of its supply chain, one identifiable person should be responsible for managing the risks of terrorism, compliance and security. This person can be part of any profit or cost center (logistics, manufacturing, purchasing, legal/regulatory, etc.) as long as they have the skill sets necessary to manage the job.

We recommend, though, that this person work within a team context drawing on members from all profit and cost centers, divisions and disciplines.

This will best be accomplished by creating a *plan of action*.

6. Action plan

Once the analysis is done and the compliance person chosen, an action plan with appropriate monitoring techniques will have to be developed. There are variations on task management programs, but we advocate a simple four-column approach that lists the action, the date to be completed, the responsible party, and the current status. The action plan flow chart needs to be accessible to all members of the team in order to align collaborative efforts.

7. Standard operating procedures

The importance of SOP's is three fold: they commit the process to a written format, which clearly outlines how a company will function in its supply chain; they then become a benchmark to meet the government's requirements of exercising due diligence and reasonable care; and they provide guidelines for subsequent personnel to follow.

In addition, these guidelines will contribute to a public company demonstrating its compliance with Sarbanes–Oxley regulations.

At various government websites (www.cbp.gov and www.bis.doc .gov) are guidelines established by agencies put forward as starting points and benchmarks for creating SOPs.

8. Training and education

A cornerstone of any compliance and security program is having all the supply chain personnel specially trained, at a minimum, in the basics of compliance and security. Among the categories that require training and education are classification, valuation, record keeping, red flag management, documentation and denied party screening.

Manage RFPs Responsibly

Every company must select vendors and providers of services to their organization. This process can be accomplished systematically following the outline below.

It is important that RFPs be done fairly, consistently, comprehensively, and with a focus on achieving results that serve your company well and create "win-win" scenarios for all parties involved.

BASIC RFP DESIGN TEMPLATE

Overview

This template provides a brief overview of how a company would go about making a selection of a service provider, consultant, or vendor for their organization.

Twelve Steps

The following 12 steps create a very basic outline of what steps an organization will follow to manage a successful RFP.

Each organization and industry vertical would vary their approach on the RFP based on the nuances related to the specifics on how they operate and what they expect to accomplish.

But following this basic outline has a 20-year track record for making RFP bids work successfully.

1. Identify stakeholders
2. Create committee
3. Develop RFP expectations: Strategic and tactical
4. Identify RFP participants
5. Create RFP template, time frame(s), and expectations for RFP actions
6. Invite "written" responses
7. Narrow the field
8. Invite "oral" presentations
9. Narrow the field to another reduced extent
10. Finalize selection and negotiate final terms
11. Agreement, SOW, or contract
12. Implementation

Identify Stakeholders

Reach inside your organization and identify who would be impacted by this RFP decision and gain their insight and participation in the RFP process.

Create a Committee

Once you identify the stakeholders, create a committee of at least three managers who will work the RFP and bring the process to a favorable conclusion.

Their participation requires a commitment of time, resources, and initiative.

Develop RFP Expectations: Strategic and Tactical

Create a list of expectations that you want to accomplish in the RFP. These are categorized into two areas:

Strategic, which are high-level goals, and tactical, which are specific actions.

For example, strategic might be

- Reduce risk and spend to our organization
- Increase sales in three divisions
- Conform to mission of the organization

Tactical might be

- Create new brochures for the company
- Train executives in the new technology
- Implement new SOPs into the operating units

Identify RFP Participants

Create a list of RFP participants and begin the scrutinizing process of being able to meet the deliverables.

This includes establishing a list of criteria for the RFP participants to meet.

Create RFP Template, Time Frame(s), and Expectations for RFP Actions

This step requires a template to be created which will be handed to the RFP participants that outlines the following:

- RFP expectations, both strategic and tactical
- Time frames and format for responses
- RFP decision-making process and any special instructions

This step can be at a very detailed or basic level depending on how much control you want to exercise over the responses to the RFP.

Invite Written Responses

The first step is to obtain a written proposal from the RFP participants in response to an overview, answers to questions asked, or allowing a total "open and creative" approach from them.

Narrow the Field

Depending on how many RFP participants you begin with, at some point you will begin to narrow the choices down to just a few.

Some organizations may start with 10 companies, then go to 7 to 3 to 1 as the process of evaluation moves forward.

Invite "Oral" Presentations

If communication capability is a big part of the responsibilities of the RFP participant in the delivery of services to your organization, we recommend that you have them come in and provide a "dog and pony" PowerPoint presentation.

This will demonstrate their prowess in communicating and allow an interface for questions, mining, scrutiny, and evaluation.

Narrow the Field Again

Move the RFP field to only one to four players. Have them finalize proposals, pricing, and terms and begin to make the final selection.

Finalize Selection and Negotiate Final Terms

Make a final choice and thoroughly understand the final terms you are negotiating. This becomes a very granular conversation and exchange as you make sure that your expectations and deliverables are being met.

Agreement, SOW, or Contract

This may be the time to bring in legal expertise to help assure legal compliance in the contract with the vendor or supplier to finalize an agreement, statement of work, or a contract.

Implementation

This phase makes sure that there is a smooth transition from contract through to execution of the new provider.

It must allow sufficient time for proper implementation and work through an "action plan" that clearly outlines responsibility and accountability of all parties.

Implementation should allow for a business review, sometimes referred to as a Quarterly Business Review (QBR) to make sure that the "action plan" is on target and all expectations and deliverables are being met.

Summary

Follow these guidelines and it becomes an excellent foundation for managing RFPs. Remember to be fair, responsible, and comprehensive to all the RFP participants and the RFP process.

> There is only one boss. The customer. And he can fire everybody in the company from the chairman on down, simply by spending his money somewhere else.
>
> **Sam Walton**
> *Founder of Wal-Mart*

Glossary

Ad Valorem: According to the value. For example, an import duty rate of 10% ad valorem means 10% of the value of the goods.

Agent: An independent person or corporation acting as a representative, usually in a foreign market, who attempts to sell products for an overseas seller (principal) and earns a commission on successful sales. Agents are not normally involved in delivery or servicing of product.

Air Waybill (AWB): The document that covers transport by air. It is issued by the carrier, whether an airline or a freight forwarder, as a nonnegotiable document serving as a receipt to the consignor for the goods and containing the conditions of transport. It also shows the details of the consignee so that they can be contacted on arrival of the goods.

- HAWB: House AWB issued by a freight forwarder acting as a carrier.
- MAWB: The term used for the AWB issued on airline's stationery to a freight forwarder for all of the goods covered by one or more House AWBs on the one flight going from one loading airport to one destination airport.

Applicant: The buyer who has requested his or her bank to arrange an L/C on his behalf. In some countries where the buyer may have trouble arranging an import license, the applicant may be a third party acting on behalf of the buyer.

BAF: Bunker adjustment factor; an adjustment to shipping companies' freight rates to take into account fluctuations in the cost of fuel oil (bunkers) for their ships.

Bank Guarantee: A document issued by a bank acting as a guarantor for their customer. The bank's guarantee is accepted because of their status and creditworthiness compared to that of their customer. Often used in conjunction with major projects, in the form of bid bonds, performance bonds, and warranty bonds, commonly for 10% of the contract value, all of which provide the buyer with a measure of comfort should the seller not fulfill his or her obligations at various stages of the contract.

Beneficiary: The seller in whose favor an L/C is issued (i.e., the person who will "benefit" from the L/C). (See also Letter of Credit.)

Bill of Exchange: An unconditional order in writing issued by the seller (drawer) instructing the buyer (drawee) to pay the seller's bank (payee) a specified amount (normally the full invoice value) on demand (at sight) or at a fixed or determinable future time. A suitable form can be obtained from the seller's bank or drawn up on a blank sheet of paper.

Bill of Lading (B/L): The document that covers transport by sea. Signed by the carrier, whether a shipping line or a freight forwarder, it serves as a receipt to the consignor for the goods, as evidence of the contract of transport containing the conditions of transport, and as a document of title by which possession of the goods can be transferred. Typically, a B/L is issued in a set of three signed originals or negotiables, one of which must be presented to claim the goods upon which the others become void.

- Combined Transport/Multimodal B/L: A B/L covering transport by shipping container from an inland place prior to the loading port to an inland place beyond the destination port. Most freight forwarders and shipping companies title their B/Ls as "Bill of Lading for Combined Transport or Port-to-Port shipment" or similar.
- Congen B/L: A standard form of bill of lading used in shipments by chartered ship.
- Clean B/L: A bill of lading indicating that the goods were received by the carrier in good order and condition without any clauses declaring a defective condition in the goods and/or their packing.
- Dirty/Foul/Claused B/L: A bill of lading with any clauses declaring a defective condition in the goods and/or their packing. Almost invariably not acceptable to banks for presentation under L/Cs and almost always not acceptable to the buyer. (See also Clean Bill of Lading.)
- House B/L: A bill of lading issued by a freight forwarder acting as a carrier. The terms and conditions of the contract may well be different to the terms and conditions contained on the shipping company's B/L, which can in

extraordinary circumstances lead to legal complications should a dispute arise.

- Master B/L: The term used for the B/L issued by a shipping company to a freight forwarder for all of the goods covered by one or more House B/Ls on the one ship going from one loading port to one destination port.
- Ocean B/L: A B/L covering port-to-port shipment. Typically banks continue to use this term on L/Cs even though the majority of international shipments are containerized. (See also Multimodal B/L.)
- On Board/Shipped On Board B/L: A B/L evidencing that the goods were not only received by the carrier but were actually loaded on board in good order and condition. "Shipped" indicates that not only were the goods on board, but that the ship has departed the port.
- Order B/L: A negotiable B/L, in which the goods are consigned "to order of" a particular party, often the shipper, in which case the consignee is mostly shown simply as "to order."
- Straight B/L: A nonnegotiable B/L in which the goods are consigned directly to a named consignee.

Box: Colloquial term for a shipping container.

Breakbulk: Noncontainerized cargo.

BSRA: Basic Service Rate Additional; the charge levied by shipping companies to importers for LCL cargo, including the port charges, transport to an unpacking depot (see CFS), subsequent sorting and storage of the goods, and finally loading onto a vehicle collecting the goods for delivery to the buyer.

C&F: Cost and Freight (named port of shipment)—INCOTerms
This abbreviation was changed in 1990 to CFR, but is still commonly used.

CAF: Currency Adjustment Factor; an adjustment to shipping companies' freight rates to take into account the effect over time of fluctuations in currency exchange rates.

Carnet: A document, normally issued by a Chamber of Commerce that is a member of the International Chamber of Commerce (ICC) to enable the holder to temporarily take merchandise into certain countries, as samples or for display purposes, without the need to pay import duty or pay a bond for the duty. The issuer will require the holder to give them security by way of a bank guarantee.

Cash against Documents (CAD): An arrangement whereby the buyer pays for goods as soon as the buyer receives the seller's documents. There is normally an intermediary involved (i.e., a bank or an agent acting on behalf of the seller) to ensure that the transaction takes place smoothly.

Certificate: A general term for any document issued by the seller or another party certifying to some action having taken place or some fact about the goods.

Certificate of Origin: A certificate stating the country of origin of the goods. Depending on the importing country's requirements, this can be as simple as being issued by the seller or the manufacturer. In most cases however, it is required to be issued by a Chamber of Commerce in the country of origin.

CFR: Cost and Freight (named port of destination)—INCOTerms

The seller must pay the costs and freight necessary to bring the goods to the named destination but the risk of loss of or damage to the goods is transferred from the seller to the buyer when the goods pass the ship's rail in the port of shipment. The seller is responsible to clear the goods for export. This term very specifically requires the carriage of the goods in a "seagoing vessel."

CIF: Cost, Insurance, and Freight (named port of destination)—INCOTerms

This term is similar to CFR but with the addition that the seller has to procure marine insurance against the buyer's risk of loss of or damage to the goods. This term very specifically requires the carriage of the goods in a "seagoing vessel."

CIP: Cost and Insurance Paid to (named place of destination)—INCOTerms

This term is similar to CPT but with the addition that the seller has to procure marine insurance against the buyer's risk of loss of or damage to the goods covering that period until the goods have been delivered from the carrier to the buyer. Being based on FCA, this term may be used for any mode of transport.

CFS: Container Freight Station; place or depot where individual LCL cargo is loaded into, and unloaded from, containers.

Charter Party: A written contract between a ship owner and a charterer who rents use of the ship or part of its freight capacity. A voyage charter party is a contract covering transport of goods from one or more ports to one or more ports and will detail the costs and responsibilities involved.

Commercial Invoice: A document issued by the seller and addressed to the buyer giving details of the individual transaction, including complete description of the goods, prices, currency, delivery and payment terms, and so on. This is generally used by the customs authorities in the importing country to assess customs duties payable.

Conference: A group of shipping companies who have associated to offer regular services on specific routes at published rates. Sometimes referred to as liner shipping. Nonconference shipping lines are sometimes referred to as independent or outsiders.

Consignee: The party shown on the bill of lading or air waybill to whom the shipment is consigned. Need not always be the buyer, and in some countries will be the buyer's bank. See also Bill of Lading— Order B/L and Notify Party.

Consolidation: Where a freight forwarder groups, or consolidates, one or more shipments for one or more shippers to the one destination as one overall shipment. (See also House B/L and Master B/L.)

Consular Invoice: The seller's commercial invoice certified, for a fee, in the exporting country by the consular representative of the importing country. Now required only by a handful of countries.

Container Ship: Ship designed to take International Standards Organization (ISO) containers in vertical cells within the ship's holds as well as on the deck. These ships generally rely on infrastructure on the wharf to load and unload the containers.

Conventional Ship: Ship designed with holds that can load almost any type of loose cargo, such as drums, sacks, crates, pallets, and so on. These ships are designed with their own derricks for loading and unloading.

CPT: Carriage Paid to (named place of destination)—INCOTerms
   The seller must pay the costs and freight necessary to bring the goods to the named destination but the risk of loss of or damage to the goods is transferred from the seller to the buyer when the goods have been delivered into the custody of the carrier. Being based on FCA, this term may be used for any mode of transport.

Customs Broker: A person or corporation licensed by the Australian Customs Service to handle on behalf of importers the process of clearing goods through customs.

Customs Duty: A tax, duty, or tariff levied at the time of import upon goods entering a country. Usually based on the value of the goods (ad valorem), on the physical nature of the goods such as quantity or weight, or on a combination of the value and other factors.

CY: Container Yard; place or depot where individual containers are held prior to loading on board a ship and after unloading from the ship. Can be inland or at the dockside.

DAF: Delivered at Frontier (named place)—INCOTerms 2000

The seller must pay the costs and freight to bring the goods to a land frontier, but before the customs border of the adjoining country. This term is for land transport only.

DDP: Delivered Duty Paid (named place of destination)—INCOTerms

The seller fulfills his or her obligation to deliver when the goods have been made available at an agreed point at the named place in the country of importation, often the buyer's premises. The seller has to bear the risks and all costs, including duties, taxes, and other charges of delivering the goods thereto, cleared for importation. This term should not be used if the seller is unable directly or indirectly to obtain any necessary import license or approval. This term may be used for all modes of transport.

DDU: Delivered Duty Unpaid (named place of destination)—INCOTerms 2000

The seller fulfills his or her obligation to deliver when the goods have been made available at an agreed point at the named place in the country of importation. The seller has to bear the risks and all costs and other charges of delivering the goods thereto, but not including duties and taxes. The buyer is responsible for customs clearance, and if he or she fails to do this, is responsible for the consequences. This term may be used for all modes of transport.

Documentary Collection: A method whereby the seller uses the services of his or her bank to ensure that the buyer only receives the shipping documents under conditions specified by the seller (i.e., upon payment or upon acceptance) of the seller's bill of exchange. (See also Bill of Exchange, Cash Against Documents and URC522.)

Documentary Credit: The officially correct term for Letter of Credit. The UCP500 only mentions "Documentary Credit" not "Letter of Credit." (See also Letter of Credit and UCP500.)

Demurrage: Extra charges paid to a carrier when loading and/or unloading has not been completed within the specified time.

DEQ: Delivered ex Quay (named port of destination)—INCOTerms 2000
Similar to DES but the seller must also arrange discharge onto the quay or wharf.

DES: Delivered ex Ship (named port of destination)—INCOTerms 2000
The seller makes the goods available to the buyer on board the ship at the destination port and is responsible for all costs and risks until that point, as well as arrival within the given period. Typically, this term would be used for bulk cargo on a chartered ship.

Documents against Acceptance (D/A): See Documentary Collection.

Documents against Payment (D/P): See Documentary Collection.

Draft: See Bill of Exchange.

Drawee: See Bill of Exchange.

Drawer: See Bill of Exchange.

Dumping: The practice of selling goods in a foreign market at a price lower than they would be sold for in the home market to gain a competitive advantage over other suppliers. If this is shown to be injurious to locally based suppliers in the foreign market, the government of that country may impose remedies by way of antidumping duties.

Duty Drawback: If goods that have been imported, and upon which customs duty has been paid, are exported or have been used in the manufacture of goods that have been exported, then the exporter may be entitled to a refund of the original import duty paid.

Exchange Rate: The price of one currency in the terms of another.

Export: To send goods from a country to an overseas destination.

EXW: Ex Works (named place)—INCOTerms
The seller's only responsibility is to make the goods available at his or her premises (i.e., works or factory). The buyer bears the full cost and risk involved in bringing the goods from there to the desired destination and the buyer must be able to carry out any required export formalities. The term represents the minimum obligation for the seller.

FCA: Free Carrier (named place)—INCOTerms
The seller fulfills his or her obligation to deliver when he or she has handed over the goods, cleared for export, into the charge of a carrier or another person named by the buyer at the named

place or point. This term may be used for any mode of transport, including multimodal transport.

FAK: Freight All Kinds; is a general description of the goods on a master B/L covered under the one freight rate regardless of the nature of the individual goods.

FAS: Free Alongside Ship (named port of shipment)—INCOTerms

The seller fulfills his or her obligation to deliver when the goods are placed alongside the vessel at the named port of shipment. This means that the buyer has to bear all costs and risks of loss of or damage to the goods from that point. The seller is responsible to clear the goods for export. This term can only be used for sea or inland waterway transport and its correct use is only when using a chartered ship or when goods are not containerized.

FCL: Full Container Load; generally but not always indicating that goods in the container are from one seller who packed the container going to one buyer who will unpack the container.

FI: (Free In)

In the international ocean freight terminology, the word "Free" means "not included"; that is, if FI, then the shipper is responsible for the cost of loading goods onto a vessel for the international shipping overseas.

FO: (Free Out)

FO is the international shipping term in ocean freight that indicates that the consignee (recipient) is responsible for the cost of unloading cargo from the vessel at the destination.

FIO: (Free In and Out)

The international shipping term used in the ocean freight industry meaning that the carrier is *not* responsible for the cost of loading and unloading gods onto/from the vessel.

FIS: Free into Store

An unofficial trade term utilized in certain verticals, indicating that the seller's price includes all costs up to delivery to the buyer. This is similar in effect to DDP.

Flat Rack: A device designed for cargos that will not fit into containers to be shipped on container ships. Consists of a base and two ends of the same dimensions as an ISO container.

FOB: Free On Board (named port of shipment)—INCOTerms

The seller fulfills his or her obligation to deliver when the goods have passed over the ship's rail at the named port of shipment. This means that the buyer has to bear all costs and risks of loss of or damage to the goods from that point. The seller is responsible to clear the goods for export. This term can only be used for sea or inland waterway transport. This is probably the most commonly misused term in international trade. Its correct use now is only where the ship's rail is relevant to the transaction, such as when using a chartered ship or when goods are not containerized. Obviously it cannot apply to airfreight.

Force Majeure: A clause in a contract which protects both parties in the event that part of the contract cannot be complied with due to causes outside the control of the parties and could not have been avoided by exercising due care. For example, floods, earthquakes, civil unrest, and so on.

Freight Forwarder: A person or corporation who arranges transport of goods on behalf of either the seller or buyer. In many cases the freight forwarder will also consolidate several small shipments into one larger one to take advantage of better freight rates. In most cases the freight forwarder will assume the legal liabilities of acting as a carrier.

Gross Weight: The total weight of a shipment of goods, including their packaging, such as crates and pallets.

Groupage: See Consolidation.

Hazardous Goods: Certain cargoes, as prescribed by the UN, such as explosive, radioactive, poisonous, and flammable goods, which must be declared to the carrier before being loaded onto ships or aircraft. The penalties for misdeclaring or failing to declare hazardous or dangerous cargo are extremely high.

Import: To bring goods from overseas into one's country.

INCOTerms 2000 and 2010: A set of rules for the interpretation of the most commonly used trade terms in foreign trade, recognized throughout the world, and issued by the International Chamber of Commerce (http://www.iccwbo.org/incoterms/id3040/index .html).

The 2010 Edition is what is more commonly referred to; however, the 2000 terms can be utilized and should then be referenced in the documentation, if that is the intent of the seller and buyer.

The 2010 INCOTerms would be considered the best option.

Insurance: A process whereby someone with a risk of something happening to their financial detriment (the assured) pays someone else (an underwriter) a fee (premium) to bear that risk on their behalf.

Insurance Certificate: A certificate issued by the insurance underwriter giving details of a particular transaction that is held insured under an insurance policy.

Insurance Policy: Contract of insurance.

Landed Cost: The total cost that an importer pays to have goods delivered into their premises. This typically includes the costs of the goods, international transport, insurance premium, port charges, customs duties, delivery charges, bank charges, and so forth.

LCL: Less than Container Load; a small amount of cargo insufficient to on its own be economically shipped as FCL. It will be combined with other LCL cargo from other shippers going to the same destination port, into an FAK FCL. (See also Consolidation.)

Letter of Credit: A conditional order in writing, issued by a buyer's bank, guaranteeing to pay the seller upon presentation of stipulated documents strictly in accordance with the credit. It is strongly recommended that every exporter and importer have a copy of *Uniform Customs and Practice for Documentary Credits*, International Chamber of Commerce publication 500, available from most major Chambers of Commerce, or from us at AUD 20.00 including postage, handling and GST, to Australian addresses only.

Letter of Credit—Confirmed: A letter of credit that has been further guaranteed by a local bank generally in the exporter's country.

Letter of Credit—Irrevocable: A credit that cannot be revoked, canceled, or amended unless the beneficiary agrees. Virtually all L/Cs issued under UCP500.

Letter of Credit—Discrepancy: Where a document does not comply strictly with the terms and conditions of an L/C.

Letter of Credit—Under Reserve: Where documents with a discrepancy or discrepancies are nevertheless negotiated against an L/C, and the negotiating bank reserves the right to take back the funds from the exporter if the discrepancy is not acceptable to either the buyer or the L/C issuing bank.

Liner terms: Freight rates that include loading/unloading charges, generally with regular shipping lines.

Manifest: A list of the various shipments being carried on a ship or aircraft.

Net Weight: The weight, or mass, of the goods themselves without any packaging.

Notify Party: The person or company to be advised by the carrier upon arrival of the goods at the destination port.

On Board/Shipped On Board: A notation on a bill of lading indicating that not only did the carrier receive the goods in good order and condition, but they were also placed on board the ship.

Open Account: The seller allows the buyer to send payment at some future time (i.e., 60 days).

Packing List: A document that details the contents, and often dimensions and weight, of each package or container.

Payee: See Bill of Exchange.

Phytosanitary Certificate: A document issued by the Department of Agriculture, Fisheries and Forestry for exports from Australia of plants or plant products.

Port charges: See APCA, BSRA, and PSC.

Prepayment: The buyer pays the seller for the goods prior to shipment.

Pro Forma Invoice: A sample invoice issued by the exporter before shipment, which the importer may require to arrange import approvals or apply for a letter of credit. It can also be used as an offer to sell goods.

PSC: Port Service Charge; similar to APCA.

Reefer: Colloquial for a refrigerated container.

RO-RO: A "roll-on/roll-off" ship, where loaded transport vehicles are driven onto it, such as a car ferry, or where containerized and other cargo is loaded into it by forklifts or similar equipment.

Shipping Marks: Specific markings on packages to identify them apart from other packages and to identify them on the relevant documents.

Sight Draft: A bill of exchange drawn "at sight" meaning that as soon as the drawee accepts the bill it falls due for payment. (See also Bill of Exchange.)

STC: Said to Contain; often placed before the description of goods on a bill of lading because the carrier does not know the nature or quantity of goods actually placed in the packages or the containers.

SWIFT: Society for Worldwide Interbank Financial Telecommunications; whereby banks can electronically transfer funds, issue L/Cs, and so on.

T/T: Telegraphic Transfer; an electronic means of transferring funds between banks generally using SWIFT.

Tare: The weight of packaging or a container without the goods.

Tenor: The period of time before a bill of exchange falls due for payment.

Term Draft: A bill of exchange drawn for a period other than at sight or on demand.

TEU: Twenty-Foot Equivalent Unit; the means of describing the carrying capacity of a train or ship. For example, a 40-foot container takes up the space of two TEUs.

THC: Terminal handling Charge; levied by CY and CFS operators for goods passing through their operations.

To Order: (See Bill of Lading, Order B/L.)

Transshipment: Goods are transferred from one ship to another at an intermediate port. Can also refer to goods being transferred from one method of transport to another.

UCP500: Uniform Customs and Practice for Documentary Credits, International Chamber of Commerce publication 500, which lays out guidelines for banks to follow when dealing with L/Cs. (See also Letter of Credit.)

URC522: Uniform Rules for Collections, International Chamber of Commerce publication 522, which lays out guidelines for banks to follow when handling collections. (See also Collections.)

Value for Duty: The value of an import declared to the customs upon which customs duty will be calculated. In Australia, the value of the goods at the time of export from the exporting country, thus generally the FOB value, and using the exchange rate at the date of export. Many other countries use the CIF value at the time or declaration in the importing country.

Volumetric: A notional or calculated weight for bulky goods sent by air. Generally stated as 6000 cm^3 = 1 kg, meaning that the total volume in cubic centimeters is divided by 6000 to give an equivalent weight in kilograms. The airline or forwarder will charge whichever is the greater of the actual weight and volumetric weight. Also shown sometimes as 167 kg = 1 cbm.

Wharfage: The accommodations provided at a wharf for the loading, unloading, or storage of goods. Also referred to as the payment made for accommodations provided at a wharf.

The business risk is not taking any risk … In a world that is changing really quickly, the only strategy that is guaranteed to fail is not taking risks.

Mark Zuckerberg
Founder, Facebook

Appendix

INTERNATIONAL MARKETING PLAN

Every chapter in this book prepared you for handling business in foreign markets. What is left is to construct a business plan, which is outlined as a sidebar in this appendix.

It will help you prepare to utilize all this aforementioned knowledge and bring it to immediate value.

The purpose of the International Marketing Plan workbook is to prepare your business to enter the international marketplace. Ask yourself: Should I expand my company through exporting? Do I have any products or services I can export? This workbook will lead you step-by-step through the process of exporting your product to an international market.

The workbook is divided into sections. Each section should be reviewed before you start the next. After you have completed the entire section, you will be ready to develop an international marketing plan to export your product. This section works as one area following another by following the guidelines and steps in developing an export strategy and marketing plan.

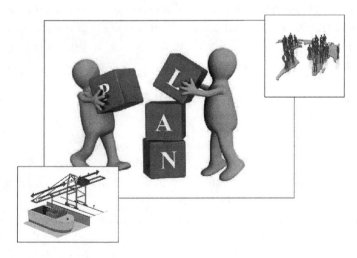

Planning

Why complete this workbook and write a plan?

Five reasons why it will be worth your time and effort:

1. Careful completion of this workbook will help evaluate your level of commitment to exporting.
2. The completed workbook can help you assess your products' potential for the global market.
3. The workbook gives you a tool to help you better manage your international business operations successfully.
4. The completed workbook will help you communicate your business ideas to persons outside your company. It is an excellent starting point for developing an international financing proposal.
5. With a plan the business is able to stay focused on primary objectives and has a measuring tool for results as each step is achieved.

Can't I hire someone to do this for me?

No! Nobody will do your thinking or make decisions for you. This is *your* business. If the marketing plan is to be useful, it must reflect *your* ideas and efforts.

Why is planning so important?

The planning process forces you to look at your future business operations and anticipate what will happen. This process better prepares you for the future and makes you more knowledgeable about your business. Planning is vital for marketing your product in an international marketplace and at home.

Any firm considering entering into international business transactions must understand that doing business internationally is not a simple task. It is stimulating and potentially profitable in the long term but requires much preparation and research prior to the first transaction.

In considering products or services for the international market, a business needs to be

1. Successful in its present domestic operation.
2. Willing to commit its resources of time, people, and capital to the export program. Entry into international markets may take as long as 2 years of cash outflow to generate profit.
3. Sensitive and aware of the cultural differences in doing business in other countries.

Approach your export operations in the same way you would your domestic operations—using sound business fundamentals. Developing an international marketing plan helps you assess your present market situation, business goals, and commitment. This will increase your opportunities for success.

A marketing plan is a process, not a product. It must be revised on a continual basis as your knowledge about international markets increases. You will be surprised how much easier it is to update a marketing plan after the first one is written. Planning is a continuous process. Plus, after a revision or two, you will know more about your international business market opportunities to export products.

Goal Setting

Identifying business goals can be an exciting and often challenging process. It is, however, an important step in planning your entry into the international marketplace. The following exercise is an additional step to help clarify your short- and long-term goals.

Step 1: Define long-term goals.

A. What are your long-term goals for this business in the next 5 years?
   Examples: Increase export sales by ___% annually or ___% market share or ___% profitability or return on assets.

_____

_____

_____

_____

_____

_____

_____

_____

B. How will the international trade market help you reach your long-term goals?

_____

_____

_____

_____

_____

_____

_____

_____

Step 2: Define short-term goals.

A. Select one or two target markets, research product standards and certification requirements, and make modifications, if needed, to get product export ready.

_____

_____

_____

_____

_____

_____

_____

_____

B. What are your 2-year goals for your international business products/services?

Example: Modify product for metric definition; expand international opportunities from initial penetration of a market to other similar markets.

_____

_____

_____

_____

_____

_____

_____

_____

Step 3: Develop an action plan with timelines to reach your short-term goals.

_____

_____

_____

_____

_____

_____

_____

_____

_____

_____

Identifying Products with Export Potential

List below the products your company sells that you believe have export potential. Write down why you believe each product will be successful in the international marketplace. The reasons should be based on your current knowledge rather than any research.

Products/Services	Reasons for Export Success
1.	1.
2.	2.
3.	3.

Based on reasons for export success, select one or more products you believe might have the best prospects for exporting.

Decision Point: These products have export potential.
    If YES, go on to next steps.   Yes   No

Step 1: Select the most exportable products to be offered internationally.

To identify products with export potential, you need to consider products that are sold successfully in the domestic market. The product should fill a targeted need for the purchaser in export markets according to price, value to customer/country, and market demand.

What are the major products your business sells?

1. _____
2. _____
3. _____

What product(s) do you feel have the best potential for international trade?

1. _____
2. _____
3. _____

Step 2: Evaluate the product(s) to be offered internationally.

What makes your product(s) attractive for an overseas market?

1. _____
2. _____
3. _____

Why do you believe international buyers will purchase your company's products?

1. _____
2. _____
3. _____

Determining Your Company's Export Readiness

Pros and Cons of Market Expansion

Brainstorm a list of pros and cons for expanding your market internationally. Based on your current assumptions about your company, your company's products, and any market knowledge, determine your probability of success in the international market.

Pros	Cons
1.	1.
2.	2.
3.	3.
4.	4.
5.	5.

Pros and Cons of Market Expansion

0%	25%	50%	75%	100%

Your Business/Company Analysis

Step 1: Why is your business successful in the domestic market? Give specific reasons. What is your company's annual growth rate?

1. _____
2. _____
3. _____

Step 2: What are the competitive advantages of your products or business over the domestic and international businesses?

List them:

1. _____
2. _____
3. _____

Step 3: What is your level of commitment and that of your company's top management to expanding into international markets? How much preparation time, planning, and resources are you willing to commit to implementing an export program?

1. _____
2. _____
3. _____

Industry Analysis

Step 1: Find export data available on your industry.

Go online to the U.S. Department of Commerce's website (www.export .gov) or search for trade statistics on Industry Canada's website (http:// strategis.ic.gc.ca/sc_mrkti/ibin/compare.html).

1. _____
2. _____
3. _____

Step 2: Research how competitive your industry is in the global markets.

Locate industry sector reports available at www.export.gov, evaluate import-export statistics from the Bureau of Census (www.census.gov), or contact your trade association or the nearest U.S. Export Assistance Center.

1. _____

2. _____

3. _____

Step 3: Find your industry's growth potential internationally.

Talk to companies in your industry or trade association, read industry-specific magazines, attend a national trade fair, and look for industry reports at the website www.export.gov.

1. _____

2. _____

3. _____

Step 4: Research federal or state government market studies that have been conducted on your industry's potential international markets.

Obtain information available through the U.S. Department of Commerce at www.export.gov or contact your local USEAC, SBA, or SBDC office or your trade association.

1. _____

2. _____

3. _____

Developing Your Export Marketing Plan

Read all material in this section thoroughly.

Step 1: Select the best countries in which to market your product.

Since the number of world markets to be considered by a company is very large, it is neither possible nor advisable to research them all. Thus, your firm's time and money will be spent most effectively by using a sequential screening process.

Your first step in this process is to select the more commercially attractive countries for your product. Preliminary screening involves defining the physical, political, economic, and cultural environment. You can find country research at www.export.gov; the website has Country Commercial Guides for each country where there is a Foreign Commercial Service presence. In addition, the Department of State has background reports on each country at www.state.gov, as does the Central Intelligence Agency's *World Factbook*, which can be accessed at www.cia.gov.

1. Select three countries you think have the best market potential for your product
2. Review the market factors for each country
3. Research data/information on each country
4. Rate each factor on a scale of 1–5 with 5 being the best
5. Select a target market country (C) based on your ratings (R)

Market Factor Assessment	Country	Rating	Country	Rating
Demographic/Physical Environment				
• Population size, growth, density				
• Urban and rural distribution				
• Climate and weather variations				
• Shipping distance				
• Product-significant demographics				
• Physical distribution and communication network				
• Natural resources				
Political Environment				
• System of government				
• Political stability and continuity				
• Ideological orientation				
• Government involvement in business				
• Attitudes toward foreign business (trade restrictions, tariffs)				
Competitive Environment				
• Uniqueness of your product/service				
• Pricing of competitive products (nontariff barriers, bilateral trade) agreements)				
• National economic and development priorities				
• Regulatory or quality standards for imports				

(Continued)

Market Factor Assessment	Country	Rating	Country	Rating
Economic Environment				
• Overall level of development				
• Economic growth; GNP, industrial sector				
• Role of foreign trade in the economy				
• Currency: inflation rate, availability, controls, stability of exchange rate				
• Balance of payments				
• Per capita income and distribution				
• Disposable income and expenditure patterns				
Social/Cultural Environment				
• Literary rate, educational level				
• Existence of middle class				
• Similarities and differences in relation to home market				
• Language and other cultural considerations				
Market Access				
• Limitations on trade: high levels, quotas				
• Documentation and import regulations				
• Local standards, practices, and other nontariff barriers				
• Patents and trademark protection				
• Preferential treaties				
• Legal considerations for investment, taxation, repatriation, employment, code of laws				
Product Potential				
• Customer needs and desires				
• Local production, imports, consumption				
• Exposure to and acceptance of product				
• Availability of linking products				
• Industry-specific key indicators of demand				
• Attitudes toward products of foreign demand				
• Competitive offerings				

(Continued)

Market Factor Assessment	Country	Rating	Country	Rating
Local Distribution and Production				
• Availability of intermediaries				
• Regional and local transportation facilities				
• Availability of manpower				
• Conditions for local manufacture				

Indicators of population, income levels, and consumption patterns should be considered. In addition, statistics on local production trends, along with imports and exports of the product category, are helpful for assessing industry market potential. Often, an industry will have a few key indicators or measures that will help determine the industry strength and demand within an international market. A manufacturer of medical equipment, for example, may use the number of hospital beds, the number of surgeries, and public expenditures for health care as indicators to assess the potential for this products.

Why do you believe international buyers will purchase your company's products?

_____

_____

Step 2: Research how competitive your industry is in the global markets.

Much of this information can be obtained from an industry trade association for your particular industry.

What is your present U.S. market percentage?

_____

_____

What are the projected sales for similar products in your chosen international markets for the coming year?

_____

_____

_____

What sales volume will you project for your products in these international markets for the coming year?

_____

_____

_____

What is the projected growth in these international markets over the next 5 years?

_____

_____

_____

Step 3: Identify customers within your chosen markets.

What companies, agents, or distributors have purchased similar products?

_____

_____

What companies, agents, or distributors have made recent requests for information on similar products?

_____

_____

What companies, agents, or distributors would most likely be prospective customers for your export products?

_____

_____

Step 4: Determine method of exporting.

How do other U.S. firms sell in the markets you have chosen?

_____

_____

Will you sell direct to the customer?
  1. Who will represent your firm?

_____

_____

  2. Who will service the customers' needs?

_____

_____

Step 5: Building a distributor or agent relationship.

Plan to travel to the country in question as many times as is necessary to build a successful relationship.

Will you appoint a rep or distributor to handle your export market? Consider legal advice from the Export Legal Assistance Network (ELAN).

A free initial consultation is available by request through a U.S. Export Assistance Center.

---

1. What facilities does the agent or distributor need to service the market?

---

2. What type of client should your agent or distributor be familiar with in order to sell your product?

---

3. What territory should the agent or distributor cover?

---

4. What financial strength should the agent or distributor have?

---

5. What other competitive or noncompetitive lines are acceptable or not acceptable for the agent or distributor to carry?

---

6. How many sales representatives does the agent or distributor need and how often will they cover the territory?

Will you use an export management company (EMC) to do your marketing and distribution for you?

Yes   No

EMCs do not have to represent your company exclusively on a worldwide basis. Rather, they sometimes can represent you in specific regional markets. For example, you might contract with an EMC to sell your products in Latin American markets, while you continue to handle direct export sales to Europe and Asia.

If yes, have you development an acceptable sales and marketing plan with realistic goals you agree to?

Yes   No

Comments:

_____

_____

Marketing Your Product/Service

Given the market potential for your products in international markets, how is your product or service distinguished from others—attractive or competitive?

1. What are your product's advantages?

_____

_____

2. What are your product's disadvantages?

_____

_____

3. What are your competitors' products' advantages?

_____

_____

4. What are your competitors' products' disadvantages?

_____

_____

What needs does your product fill in a foreign market?

_____

_____

What competitive products are sold abroad and to whom?

_____

_____

How complex is your product? What skills or special training are required to
  1. Install your product?

_____

_____

  2. Use your product?

_____

_____

  3. Maintain your product?

_____

_____

4. Service your product?

_____

_____

What options and accessories are available?

_____

_____

_____

1. Has an aftermarket been developed for your product?

_____

_____

2. What other equipment does the buyer need to use your product?

_____

_____

3. What complementary goods does your product require?

_____

_____

If your product is an industrial good:
1. What firms are likely to use it?

_____

_____

2. What is the useful life of your product?

_____

_____

3. Is use or life of product affected by climate? If so, how?

_____

_____

4. Will geography affect product purchase; for example, transportation problems?

_____

_____

5. Will the product be restricted abroad; for example, tariffs, quotas, or nontariff barriers?

_____

_____

If your product is a consumer good:

1. Who will consume it? How frequently will the product be bought?

    _____

    _____

2. Is consumption affected by climate?

    _____

    _____

3. Is consumption affected by geography; for example, transportation problems?

    _____

    _____

4. Will there be product-related requirements; for example, product certification, testing, special government approval, or quotas?

    _____

    _____

5. Does your product conflict with traditions, habits, or beliefs of customers abroad?

    _____

    _____

Support Functions

To achieve efficient sales offerings to buyers in the targeted markets, you should address several concerns regarding products, literature, and customer relations.

Step 1: Identify product concerns.

Can the potential buyer see a functioning model or sample of your products that is substantially the same as would be received from production?

Yes   No

Comments:

_____

_____

_____

_____

What product labelling requirements must be met? (metric measurements, AC, or DC electrical, voltage, etc.). Keep in mind that the European Union countries now requires three languages on all new packaging, Mexico requires labels in Spanish, while Canada requires labels in French and English, under the North American Free Trade Agreement.

When and how can product conversion requirements be obtained?

Can product be delivered on time as ordered?

Yes   No

This is especially important if letters of credit are used as a payment method.

Comments:

Step 2: Identify literature concerns.

If required, can you produce product literature in a language other than English?

Yes   No

Do you need a product literature translator to handle the technical language?

Yes   No

What special concerns should be addressed in sales literature to ensure quality and informative representation of your product? Keep in mind that translations should reflect the linguistic nuances of the country where the literature will be used.

Step 3: Identify customer relations concerns.

What are delivery times and method of shipment?

What are payment terms? Will financing be necessary to support either the preshipment (production) or postshipment (accounts receivable) working capital needed for these orders? If so, are you aware of export financing programs offered by the SBA and the Export-Import Bank?

_____

_____

What are the warranty terms? Will inspection/acceptance be required?

_____

_____

Who will service the product when needed?

_____

_____

How will you communicate with your customer; through a local agent or fax? Via Internet?

_____

_____

Are you prepared to give the same order and delivery preferences to your international customers that you give to your domestic customers?

Yes   No

MARKETING STRATEGY

In international sales, the chosen "terms of sale" are most important. Where should you make the product available; at your plant, at the port of exit, landed at the port of importation, or delivered free and clear to the customer's door? The answer to this question involves determining what the market requires and how much risk you are willing to take.

Terms of sale have internationally accepted definitions; learn to be familiar with the most commonly used types and be prepared to include them in quotations. For definitions of INCO terms, see www.iccwbo.org /INCOTerms/faq.asp.

Pricing strategy depends on "terms of sale" and also considers value-added services of bringing the product to the international market.

Step 1: Define international pricing strategy.

How do you calculate the landed (in country) price for each product?

_____

_____

What factors have you considered in setting prices?

_____

_____

Which products' sales are very sensitive to price changes?

_____

_____

How important is pricing in your overall marketing strategy?

_____

_____

What are your discount policies?

_____

_____

What terms of sale are best for your export product?

_____

_____

Step 2: Define promotional strategy.

What advertising materials will you use?

_____

_____

What trade shows or trade missions will you participate in, if any?

_____

_____

What time of year and how often will foreign travel be made to customer markets?

_____

_____

Step 3: Define customer services.

What special customer services do you offer?

_____

_____

What types of payment options do you offer?

_____

_____

How do you handle merchandise that customers return?

_____

_____

Sales Forecast

Forecasting sales of your product is the starting point for your financial projections. Use realistic estimates to produce a useful sales forecast. Remember that sales forecasts show volume only. Actual cash flow will be determined by the cash cycle that includes supplier terms, delivery dates, and payment terms and methods.

Step 1: Fill in the units-sold line for markets 1, 2, and 3 for each year on the following worksheet.

Step 2: Fill in the sales price per unit for products sold in markets 1, 2, and 3.

Step 3: Calculate the total sales for each of the different markets (units sold × sales price per unit).

Step 4: Calculate the sales (all markets) for each year—add down the columns.

Step 5: Calculate the 5-year total sales for each market—add across the rows.

Sales Forecasts: First 5 Years

	1	2	3	4	5
Market 1					
Units sold					
Sale price/unit					
Total sales					
Market 2					
Units sold					
Sale price/unit					
Total sales					
Market 3					
Units sold					
Sale price/unit					
Total sales					
Total sales					
All markets					

COST OF GOODS SOLD

The cost of goods sold internationally will differ from cost of goods sold domestically if significant product alterations will be required. These changes will affect costs in terms of material and direct and indirect labor costs.

Pass Through Costs

To ascertain the costs associated with the different terms of sale, it will be necessary to consult an international freight forwarder. For example, a typical term of sale offered by a U.S. exporter is cost, insurance, and freight (CIF) port of destination. Your price can include all the costs to move the product to the port of destination and other costs necessary to complete the export transaction. However, many of these costs are incurred by the exporter to provide a service to the importer. For example, you can price your product *Ex Works* and let your customer worry about getting the product to their destination from your factory or warehouse. However, most exporters arrange many of the details (transportation, insurance, etc.) for their customers. These costs should be identified separately on the invoice and passed through with little or no markup.

A typical cost work sheet will include some of the following factors. These costs are in addition to the material and labor used in the manufacture of your product.

Export packing	Forwarding
Container loading	Export documentation
Inland freight	Consular legalization
Truck/rail unloading	Bank documentation
Wharfage	Dispatch
Handling	Bank collection
Terminal charges	Cargo insurance
Ocean freight	Other miscellaneous
Bunker surcharge	Telex
Courier mail	Demurrage
Tariffs	Import duties

To complete this worksheet, you will need to use data from the sales forecast. Certain costs related to your terms of sale may also have to be considered. For example, include cost of capital if you are extending payment terms.

Step 1: Fill in the units-sold line for markets 1, 2, and 3 for each year.

Step 2: Fill in the cost per unit for products sold in markets 1, 2, and 3.

Step 3: Calculate the total costs for each of the different markets (units sold × cost price per unit).

Step 4: Calculate the cost of goods sold—all products for each year—add down the columns.

Step 5: Calculate the 5-year cost of goods for each market—add across the rows.

Cost of Goods Sold: First 5 Years

	1	2	3	4	5
Market 1					
Units sold					
Cost per unit					
Total cost					
Market 2					
Units sold					
Cost per unit					
Total cost					
Market 3					
Units sold					
Cost per unit					
Total cost					
Cost of goods sold					
All markets					

INTERNATIONAL MARKETING EXPENSES

To determine marketing costs for your export products, you should include costs that apply only to international marketing efforts. For example, cost for domestic advertising of services that do not pertain to the international market should not be included. Examples of most typical expense categories for an export business are listed below. Some of the expenses will be first-year, start-up expenses; others will occur every year.

Step 1: Review the expenses listed below. These are expenses that will be incurred because of your international business. There may be other expense categories not listed—list them under "other expenses."

Step 2: Estimate your cost for each expense category.

Step 3: Estimate any domestic marketing expense included that is not applicable to international sales. Subtract these from the international expenses.

Step 4: Calculate the total for your international overhead expenses.

	Cost			
Expense	**Market 1**	**Market 2**	**Market 3**	**Total Year 1**
Legal fees				
Accounting fees				
Promotional material				
Travel				
Communication				
Equip/fax/internet				
Advertising allowances				
Promotional expenses				
Other expenses				
Total expenses				
Less domestic expenses included above, if any				
Total international marketing expenses				

PROJECTED INCOME STATEMENT: YEARS 1 TO 5, ALL MARKETS

You are now ready to assemble the data for your projected income statement. This statement will calculate your net profit or net loss (before income taxes) for each year.

> Step 1: Fill in the sales for each year. You already have estimated these figures; just recopy them on the work sheet.
>
> Step 2: Fill in the cost of goods sold for each year. You already have estimated these figures; just recopy them on the work sheet.
>
> Step 3: Calculate the Gross Margin for each year (Sales minus Cost of Goods Sold).
>
> Step 4: Calculate the Operating Expenses specifically associated with the international marketing program for each year.
>
> Step 5: Allocate the International Division's portion of the firm's overall domestic operating expenses (International's portion of lighting, office floor space, secretarial pool, etc.).

	1	2	3	4	5
International sales					
Cost of goods sold					
Gross margin					
International operating expenses					
Legal					
Accounting					
Advertising					
Travel					
Trade shows					
Promotional material					
Supplies					
Communication equipment					
Interest					
Insurance					
Other					
International division's domestic expense allocation					
Total international operating expense					
Net profit before income taxes					

BREAK-EVEN ANALYSIS

The break-even is the level of sales at which your total sales exactly cover your total costs, which includes nonrecurrent fixed costs and variable costs. This level of sales is called the break-even point (BEP) sales level.

In other words, above the BEP sales level, you will make a net profit. If you sell less than the BEP sales level, you will have a net loss.

To calculate the break-even point, costs must be identified as being either fixed or variable. *Fixed expenses* are those that the business will incur regardless of its sales volume—they are incurred even when a business has no sales—and include such expenses as rent, office salaries, and depreciation. *Variable expenses* change directly and proportionately with a company's sales and include such expenses as Cost of Goods Sold and sales commissions. Some expenses are semivariable in that they vary somewhat with sales activity but are not directly proportional to sales. Semivariable expenses include utilities, advertising, and administrative salaries. Semivariable expenses ideally should be broken down into their fixed and variable components for an accurate break-even analysis. Once a company's expenses have been identified as either fixed or variable, the following formula is used to determine its breakeven point:

$$\text{Break-Even Point} = \frac{\text{Total Fixed Expenses}}{1 - \dfrac{\text{Total Variable Expenses}}{\text{Sales Volume}}}$$

Note: In addition to a break-even analysis, it is highly recommended that a profit and loss analysis be generated for the first few actual international transactions. Since there are a great number of variables relating to costs of goods, real transactions are required to establish actual profitability and minimize the risk of losses.

TIMETABLE

This is a worksheet that you will need to work on periodically as you progress in the workbook. The purpose is to ensure that key tasks and objectives are identified and completed to ensure accomplishment of your states goals.

Step 1: Identify key activities.

By reviewing other portions of your marketing plan, compile a list of tasks that are vital to the successful operation of your business. Be sure to include travel to your chosen market as applicable.

Step 2: Assign responsibility for each activity.

For each identified activity, assign one person primary responsibility for the completion of that activity.

Step 3: Determine a scheduled start date.

For each activity determine the date when work will begin. You should consider how the activity fits into your overall plan as well as the availability of the person responsible.

Step 4: Determine a scheduled finish date.

For each activity determine when the activity must be completed.

Action Plan

Project/Task	Person	Start Date	Finish Date

SUMMARY

Step 1: Verify completion of previous pages.

You should have finished all the other sections in the workbook before continuing any further. You are now ready to summarize the workbook into an exporting plan for your company.

Step 2: Identify your international marketing plan audience.

What type of person are you intending to satisfy with this plan? A banker? The company's chief executive officer? The summary should briefly address all the major issues that are important to this person. You may want to have several different summaries depending on who will read the marketing plan.

Step 3: Write a one-page summary.

You will now need to write no more than a page summarizing all the previous worksheets you have completed.

Determine which sections are going to be most interesting to your reader. Write one to three sentences that summarize each of the important sections. Keep in mind that this page will probably be the first read by this person. A brief summary of the most important information should make the reader want to read the rest of your plan.

Summarize the sections in the order in which they appear in the workbook.

INTERNATIONAL MARKETING PLAN SUMMARY

_____

_____

_____

_____

_____

_____

_____

_____

PREPARING AN EXPORT PRICE QUOTATION

Setting proper export prices is crucial to a successful international program; prices must be high enough to generate a reasonable profit, yet low enough to be competitive in overseas markets. Basic pricing criteria—costs, market demand, and competition—are the same for domestic and foreign sales. However, a thorough analysis of all cost factors going into producing goods for export, plus operating expenses, result in prices that are different from domestic ones (remember freight cost, insurance, etc., are *pass through costs* identified separately and include little or no markup).

Marginal cost pricing is an aggressive marketing strategy often used in international marketing. The theory behind marginal cost concludes that if the domestic operation is making a profit, the nonrecurring annual fixed costs are being met. Therefore, only variable costs and profit margin should be used to establish the selling price for goods that will be sold in the international market (this strategy is used for domestic pricing as well). This results in a lower price for international goods yet maintains the profit margin. The risk of this strategy becomes apparent when the domestic operation becomes unprofitable and cannot cover the fixed costs, as each incremental sale could result in a larger loss for the company. This is a complex issue that can yield substantial benefits to company with manageable risks. Some effort should be made by management to understand this pricing strategy.

Cost Factors

In calculating an export price, be sure to take into account all the cost factors for which you, the exporter, are liable.

1. Calculate direct materials and labor costs involved in producing the goods for export.
2. Calculate your factory overhead costs, prorating the amount of overhead chargeable to your proposed export order.
3. Deduct any charges not attributable to the export operation, especially if export sales represent only a small part of total sales.
4. Be sure operating expenses are covered by your gross margin. Some of these expenses directly tied to your export shipments may include:

Travel expenses	Catalogs, slide shows, video presentations
Promotional material	Export advertising
Commissions	Transportation expenses (usually *pass through costs*)
Packing materials	Legal expenses[a]
Office supplies[a]	Patent and trademark fees[a]
Communications[a]	Taxes[a]
Rent[a]	Insurance[a]
Interest[a]	Provision for bad debts
Market research	Credit checks
Translation costs	Product modification
Consultant fees	Freight forwarder fees (usually *pass through costs*)

[a]These items will typically represent the expenses of the total operation, so be sure to prorate these to reflect only the operating expenses associated with your export operation.

5. Allow yourself a realistic price margin for unforeseen production costs, operating expenses, unavoidable risks, and simple mistakes that are common in any new undertaking.
6. Also allow yourself a realistic profit or markup.

Other Factors to Consider

Market demand. As in the domestic market, product demand is the key to setting prices in a foreign market. What will the market bear for a specific product or service? What will the estimated consumer price for your product be in each foreign market? If your prices seem out of line, try some simple product modifications to reduce the selling price, such as simplification of technology or alteration of product size to conform to local market norms. Also keep in mind that currency valuations alter the affordability of goods. A good pricing strategy should accommodate fluctuations in currency, although your company should quote prices in dollars to avoid the risks of currency devaluations.

Competition. As in the domestic market, few exporters are free to set prices without carefully evaluating their competitors' pricing policies. The situation is further complicated by the need to evaluate the competition's prices in each foreign market an exporter intends to enter. In a foreign market that is serviced by many competitors, an exporter may have little choice but to match the going price or even go below it to establish a market share. If, however, the exporter's product or service is new to a particular foreign market, it may be possible to set a higher price than normally charged domestically.

WORKSHEETS

Export Programs and Services

This worksheet helps you identify organizational resources that can provide programs and services to assist you in developing your international business plan and increase your export sales.

ORGANIZATIONS

Services	USDOC Office	SBDC	USEAC	Trade Associations	Colleges	World Trade Centers
Readiness to export assessment						
Market research studies						
Counseling						
Training seminars						
Education programs						
Publications						
Export guides						
Databases						
Trade shows						
Financing						
Partner search						

EXPORT COSTING WORKSHEET

Quote Preparation

Pricing is a reflection of all costs incurred and influenced by the competitiveness of the marketplace. The quotation must first determine the domestic *ex works** costs and then identify the additional costs incurred to sell overseas.

---

* *Ex works* means that the seller fulfills his or her delivery obligation to the buyer when they have made the goods available at their factory, warehouse, or other place of business.

Export Costing Worksheet

Reference Information

1. Our reference_____   2. Customer reference_____

Customer Information

3. Name_____   5. Cable address_____
4. Address_____   6. Telex no._____
_____   7. Fax no._____
_____   8. Email address_____

Product Information_____   NAICS Code_____
9. Product_____   13. Dimensions_____x_____x_____
10. No. of units_____   14. Cubic measure_____(sq.in.)
11. Net weight_____(unit)   15. Total measure_____
12. Gross weight_____   16. H.S. No._____

Ex Works Costs

17. Direct materials_____
18. Direct labor_____
19. Factory burden_____
20. Cost of goods_____
21. Selling expenses_____(should be less than domestic sales)
22. General expenses_____(includes cost of money borrowed)
23. Administrative expenses_____
24. Export marketing costs (product changes, labeling)_____
25. Profit margin_____
26. *Ex works* price_____

Additional Exporting Costs

27. Foreign sales commission (if applicable)
28. Special export packing costs (typically 1 to 1.5% above *ex works* price)
29. Special labeling and marking (to protect from moisture, theft, rough handling)
30. Inland freight to pier (normal domestic common carrier; should also carry insurance)
31. Unloading charges (include demurrage, if any)
32. Terminal charges (include wharfage, if any)
33. Consular documents (includes Shippers Export Declaration (SED), export license and/or certificate of origin)
34. Freight (port-to-port); determined by freight forwarder
35. Freight forwarder fees (*must* be included)
36. Export insurance (insurance for transit risk; also for credit risk, if credit-worthiness of buyer is unknown)
37. Cost of credit (include credit reports, letter of credit costs, amendments, if any)
38. Total additional export costs_____

Quote = *Ex Works* Price + Total of additional exporting costs

FOCUSED ASSESSMENT
PREASSESSMENT SURVEY QUESTIONNAIRE

The purpose of this document is to obtain information from the importers about their import operations over compliance with CBP laws and regulations. The contents of the preassessment survey questionnaire (PASQ) will be tailored based on the auditors' analysis, the importer's import activity, and the audit team's initial assessment of the potential risks for each of the audit areas that were identified in the preliminary assessment of risk (PAR). Auditors may adapt or modify this document as needed or may develop alternate formats. Auditors may also request copies of documentation in conjunction with the PASQ.

PREASSESSMENT SURVEY QUESTIONNAIRE
INSTRUCTIONS TO THE IMPORTER FOR COMPLETING THE PASQ Please respond to all the questions. The information you provide will assist us in focusing on the specific risks that are relative to your imported merchandise and the processes/procedures that are used to mitigate the risk of being noncompliant with CBP laws and regulations. In addition, your responses will help us to identify the individuals who are responsible for performing the procedures and the types of documentation that will be available for us to review. The audit team will review your responses and prepare supplemental questions that will be discussed with your personnel to further our understanding of your processes and procedures. This PASQ file is a Word document that may be filled in with your responses and returned to the auditors, either as a Word or a portable document format (pdf) file. We request that your *complete response* be provided to us by [insert date] so that we may prepare our questions prior to the entrance conference.
POINT OF CONTACT INFORMATION
Name(s) of the person(s) preparing the form: *If there are multiple preparers, you may identify a single person who can be contacted to obtain clarification of the responses.*
Title(s):
Phone number(s):
E-mail address(es):
Section 1—Information about [name of importer]'s organization and policy and procedures pertaining to CBP activities

1.1	Describe the company's mission statement, code of ethics/conduct, and objectives.

1.1.1	How are the mission statement, the code of ethics/conduct, and the company's objectives disseminated within the organization?
1.2	Who is responsible for assessing the risks in achieving the company's objectives? *Indicate if there is a subgroup or individual who is responsible for assessing the risk for being noncompliant with CBP laws and regulations.*
1.2.1	Describe how the risk assessment is accomplished. *Indicate, for example, when/how often the risk assessment is performed, what information is used, and what thresholds/tolerances the company considers to be acceptable.*
1.2.2	When was the last risk assessment that was performed? *Describe any significant changes that were made as a result of the risk assessment.*
1.3	Who, within your company, has the overall responsibility for ensuring compliance with CBP laws and regulations?
	• *Indicate if there is an import function or department, and describe the chain of command (e.g., identify who they report to).* • *Alternately, your company may entrust compliance to a customs broker, a customs consultant, or other outside agent. Identify them, and indicate who within your company (i.e., individuals or groups) is/are responsible for interacting with the broker, consultant, or other outside agent (i.e., providing information to them and monitoring their work).*
1.3.1	If there is an import function or department, provide the following information:
	• How is it staffed? *Indicate if an individual is assigned as the manager, and the number of employees who report to them.* • How long has the manager been assigned to his or her position? • What are the responsibilities of the manager, and how is he or she accountable? *Indicate if he or she is responsible for providing weekly activity reports and describe any performance measures.*
1.3.2	If compliance has been entrusted to a customs broker, a customs consultant, or other outside agent (i.e., no import department per se), provide the following information:
	• How long has the company engaged the current broker, consultant, or other outside agent? • Describe the processes that are used to communicate information and to monitor his or her work. *Indicate if there is a written contract or agreement.*
1.4	Who is responsible for developing and maintaining the written policies and procedures that are used to ensure compliance with CBP laws and regulations?
	• How often are the written policies and procedures updated?

Section 2—Information about the valuation of imported merchandise	
2.1	What basis of appraisement is used for the value of imported merchandise?
2.2	Who is responsible for transacting with the foreign vendors? *Identify all the individuals or groups/departments that are responsible.*
2.2.1	Describe how transactions are negotiated with foreign vendors. *Describe all the processes that are used and the conditions that apply.*
2.2.2	Describe the terms of sale that are used. *If there are different terms of sale, explain the conditions when each is used.*
2.2.3	If applicable, describe the terms/conditions when discounts or rebates are made.
2.2.4	If applicable, describe any additional expenses such as management fees or engineering services that are separately billed by the foreign vendors.
2.2.5	What documentation shows the terms of sale and prices (e.g., contracts, distribution and other similar agreements, invoices, purchase orders, bills of lading, proof of payment, correspondence between the parties, and company reports or catalogs/brochures)?
2.3	Describe the accounting procedures for recording purchases and payments.
	• What accounts are used to record *purchases* of foreign merchandise? *Identify or provide a list of vendor codes.* • What accounts are used to record *payments* that are made to foreign vendors? *Explain the methods of payment that are used (e.g., wire transfer, letters of credit).*
2.4	If applicable, what accounting data/reports are provided to the import function or department? *Indicate how often data/reports are provided (e.g., quarterly reports of price adjustments for purchases from foreign vendors).*
For risk pertaining to related-party transactions	
2.5	Describe the nature of the relationship between your company and the related foreign vendor/seller. *Indicate if your company is the exclusive US importer.*
2.5.1	Describe any financial arrangements (e.g., loans, financial assistance, and expense reimbursement) between your company and the foreign vendor/seller.

2.5.2	If applicable, explain the terms and conditions of goods that are sold to your company on consignment.
2.5.3	Describe how the prices between your company and the foreign vendor/seller/manufacturer are determined. *Identify all the sources of data that are used, and explain the accounting methodology or computational formulas where appropriate. If the transaction value is used, indicate if your company supports circumstances of sale or test values. If applicable, provide the following information:* • Describe when price adjustments are made. • Identify any additional expenses such as management fees or engineering services that are separately billed to your company.
2.5.4	Explain how transactions are accounted for. *Indicate if your company maintains its own accounting books and records.*
2.5.4.1	What intercompany accounts are used?
For risk pertaining to statutory additions	
2.6	*Assists*
2.6.1	If applicable, describe the type of assists that are provided to the foreign vendors for free or at a reduced cost (e.g., tooling, hangtags, art, or design work).
2.6.2	Who decides (or determines) that the assists will be provided? *Identify all the individuals or groups/departments that are involved in the decision.* • When is it decided that the assists will be provided? • What accounts are used to record the costs of the assists?
2.6.3	Describe the procedures that are used to ensure that the costs of the assists are included in the values that are declared to CBP. *Indicate who decides how the actual cost of the assist will be apportioned to the imported items, and explain how the apportioned cost is tracked.*
2.7	*Packing*
2.7.1	If applicable, describe the type of packing (i.e., labor or materials), containers (exclusive of instruments of international traffic), and coverings of whatever nature that is separately paid to the vendor to put the imported merchandise in condition ready for shipment to the United States.

2.7.2	Who decides (or determines) that the cost of packing will be separately charged? *Identify all the individuals or groups/departments that are involved in the decision.*
	• When is it decided that the cost of packing will be separately charged? • What accounts are used to record the costs of packing, containers, and coverings?
2.7.3	Describe the procedures that are used to ensure that the cost of the packing is included in the values that are declared to CBP.
2.8	*Commissions*
2.8.1	If applicable, describe the terms of sale with foreign vendors that require your company to separately pay for *selling agent* commissions. *Identify the vendors.*
2.8.2	Who decides (or determines) that the *selling agent* commissions will be paid directly to the intermediary?
	• When is it decided that the *selling agent* commissions will be paid directly to the intermediary? • What accounts are used to record the payment of these commissions?
2.8.3	Describe the procedures that are used to ensure that these commissions are included in the values that are declared to CBP.
2.9	*Royalty and License Fees*
2.9.1	If applicable, describe the terms of sale with foreign vendors that require your company to pay, directly or indirectly, any royalty or license fee that is related to the imported merchandise as a condition of the sale of the imported merchandise for exportation to the United States. *Identify the vendors.*
2.9.2	Who decides (or determines) that royalty or license fees will be paid as a condition of the sale?
	• When is it decided that royalty or license fees will be paid as a condition of the sale? • What accounts are used to record the payment of the royalty or license fees that are related to imported merchandise?
2.9.3	What procedures ensure that royalty or license fees are included in the values declared to CBP?

2.10	*Proceeds of Any Subsequent Resale, Disposal, or Use*
2.10.1	If applicable, describe any agreements with the foreign vendors where the proceeds of any subsequent resale, disposal, or use of the imported merchandise accrue directly or indirectly to the foreign vendor. *Identify the vendors.*
2.10.2	Who decides (or determines) that the proceeds of any subsequent resale, disposal, or use of the imported merchandise will accrue directly or indirectly to the foreign vendor? • When is it decided that the proceeds of any subsequent resale, disposal, or use of the imported merchandise will accrue directly or indirectly to the foreign vendor? • What accounts are used to record the payment of these proceeds?
2.10.3	Describe the procedures that are used to ensure that the proceeds of any subsequent resale, disposal, or use of the imported merchandise accruing directly or indirectly to the foreign vendor are included in the values that are declared to CBP.
Section 3—Information about the classification of imported merchandise	
3.1	Who is responsible for determining how imported merchandise is classified? *Identify all the individuals or groups that are responsible.*
3.1.1	What records and other information (e.g., product specifications, engineering drawings, physical items, laboratory analyses) are used to determine the classification of merchandise?
3.2	Does your company have a classification database?
3.2.1	If there is a classification database, do you archive previous versions of it? *Indicate how long the previous versions are retained.*
3.2.2	If there is a classification database, is a copy provided to the broker? *Indicate how it is provided to him or her.*
3.2.3	If there is a classification database, what procedures ensure that the information in the database is accurate?
Section 4—Information about special classification provisions HTSUS 9801	
4.1	Describe the type of merchandise that is imported under HTSUS 9801.
4.2	Who decides (or determines) that products of the United States will be returned after having been exported? *Identify all the individuals or groups/departments that are involved in the process.*

	• When is it determined that the products will be returned after having been exported? • What documentation/records are maintained for the exported items?
4.3	Describe the procedures that ensure that the exported items have not been advanced in value or improved in condition by any manufacturing process or other means while abroad.
4.4	Describe the procedures that ensure that drawback has not been claimed for the exported items.
Section 5—Information about special classification provisions HTSUS 9802	
5.1	Describe the type of merchandise that is imported under HTSUS 9802.
5.2	What documentation/records are maintained for the exported items?
5.3	**For items that are imported under HTSUS 9802.00.40/9802.00.50:** What documentation/records support the cost or value of the repair?
5.4	Describe the procedures or means (e.g., unique identifiers) that are used to ensure that the articles exported for repair or alterations are the same articles being reimported.
5.5	**For items that are imported under HTSUS 9802.00.40/9802.00.50:** Describe the procedures that ensure that the foreign operation (e.g., repair or alteration process) does not result in the exported item becoming a commercially different article with new properties and characteristics.
5.6	Describe the procedures that ensure that drawback has not been claimed for the exported items.
Section 6—Information about Generalized System of Preferences/Free Trade Agreement	
6.1	If applicable, identify the name and manufacturers identification (MID) number for all of the foreign vendors from whom items are imported under the Generalized System of Preference/Free Trade Agreement (GSP/FTA).
6.2	Describe any agreements with unrelated foreign vendors. *Indicate if the unrelated vendors are required to provide cost and production records to CBP or are legally prevented from releasing the records.*
6.3	Describe the procedures that are used to ensure that the origin of articles that are imported under the GSP (or FTA) is wholly the growth, product, or manufacture of the beneficiary developing country (BDC) (or FTA country)? *Identify who performs the procedures and when/how often the procedures are performed.*

6.3.1	What documentation/records are verified? *Indicate if copies of the documentation/records are retained on file or may be obtained upon request.*
6.4	Describe the procedures that are used to ensure the cost or value of the material that is produced in the BDC (or FTA country), plus the direct processing cost, is not less than 35% of the appraised value of the articles at the time of entry into the United States. *Identify all the individuals/groups that perform the procedures and when/how often the procedures are performed.*
6.4.1	What documentation/records are verified? *Indicate if copies of the documentation/records are retained on file or may be obtained upon request.*
6.5	What documentation is maintained on file showing that the articles are shipped directly from the BDC (or FTA country) to the United States without passing through the territory of any other country, or if passing through the territory of any other country, that the articles did not enter the retail commerce of the other country?
Section 7—Information about NAFTA	
7.1	Who is responsible for maintaining the certificates of origin from NAFTA vendors?
7.2	Describe the procedures that are used to ensure that imported items are eligible for NAFTA.
Section 8—Information about antidumping/countervailing duties (AD/CVD)	
8.1	Who decides (or determines) that items may be subject to AD/CVD? *Indicate when and how often items are reviewed.*
8.1.1	What information is used to determine whether items may be subject to AD/CVD? *Identify all the individuals or groups/departments that provide information as well as the documentation/records that are used.*
8.2	Describe the procedures that are used to ensure that the correct (true) country of origin is identified for items that are subject to AD/CVD.
8.3	Describe the procedures that are used to ensure that the correct AD/CVD case numbers are identified on the entry.

Section 9—Information about Intellectual Property Rights	
9.1	Identify all imported items for which your company has authorizations from the holders of intellectual property rights (IPR) such as trade names, trademarks, or copyrights. *Describe the item, and indicate the type of IPR.*
9.2	Who decides (or determines) that an imported item may have IPR belonging to other entities? *Indicate when and how often items are reviewed.*
	• When is it decided that an imported item may have IPR belonging to other entities? • What information is used to determine that the items have IPR belonging to other entities? *Identify all the individuals or groups/departments that provide information as well as the documentation/records that are used.*
9.3	Describe the procedures that are used to ensure that there is a valid authorization/agreement between your company and the owner of the trade name, trademark, copyright, or patent prior to the importation of the items?
9.4	What accounts are used to record royalties, proceeds, and indirect payments that are related to the use of the IPR?

REQUEST FOR DOCUMENTATION

DATE OF REQUEST:

RESPONSE DUE:

SUBJECT: *When submitted in conjunction with the PASQ, the subject matter may be "Information about the organization and policies and procedures relative to compliance with CBP laws and regulations."*

Item No.	Description of Documentation
1	A copy of the organizational chart, if there is one.
2	A copy of the written policies and procedures that are used to ensure compliance with CBP laws and regulations (e.g., an import compliance manual).
3	A copy of the general ledger (GL) working trial balance for the period ending [xxxx] and the description of the accounts that are used.
4	A copy of written accounting procedures for recording purchases and the payments.

FROM CBP INFORMED COMPLIANCE PUBLICATION: REASONABLE CARE

General Questions for All Transactions

1. If you have not retained an expert to assist you in complying with Customs requirements, do you have access to the Customs Regulations (Title 19 of the Code of Federal Regulations), the Harmonized Tariff Schedule of the United States, and the GPO publication Customs Bulletin and Decisions? Do you have access to the Customs Internet Website, Customs Bulletin Board, or other research service to permit you to establish reliable procedures and facilitate compliance with Customs laws and regulations?

2. Has a responsible and knowledgeable individual within your organization reviewed the Customs documentation prepared by you or your expert to ensure that it is full, complete, and accurate? If that documentation was prepared outside your own organization, do you have a reliable system in place to insure that you receive copies of the information as submitted to U.S. Customs and Border Protection, that it is reviewed for accuracy, and that U.S. Customs and Border Protection is timely apprised of any needed corrections?

3. If you use an expert to assist you in complying with Customs requirements, have you discussed your importations in advance with that person and have you provided that person with full, complete, and accurate information about the import transactions?

4. Are identical transactions or merchandise handled differently at different ports or U.S. Customs and Border Protection offices within the same port? If so, have you brought this to the attention of the appropriate U.S. Customs and Border Protection officials?

Questions Arranged by Topic

Merchandise Description and Tariff Classification

Basic question: Do you know or have you established a reliable procedure or program to ensure that you know what you ordered, where it was made, and what it is made of?

1. Have you provided or established reliable procedures to ensure you provide a complete and accurate description of your merchandise to U.S. Customs and Border Protection in accordance with 19 U.S.C. 1481? (Also, see 19 CFR 141.87 and 19 CFR 141.89 for special merchandise description requirements.)

2. Have you provided or established reliable procedures to ensure you provide a correct tariff classification of your merchandise to U.S. Customs and Border Protection in accordance with 19 U.S.C. 1484?

3. Have you obtained a Customs "ruling" regarding the description of the merchandise or its tariff classification (See 19 CFR Part 177), and if so, have you established reliable procedures to ensure that you have followed the ruling and brought it to U.S. Customs and Border Protection's attention?

4. Where merchandise description or tariff classification information is not immediately available, have you established a reliable procedure for providing that information, and is the procedure being followed?

5. Have you participated in a Customs preclassification of your merchandise relating to proper merchandise description and classification?

6. Have you consulted the tariff schedules, Customs informed compliance publications, court cases, and/or Customs rulings to assist you in describing and classifying the merchandise?

7. Have you consulted with a Customs "expert" (e.g., lawyer, Customs broker, accountant, or Customs consultant) to assist in the description and/or classification of the merchandise?

8. If you are claiming a conditionally free or special tariff classification/provision for your merchandise (e.g., GSP, HTS Item 9802, NAFTA), how have you verified that the merchandise qualifies for such status? Have you obtained or developed reliable procedures to obtain any required or necessary documentation to support the claim? If making a NAFTA preference claim, do you already have a NAFTA certificate of origin in your possession?

9. Is the nature of your merchandise such that a laboratory analysis or other specialized procedure is suggested to assist in proper description and classification?

10. Have you developed a reliable program or procedure to maintain and produce any required Customs entry documentation and supporting information?

Valuation

Basic questions: Do you know or have you established reliable procedures to know the price actually paid or payable for your merchandise? Do you know the terms of sale, whether there will be rebates, tie-ins, indirect costs, or additional payments, whether assists were provided or commissions or royalties paid? Are amounts actual or estimated? Are you and the supplier related parties?

1. Have you provided or established reliable procedures to provide U.S. Customs and Border Protection with a proper declared value for your merchandise in accordance with 19 U.S.C. 1484 and 19 U.S.C. 1401a?

2. Have you obtained a Customs "ruling" regarding the valuation of the merchandise (See 19 CFR Part 177), and if so, have you established reliable procedures to ensure that you have followed the ruling and brought it to U.S. Customs and Border Protection attention?

3. Have you consulted the Customs valuation laws and regulations, Customs Valuation Encyclopedia, Customs informed compliance publications, court cases, and Customs rulings to assist you in valuing merchandise?

4. Have you consulted with a Customs "expert" (e.g., lawyer, accountant, Customs broker, Customs consultant) to assist in the valuation of the merchandise?

5. If you purchased the merchandise from a "related" seller, have you established procedures to ensure that you have reported that fact upon entry and taken measures or established reliable procedures to ensure that value reported to U.S. Customs and Border Protection meets one of the "related party" tests?

6. Have you taken measures or established reliable procedures to ensure that all of the legally required costs or payments associated with the imported merchandise have been reported to U.S. Customs and Border Protection (e.g., assists, all commissions, indirect payments or rebates, or royalties)?

7. If you are declaring a value based on a transaction in which you were/are not the buyer, have you substantiated that the transaction is a bona fide sale at arm's length and that the merchandise was clearly destined to the United States at the time of sale?

8. If you are claiming a conditionally free or special tariff classification/provision for your merchandise (e.g., GSP, HTS Item 9802, NAFTA), have you established a reliable system or program to ensure that you reported the required value information and obtained any required or necessary documentation to support the claim?

9. Have you established a reliable program or procedure to produce any required entry documentation and supporting information?

Country of Origin/Marking/Quota

Basic question: Have you taken reliable measures to ascertain the correct country of origin for the imported merchandise?

1. Have you established reliable procedures to ensure that you report the correct country of origin on Customs entry documents?

2. Have you established reliable procedures to verify or ensure that the merchandise is properly marked upon entry with the correct country of origin (if required) in accordance with 19 U.S.C. 1304 and any other applicable special marking requirement (watches, gold, textile labeling, etc.)?

3. Have you obtained a Customs "ruling" regarding the proper marking and country of origin of the merchandise (See 19 CFR Part 177), and if so, have you established reliable procedures to ensure that you followed the ruling and brought it to U.S. Customs and Border Protection's attention?

4. Have you consulted with a Customs "expert" (e.g., lawyer, accountant, Customs broker, Customs consultant) regarding the correct country of origin/proper marking of your merchandise?

5. Have you taken reliable and adequate measures to communicate Customs country of origin marking requirements to your foreign supplier prior to importation of your merchandise?

6. If you are claiming a change in the origin of the merchandise or claiming that the goods are of U.S. origin, have you taken required measures to substantiate your claim (e.g., do you have U.S. milling certificates or manufacturer's affidavits attesting to the production in the United States)?

7. If you are importing textiles or apparel, have you developed reliable procedures to ensure that you have ascertained the correct country of origin in accordance with 19 U.S.C. 3592 (Section 334, Pub. Law

103-465) and assured yourself that no illegal transshipment or false or fraudulent practices were involved?

8. Do you know how your goods are made from raw materials to finished goods, by whom, and where?

9. Have you checked with U.S. Customs and Border Protection and developed a reliable procedure or system to ensure that the quota category is correct?

10. Have you checked or developed reliable procedures to check the Status Report on Current Import Quotas (Restraint Levels) issued by U.S. Customs and Border Protection to determine if your goods are subject to a quota category which has part categories?

11. Have you taken reliable measures to ensure that you have obtained the correct visas for your goods if they are subject to visa categories?

12. In the case of textile articles, have you prepared or developed a reliable program to prepare the proper country declaration for each entry (i.e., a single country declaration, if wholly obtained/produced, or a multicountry declaration, if raw materials from one country were produced into goods in a second)?

13. Have you established a reliable maintenance program or procedure to ensure you can produce any required entry documentation and supporting information, including any required certificates of origin?

Intellectual Property Rights

Basic question: Have you determined or established a reliable procedure to permit you to determine whether your merchandise or its packaging bear or use any trademarks or copyrighted matter or are patented, and if so, that you have a legal right to import those items into, and/or use those items in, the United States?

1. If you are importing goods or packaging bearing a trademark registered in the United States, have you checked or established a reliable procedure to ensure that it is genuine and not restricted from importation under the gray-market or parallel import requirements of U.S. law (see 19 CFR 133.21), or that you have permission from the trademark holder to import such merchandise?

2. If you are importing goods or packaging which consist of, or contain registered copyrighted material, have you checked or established

a reliable procedure to ensure that it is authorized and genuine? If you are importing sound recordings of live performances, were the recordings authorized?

3. Have you checked or developed a reliable procedure to see if your merchandise is subject to an International Trade Commission or court ordered exclusion order?

4. Have you established a reliable procedure to ensure that you maintain and can produce any required entry documentation and supporting information?

Miscellaneous Questions

1. Have you taken measures or developed reliable procedures to ensure that your merchandise complies with other agency requirements (e.g., FDA, EPA/DOT, CPSC, FTC, Agriculture) prior to or upon entry, including the procurement of any necessary licenses or permits?

2. Have you taken measures or developed reliable procedures to check to see if your goods are subject to a Commerce Department dumping or countervailing duty investigation or determination, and if so, have you complied or developed reliable procedures to ensure compliance with Customs reporting requirements upon entry (e.g., 19 CFR 141.61)?

3. Is your merchandise subject to quota/visa requirements, and if so, have you provided or developed a reliable procedure to provide a correct visa for the goods upon entry?

4. Have you taken reliable measures to ensure and verify that you are filing the correct type of Customs entry (e.g., TIB, T&E, consumption entry, mail entry), as well as ensure that you have the right to make entry under the Customs Regulations?

ELEMENT 1: Management Commitment				Initials_____Date_____
	Y	N	U	Comments
Is management commitment communicated on an ongoing basis by the following? A. Company publications B. Company awareness posters C. Daily operating procedures D. Other means, e.g., bulletin boards, in meetings				
Does management issue a formal Management Commitment Statement that communicates a clear commitment to export controls?				
Is the formal statement distributed to all employees and contractors?				
Who is responsible for the distribution of the statement?				
Is there a distribution list of those who should receive the statement?				
What method of communication is used (letter, email, intranet, etc.)?				
Does the distribution of the statement include an employee-signed receipt and a personal commitment to comply?				
Is the formal statement from current senior management communicated in a manner that is consistent with management priority correspondence?				
Does the formal statement explain why corporate commitment is important from your company's perspective?				
Does the formal statement contain a policy statement that no sales will be made contrary to the EAR?				
Does the formal statement convey the dual-use risk of the items to be exported?				

ELEMENT 1: Management Commitment	Y	N	U	Initials_____ Date_____ **Comments**
Does the formal statement emphasize end-use/end-user prohibitions? Proliferation activities of concerns • Nuclear • Certain rocket systems and unmanned air vehicles (UAVs) • Chemical and biological weapons				
Does the formal statement contain a description of the penalties that are applied in instances of compliance failure? • Imposed by the Department of Commerce • Imposed by your company				
Does the formal statement include the name, position, and contact information, such as the e-mail address and telephone number of the person(s) to contact with questions concerning the legitimacy of a transaction or possible violations?				
What management records will be maintained to verify compliance with procedures and processes (including the formal statement)?				
Who is responsible for keeping each of the management records?				
How long must the records be retained?				
Where will the records be maintained?				
In what format will the records be retained?				
Are adequate resources (i.e., time, money, people) dedicated to the implementation and maintenance of the EMCP?				
Is management directly involved through regularly scheduled meetings with various units that are responsible for roles within the EMCP?				
Is management involved in the auditing process?				
Has management implemented a team of EMCP managers who meet frequently to review the challenges, procedures, and processes and who serve as the connection to the employees who perform the EMCP responsibilities?				

ELEMENT 1: Management Commitment				Initials _____ Date _____
	Y	N	U	Comments
Does the statement describe where employees can locate the EMCP Manual (on the company intranet or a specific person and location of hard copies)?				
Are there written procedures to ensure a consistent, operational implementation of this element?				
Is a person designated to update this element, including the Management Commitment Statement, when management changes, or at least annually? (Note the name of the person in the comments section.)				
Who are the other employees who are held accountable for specific responsibilities under this element? For example: • Company officials charged with EMCP oversight and ongoing commitment to the program • Management team members who are responsible for connecting with all the responsible employees in the EMCP • Persons who are charged with ensuring that the EMCP is functioning as directed by management				
If the primary responsible person is unable to perform the responsibilities, is a secondary person designated to back up the primary designee? (If not, is a procedure in place to eliminate the vulnerabilities of an untrained person proceeding with tasks that might lead to violations of the EAR?)				
Do the responsible persons understand the interconnection of their roles with other EMCP processes and where they fit in the overall export compliance system?				
Is the message of management commitment conveyed in employee training through the following? • Orientation programs • Refresher training • Electronic training modules • Employee procedure manuals • Other				

ELEMENT 1: Management Commitment				Initials_____Date_____
	Y	N	U	Comments
Is management involved in EMCP training to emphasize management commitment to the program?				
Determination:				

ELEMENTS 2 and 5: Risk Assessment and Cradle-to-Grave Export Compliance Security and Screening				Initials_____ Date_____
	Y	**N**	**U**	**Comments**
Are there written procedures for ensuring compliance with product and country export restrictions?				
Do procedures include reexport guidelines or any special instructions?				
Is there a written procedure that describes how items are classified under ECCNs on the CCL? A. Does a technical expert within the company classify the items? B. If your company does not manufacture the item, does the manufacturer of the item classify it? C. Is there a written procedure that describes when a classification will be submitted to the BIS and who will be responsible for it? D. Is there a written procedure that describes the process for seeking commodity jurisdiction determinations?				
Is an individual designated to ensure that the product/country license determination guidance is current and updated?				
Is there a distribution procedure to ensure that all appropriate users receive the guidance and instructions for use?				
Is there a list that indicates the name of the persons who are responsible for using the guidance?				
Is a matrix or decision table for product/country license determinations used? Are the instructions provided easily understood and applied?				
Do the instructions provided specify who, when, where, and how to check each shipment against the matrix?				
Does the matrix/table display ECCNs and product descriptions?				
Appropriate shipping authorizations: (a) license required, (b) license exception (specify which), or (c) NLR?				
Does the matrix communicate license exception parameters/restrictions?				
Are license conditions and restrictions included within the matrix/table?				
Does the matrix/table cross-reference items to be exported with license exceptions that are normally available (based on item description and end destination)?				

ELEMENTS 2 and 5: Risk Assessment and Cradle-to-Grave Export Compliance Security and Screening	Y	N	U	Initials_____ Date_____
				Comments
Does the matrix/table clearly define which license exceptions are normally available for each item? (Also, clearly state which license exceptions may not be used due to general prohibitions)				
Are embargoed destinations displayed?				
Is the country information in the table up to date?				
Are item restrictions displayed? (i.e., technical parameter limitations, end-user limitations)				
Is the matrix automated? Is a person designated for updating the tool?				
Are reporting prompts built into the matrix/table?				
Are Wassenaar reports required? Does the matrix/table denote when they are required?				
Is the matrix manually implemented? If so, is a person designated to update the tool?				
Is there a *hold* function to prevent shipments from being further processed, if needed?				
Is there a procedure to distribute and verify the receipt of license conditions?				
Is there someone who is designated to distribute and follow-up with the acknowledgment verification?				
Is there a response deadline that is defined when the conditions are distributed?				
Are there written procedures to ensure that checks and safeguards are in place within the internal process flows? And are there assigned personnel who are responsible for all the checks?				
Are the order process and all linking internal flows displayed visually in a series of flow charts?				
Is there a narrative that describes the total flow process?				

ELEMENTS 2 and 5: Risk Assessment and Cradle-to-Grave Export Compliance Security and Screening				Initials_____Date_____
	Y	N	U	Comments
Are the following checks included in the internal process?				
• Preorder entry screen checks that are performed (i.e., know-your-customer red flags)				
• DPL				
• Entity List				
• Unverified List				
• SDNs List				
• Boycott language				
• Nuclear end uses				
• Certain rocket systems and UAVs' end uses				
• Chemical and biological weapons' end uses				
• Product/country licensing determination				
• Diversion risk check				
Do the order process and other linking processes include a description of administrative control over the following documents? A. Shipper's export declarations (SED)/AES records B. Shipper's Letter of Instruction (SLI) C. Airway bills (AWB) and/or bills of lading D. Invoices				
Does the procedure explain the order process and other linking processes from the receipt of order to actual shipment?				
Does the procedure include who is responsible for each screen check throughout the flow?				
Does the procedure describe when, how often, and what screening is performed?				
Are hold/cancel functions implemented?				
Does the procedure clearly indicate who has the authority to make classification decisions?				
Are supervisory or EMCP administrator sign-off procedures implemented at high-risk points?				
Does the company have an ongoing procedure for monitoring the compliance of consignees, end users, and other parties who are involved in export transactions?				
Determination:				

ELEMENTS 2 and 5: Risk Assessment and Cradle-to-Grave Export Compliance Security and Screening				Initials_____Date_____
Review orders/transactions against the DPL	Y	N	U	Comments
Is there a written procedure to ensure the screening of orders/shipments to customers covering the servicing, training, and sales of items against the DPL?				
Are the personnel/positions who are responsible for DPL screening identified (consider domestic and international designee)?				
Is there a procedure to stop orders if a customer and/or other parties are found on the DPL?				
Is there a procedure to report all the names of the customers and/or the other parties who are found on the DPL?				
Do the procedures include a process for what is used to perform the screening? And if distribution of hard copies is required, who is responsible for their update and distribution?				
Is the DPL checked against your customer base? A. Are both the customer name and the principal checked? B. Is there a method for keeping the customer base current? C. Is there a method for screening new customers?				
Is the DPL checked on a transaction-by-transaction basis? A. Is the name of the ordering party's firm and principal checked? B. Is the end user's identity available? If so, is a DPL check done on the end user? C. Is the check performed at the time that an order is accepted and/or received? D. Is the check performed at the time of shipment? E. Is the check performed against backlog orders when a new or updated DPL is published?				
Does the documentation of screen (whether hard copy or electronic signature) include the following? A. The name of individuals performing the checks. B. Dates that the screen checks are performed. C. Date of current denied person's information that is used to perform the check. D. Is the date of the DPL used to check the transaction that is documented? Is it current?				

ELEMENTS 2 and 5: Risk Assessment and Cradle-to-Grave Export Compliance Security and Screening				Initials_____Date_____
Review orders/transactions against the DPL	Y	N	U	Comments

Are other trade-related sanctions, embargoes, and debarments imposed by agencies other than the Department of Commerce checked?
 	
A. *Department of Treasury (OFAC)*
   1. SDTs?
   2. SDNs and FTOs?
 	
B. *Department of State*
   1. Trade-related sanctions (Bureau of Politico-Military Affairs)?
   2. Suspensions and debarments (Center for Defense Trade, Office of Defense Trade Controls)?				

Are domestic transactions screened against the DPL?				
Determination:				

ELEMENTS 2 and 5: Risk Assessment and Cradle-to-Grave Export Compliance Security and Screening				Initials_____Date_____
Diversion Risk Profile (DRP) See EAR Part 732, Supplements 1 and 3	Y	N	U	**Comments**
Are there procedures to screen orders for diversion risk red flag indicators?				
Is a checklist used based upon the red flag indicators?				
Does the written screening procedure identify the responsible individuals who perform the screen checks?				
Is the DRP considered at all the phases of the order processing system?				
Is a transaction-based DRP performed?				
Is a customer-based DRP performed?				
Is a checklist documented and maintained on file for each and every order?				
Is a checklist documented and maintained on file in the customer profile?				
Is the customer base checked at least annually against the red flag indicators or when a customer's activities change?				
General Prohibition 6—Prohibits the export/reexport of items to embargoed destinations without proper license authority. Are embargoed-destination prohibitions communicated on the product/country matrix and part of the red flag indicators?				
General Prohibition 10—Prohibits an exporter from proceeding with transactions with knowledge that a violation has occurred or is about to occur. Is there anything that is suspect regarding the legitimacy of the transactions?				
Determination:				

ELEMENTS 2 and 5: Risk Assessment and Cradle-to-Grave Export Compliance Security and Screening Prohibited nuclear end uses/users, EAR, Section 744.2	Y	N	U	Initials_____Date_____ Comments
Are there written procedures for reviewing the exports and reexports of all the items that are subject to the EAR to determine, prior to exporting, whether they might be destined to be used directly or indirectly in any one or more of the prohibited nuclear activities?				
Are the personnel/positions who are responsible for ensuring the screening of customers and their activities against the prohibited end uses identified?				
Does the procedure describe when the nuclear screen should be performed?				
A. Is your nuclear screen completed on a transaction-by-transaction basis? B. Is the screen conducted against an established customer base? If yes, is there a procedure for screening each new customer before he or she is added to that customer base? C. Is the nuclear screen completed before a new customer is approved?				
Is there a list of all the employees who are responsible for performing the nuclear screening?				
Does the check include documentation with the signature/initials of the person performing the check, and the date performed, to verify the consistent operational performance of the check?				
Is the customer base checked and the check documented at least annually in the customer profiles (see EMCP guidelines, diversion risk screen)?				
Is it clear who is responsible for the annual check?				
Is there a procedure to verify that all responsible employees are performing the screening?				
Are nuclear checklists (and/or other tools) distributed to appropriate export-control personnel for easy, efficient performance of the review?				
Have export/sales personnel been instructed on how to recognize situations that may involve prohibited nuclear end-use activities?				
Does the procedure include what to do if it is known that an item is destined to a nuclear end use/end user?				
Determination:				

ELEMENTS 2 and 5: Risk Assessment and Cradle-to-Grave Export Compliance Security and Screening				Initials _____Date_____
Rocket systems and UAVs' prohibited missile end uses/users, EAR, Section 744.3	**Y**	**N**	**U**	**Comments**
Are there written procedures for reviewing the exports and reexports of all the items that are subject to the EAR to determine, prior to exporting, whether the items are destined for a prohibited end use?				
Are the personnel/positions who are responsible for ensuring the screening of customers and their activities against the prohibited end users/users identified?				
Does the procedure describe when the missile systems and the UAV screening should be performed?				
Does the procedure include a check against the Entity List?				
If yes, is there a procedure to maintain the documented Entity List screen decisions on file to verify consistent operational review?				
A. Is your rocket/UAV screen completed on a transaction-by-transaction basis? B. Is the screen conducted against an established customer base? If yes, is there a procedure for screening each new customer before he or she is added to that customer base? C. Is the rocket/UAV screen completed before the new customer is approved?				
Does the check include documentation with the signature/initials of the person performing the check, and the date performed, to verify the consistent operational performance of the check?				
Is the customer base checked and the check documented at least annually in the customer profiles?				
Is it clear who is responsible for the annual check?				
Is there a list of all the employees who are responsible for the annual check?				
Is there a procedure to verify that all the responsible employees are performing the screening?				
Are the missile system and UAV checklists (and/or other tools) distributed to appropriate export-control personnel for easy, efficient performance of the review?				
Have export/sales personnel been instructed on how to recognize prohibited missile systems and UAVs' end-use activities?				
Does the procedure include what to do if it is known that an item is destined to a prohibited end use/user?				
Determination:				

ELEMENTS 2 and 5: Risk Assessment and Cradle-to-Grave Export Compliance Security and Screening Prohibited chemical and biological weapons (CBW) end uses/users, EAR, Section 744.4	Y	N	U	Initials_____Date _____ Comments
Are there written procedures for reviewing the exports and reexports of all the items that are subject to the EAR for license requirements, prior to exporting, if the item can be used in the design, development, production, stockpiling, or use of CBW?				
Are the personnel/positions who are responsible for ensuring the screening of customers and their activities against the prohibited end uses/ users identified?				
Does the procedure describe when the CBW screen should be performed?				
A. Is your CBW screen completed on a transaction-by-transaction basis? B. Is the screen conducted against an established customer base? If yes, is there a procedure for screening each new customer before he or she is added to that customer base? C. Is your CBW screen completed before the new customer is approved?				
Does the check include documentation with the signature/initials of the person performing the check, and the date when the check is performed, to verify the consistent operational performance of the check?				
Is the customer base checked and the check documented at least annually in the customer profiles?				
Is it clear who is responsible for the annual check?				
Is there a list of all the employees who are responsible for performing CBW screening?				
Is there a procedure to verify that all the responsible employees are performing the screening?				
Are CBW checklists (and/or other tools) distributed to appropriate export-control personnel for easy, efficient performance of the review?				
Have export/sales personnel been instructed on how to recognize prohibited CBW end-use activities?				
Does the procedure include what to do if it is known that an item is destined to a prohibited end use/ end user?				
Determination:				

ELEMENTS 2 and 5: Risk Assessment and Cradle-to-Grave Export Compliance Security and Screening Review orders/transactions against antiboycott compliance red flags	Y	N	U	Initials_____Date _____ Comments
Is there a written procedure to screen transactions and orders/shipping documents for restrictive trade practice or boycott language that is included in Part 760 of the EAR?				
Are the personnel/positions who are responsible for performing this screen identified?				
Is the antiboycott screening performed by using a profile checklist?				
Does the checklist include the following? A. The firm's name? (as a *consignee*) B. Names/initials of personnel performing the screen check C. Date that the screen check is performed				
Is there a procedure to hold orders if there is a red flag during the processing of orders?				
Is a person designated to resolve red flags or report them to the BIS Office of Antiboycott Compliance?				
Have all the units that might possibly come into contact with the red flags been trained to identify the red flags?				
Are antiboycott red flags included in the training materials?				
Determination:				

ELEMENTS 2 and 5: Risk Assessment and Cradle-to-Grave Export Compliance Security and Screening				Initials_____Date_____
Review customers and other parties against the Entity List	Y	N	U	**Comments**
Is there a written procedure to screen transactions against the Entity List to determine whether there are any license requirements, in addition to normal license requirements, for the exports or reexports of specified items to specified end users, based on the BIS's determination that there is an unacceptable risk of use in, or diversion to, prohibited proliferation activities?				
Is the screening documented, including the following? A. The firm's name B. Names/initials of individuals performing the check C. Date that the checks are performed D. Is the screen check combined and performed with another check (e.g., DPL check)				
Is the Federal Register monitored daily for the addition of new entities to the Entity List?				
If matches occur, is there a hold function that is implemented within the order processing system that stops the order until a decision is made as to license requirements?				
Determination:				

ELEMENT 3: A Formal Written EMCP				Initials_____Date_____
	Y	N	U	**Comments**
Are there written procedures that describe how information will flow among all the elements to help ensure EMCP effectiveness and accountability?				
Is the written EMCP developed and maintained with input from all the corporate stakeholders in the export process?				
Do the written procedures clearly describe detailed step-by-step processes that employees are expected to follow? And are contingencies addressed?				
Are the written procedures reviewed for update at least annually and when major changes occur?				
Are the written and operational procedures consistent?				
Has an administrator been designated for oversight of the EMCP?				
Is there a table that identifies individuals, their positions, addresses, telephone numbers, e-mail addresses, and their respective export transaction and compliance responsibilities?				
Does it include all domestic sites?				
Does it include all international sites?				
Is a person designated as responsible for the management and maintenance of this element?				
Is a person assigned the responsibility for the distribution of information that is related to this element?				
Is a person assigned to retain the records?				
Is the length of time the records are to be retained included?				
Is the location of where the records are to be retained included?				
Is the format of the records to be retained included?				
If the primary responsible persons are unable to perform the assigned responsibilities, are secondary persons designated to back up the primary designees?				
Where there are no backup designees, are there procedures in place to prevent untrained/unauthorized personnel from taking action?				
Are all EMCP tasks clearly summarized in this element and consistent with detailed information in other corresponding elements?				
Does each employee designated with tasks understand the importance of his or her role that is related to the overall export compliance system?				
Do the responsible persons understand how the processes that they are responsible for connect to the *next* process? ("...and then what happens next?")				
Do all the appropriate personnel have the ability to hold a questionable transaction?				
Are the necessary systems to allow employees to perform their tasks readily available to them?				

ELEMENT 3: A Formal Written EMCP				Initials _____ Date _____
	Y	N	U	Comments
Is the training for the understanding and use of the EMCP provided on a regular basis to the necessary employees? And are the records of the training kept?				
Based on an organization chart and the assignment of tasks, does it appear that there are conflicts of interest in the chain of command and the tasks to be performed?				
Determination:				

ELEMENT 4: Training				Initials_____Date_____
	Y	N	U	Comments
Are there written procedures that describe an ongoing program of export transaction/compliance training and education?				
Do the written procedures clearly describe detailed step-by-step processes that employees are expected to follow?				
Is a qualified individual designated to conduct training and to update the training materials? (Note the name of the person in the comments section.)				
If the primary responsible person is unable to perform the responsibilities, is a secondary person designated to back up the primary designee? (If not, is a procedure in place to eliminate the vulnerabilities of an untrained person proceeding with tasks that might lead to violations of the EAR?)				
Is there a schedule to conduct training (including the date, time, and place)?				
Does the training component of the EMCP include what training materials are used (modules, videos, and manuals)?				
Are the training materials accurate, consistent, and current with the operational company policy, procedures, and processes? (If not, note what corrective actions are needed in the comments section.)				
Are attendance logs used for documentation, which includes the agenda, date, trainer, trainees, and subjects?				
Is the frequency of training defined?				
Is a list of employees/positions who should receive export control/compliance training defined?				
Are the responsible persons trained to understand the interconnection of their roles with other EMCP processes and where they fit in the overall export transaction/ compliance program?				
Is the list of employees/positions to be trained consistent with other elements?				
Is a person identified and responsible for keeping the training records?				
Is the location of where these training records are to be maintained included?				
Is the format of how these training records will be maintained noted?				

ELEMENT 4: Training				Initials_____Date_____
	Y	N	U	Comments
Do the training methods include the following?				
• Orientation for new employees				
• Formal (structured setting, agenda, modules that are used)				
• Informal (less structured basis, verbal, daily, on-the-job exchanges)				
• Circulation of written memoranda and e-mails to a small number of personnel, (usually group-specific instruction)				
• Refresher courses and update sessions that are scheduled				
• Employee desk procedure manuals				
• Backup personnel training				
Does the content of training materials include the following?				
• Organizational structure of export-related departments and functions				
• Message of management commitment—policy statement				
• The role of the EMCP administrator and key contacts				
• US export/reexport regulatory requirements				
• EMCP company operating procedures				
• The purpose and scope of export controls				
• Licenses and conditions/license exceptions and parameters				
• Regulatory changes and new requirements				
• Destination restrictions				
• Item restrictions				
• End-use and end-user prohibitions				
• How to perform and *document* screens and checklists				
• Various process flows for each element				
• New customer review procedures				
• Identification and description of noncompliance				
Determination:				

ELEMENT 6: Recordkeeping (EAR, Part 762)	Y	N	U	Initials_____Date_____ Comments
Are there written procedures to comply with recordkeeping requirements?				
Do the written procedures clearly describe detailed step-by-step processes that employees are expected to follow?				
Are all the records in each process included in the records that are maintained?				
Are the written procedures reviewed for update at least annually and when significant changes occur?				
Are the written and operational procedures consistent?				
Is there a designated employee who is responsible for the management and maintenance of this element? Is his or her name and contact information provided?				
Identify all the other employees who are held accountable for specific responsibilities under this recordkeeping element.				
Do the designated employees know who is responsible for the next action to be taken in the process?				
If the primary responsible person is unable to perform the responsibilities, is a secondary person designated to back up the primary designee?				
Where there are no backup designees, are there procedures in place to prevent untrained/unauthorized personnel from taking action?				
Do employees understand the importance of their roles that are related to the overall recordkeeping requirement?				
Do employees have the appropriate budgetary, staff, and supporting resources to perform their responsibilities?				
Do employees have access to all the appropriate systems, tools, databases, and records to perform their responsibilities and ensure compliance with recordkeeping procedures?				
Is appropriate and specific training provided regarding this element?				
Is the training included on an annual schedule of employee training?				
Have the appropriate parties who will retain the records been identified? Are their names and contact information provided?				
Has the length of time for record retention been identified?				
Have secure physical and electronic storage locations for records been identified for the retention of records?				
Have determinations been made regarding the formats that all of the different types of records will be retained in?				
Is there a list of records that are to be maintained (see guidelines and below for checklists)?				

ELEMENT 6: Recordkeeping (EAR, Part 762)	Y	N	U	Initials_____Date_____ Comments
Does the procedure include a list of records to maintain, including the following *administrative records*? • Commodity classification records. • Commodity jurisdiction letters. • Advisory opinion letters. • Copy of the EMCP. • BIS 748P, Multipurpose Application Form. • BIS 748P-A, Item Appendix. • BIS 748P-B, End-User Appendix. • BIS 711 Statement by Ultimate Consignee and Purchaser. • Electronic version BIS 748P, SNAP ACCN Number. • Accompanying attachments, riders, or conditions; international import certificates. • End-user certificates. • License Exception TSR Written Assurance. • AES Electronic Filing Authorization. • High-performance computer records. • Transmittal and acknowledgement of license condition. • Log administering control over use of export/reexport license. • Is a log maintained to ensure return or commodities that are previously exported under License Exception TMP? • Is a log maintained to ensure that License Exception LVS limits are not exceeded? • Humanitarian Donations GFT Records.				

Are there instructions for the accurate completion and filing of the following *transaction records*?
 	
A. Commercial invoices?
B. AES electronic filing authorization
    1. Description of items(s)
    2. ECCN(s)
    3. License number
    4. License exception symbols or exemptions
    5. Schedule B number(s)
C. AWBs and/or bills of lading value of shipments				

Is there conformity regarding the above documents?				
Determination:				

ELEMENT 7: Audits/Assessments				Initials_____ Date_____
	Y	N	U	Comments
Are written procedures established to verify ongoing compliance?				
Is there a qualified individual (or auditing group) who is designated to conduct internal audits?				
Is there a potential conflict of interest between the auditor and the division being audited?				
Is there a schedule for audits? Are internal reviews performed annually, every six months, quarterly, etc.?				
Is there a step-by-step description of the audit process?				
Is a standard audit module or self-assessment tool used?				
If yes, does the audit module or self-assessment tool evaluate corporate management commitment in all aspects of the audit, not just in the written policy statement element?				
If yes, does the audit module or self-assessment tool evaluate formalized, written EMCP procedures compared to operational procedures?				
If yes, does the audit module or self-assessment tool evaluate the accuracy and conformity of export transaction documents by random sampling or 100% verification?				
If yes, does the audit module or self-assessment tool evaluate whether there is a current, accurate product/license determination matrix that is consistent with the current EAR and Federal Register notices?				
If yes, does the audit module or self-assessment tool evaluate whether correct export authorizations were used for each transaction?				
If yes, does the audit module or self-assessment tool evaluate the maintenance of documents, as required in the written EMCP?				
If yes, does the audit module or self-assessment tool evaluate whether internal control screens were performed and documented, as required in the EMCP?				
If yes, does the audit module or self-assessment tool evaluate whether there are flow charts of the various processes for each element?				
If yes, does the audit module or self-assessment tool evaluate what is used to provide verification that the audits were conducted?				

ELEMENT 7: Audits/Assessments				Initials _____ Date_____
	Y	N	U	Comments
If yes, does the audit module or self-assessment tool evaluate whether there is a procedure to stop/hold transactions if problems arise?				
If yes, does the audit module or self-assessment tool evaluate whether all key export-related personnel are interviewed?				
If yes, does the audit module or self-assessment tool evaluate whether there are clear, open communications between all export-related divisions?				
If yes, does the audit module or self-assessment tool evaluate whether there is daily oversight over the performance of export control checks?				
If yes, does the audit module or self-assessment tool include a sampling of the completed screens that are performed during the order processing and/or new (or annual) customer screening?				
If yes, does the audit module or self-assessment tool evaluate whether the export control procedures and the EMCP manual are consistent with EAR changes that have been published?				
If yes, does the audit module or self-assessment tool evaluate whether the company's training module and procedures are current with EAR and Federal Register notices?				
Is there a written report of each internal audit?				
Are there written results of the review?				
Is the appropriate manager notified, if action is needed?				
Are spot checks/informal self-assessments performed? Are they documented?				
Is there evidence of a conflict of interest between the reviewer and the division being reviewed?				
Are records of past audits maintained to monitor repeated deficiencies?				
Is there a *best practice* that should be shared with other divisions in the company to improve the effectiveness and efficiency of export controls and promote the consistency of procedures?				
Are other departments aware of their export control–related responsibilities, e.g., legal, human resources, information management?				
Determination:				

ELEMENTS 8 and 9: Reporting, Escalation, and Corrective Action				Initials_____Date_____
	Y	N	U	Comments
Are there internal procedures in place to notify management within the company if a party is determined to be in noncompliance? Is the contact information provided for each official in the chain?				
Do the company policy/guidelines address the accountability and consequences for noncompliant activity? Are the appropriate incentives, rewards, requirements, and penalties in place, and is an appropriate business culture of compliance being fostered to facilitate the notification of any possible noncompliance?				
Are there internal procedures in place to notify the appropriate USG officials (e.g., Export Administration's Office of Exporter Services, Export Enforcement) when noncompliance is determined?				
Has a central corporate point of contact been defined for all communications with the USG?				
Is the management chain clearly defined for voluntary self-disclosures (VSDs), and are there clear guidelines for VSDs?				
Do all employees receive export-control awareness training (including for potential deemed exports and hand-carry scenarios)? Does this training detail the reporting, escalation, and corrective action requirements?				
Is there a 24-hour mechanism for notifying compliance management of possible export violations or problems?				
Does the company have an anonymous reporting mechanism for employees?				
Do compliance guidelines provide defined criteria for when a formal internal investigation is required? If yes, are the procedures to be followed defined? Are the reporting and documentation requirements defined?				
Do compliance guidelines include the policy and procedures for follow-up reporting to management and the reporting employee? Is there a process for evaluating the lessons that are learned?				
Determination:				

WEBSITES

www.cbp.gov/ace
www.cbp.gov/trade/ace/training-and-reference-guides
www.apps.cbp.gov/csms
www.cpb.gov/trade/automated/ace-faq
www.cbp.gov/aceoutreach
www.census.gov/foreign-trade/outreach
http://www.cpsc.gov/en/Regulations-Laws—Standards/Regulations
-Mandatory-Standards-Bans/

Index

Author

Thomas A. Cook is the managing director of Blue Tiger International (bluetigerintl.com), a premier international business consulting company on supply chain management, trade compliance, purchasing, sales and business development, global trade, and logistics.

Tom was the former CEO of American River International in New York and Apex Global Logistics Supply Chain Operation in Los Angeles.

He has over 30 years of experience in assisting companies all over the world managing their global operations.

He is a member of the NY District Export Council, sits on the boards of numerous corporations, and is considered a leader in the business verticals he works in.

Tom has been engaged by the AMA since 1981. He has been a course developer and leader/instructor in a host of areas, such as, but not limited to, project management, import and export, global supply chain, purchasing, risk management, negotiation skills, sales, marketing, and business development.

He has now authored over 15 books on global trade and is in the middle of an eight-book series titled *The Global Warrior ... Advancing on the Necessary Skill Sets to Compete Effectively in Global Trade.*

He has also authored books on sales management, customer service, purchasing and growth in world markets.

Tom has been or is involved with a number of organizations in education and training in a number of industry verticals, such as, but not limited to, ISM, CCSMP, TIA, AFA, U.S. Chamber of Commerce, Department of Commerce, Conference Board, SUNY, Dale Carnegie, Cal State Long Beach, and NYIT.

Tom is also the director of the National Institute of World Trade (niwt.org), a 30-year-old educational and training organization based in New York.

Tom is a former U.S. Naval and Merchant Marine Officer. He holds a BS and MS degree in business from SUNY Fort Schuyler, Maritime College.

Tom can be reached at tomcook@bluetigerintl.com or 516-359-6232.

Tom is also the founder of the "Soldier on at Home" organization, assisting wounded combat veterans and dogs along with funding dog training for Veterans with PTSD. www.soldieronathome.org.

APPRECIATION FOR THEIR CONTRIBUTIONS

Kelly Raia, in particular, for her contribution on the regulatory and trade compliance section and for assisting in editing, formatting, and material gain

Department of Commerce

American Shipper Magazine

National Cargo Bureau

If we don't change, we don't grow. If we don't grow, we aren't really living.

Gail Sheehy